John Ridd '88

A Manager's Guide to Ergonomics in the Electronic Office

A Manager's Guide to Ergonomics in the Electronic Office

Marvin J. Dainoff

Marilyn Hecht Dainoff

JOHN WILEY & SONS
Chichester · New York · Brisbane · Toronto · Singapore

Copyright © 1987 by John Wiley & Sons Ltd.

First published 1986 © Holt, Rinehart and Winston of Canada, Ltd under the title People and Productivity: A Manager's Guide to Erogonomics in the Electronic Office

All rights reserved.

No part of this book may be reproduced by any means, or transmitted, or translated into a machine language without the written permission of the publisher.

Library of Congress Cataloging in Publication Data:

Dainoff, M. J.
  A manager's guide to erogonomics in the electronic office.
    1. Office practice—Automation—Psychological aspects.
2. Video display terminals—Hygienic aspects.   3. Human engineering.   4. Work environment.   I. Dainoff, Marilyn Hecht.   II. Title.
HF5547.5.D32   1986   658.3'044   86-32493
ISBN 0 471 91423 1

British Library Cataloguing in Publication Data available

Printed and bound in Great Britain

Acknowledgements

Many dear friends, colleagues, and members of our families have contributed their time, patience, and support in helping us with this book. Although we cannot list them all here, we owe them a tremendous debt.

We wish to express our thanks to the following:

At NIOSH-Taft Laboratories, in Cincinnati, the research team that worked so hard to produce the work that, in effect, launched this book: Michael Smith, Diane Secrest, Laurie Fraser, B.J. Taylor, and Carol Pustinger.

At the Miami University Center for Ergonomic Research in Oxford, Ohio, the research team that continues to work and inspire: Prof. Leonard Mark, Ray Daley, David Vogele, and Robert Moritz, and our programming consultant Edward Fullman.

To the people at Holt, Rinehart and Winston of Canada — particularly our editor, Jocelyn Klemm, who has supported us with unfailing good humor and wisdom; and our meticulous copy editor, Kathryn Dean. Our relationships with both were enjoyable and iterative, in the best sense. Our thanks also to Pat Slowey and Chris Marvin.

To our anonymous but diligent reviewers who obviously devoted much energy and thought to our work and who made many valuable suggestions.

To Debbie Johnson, Ray Daley, and Barbara G.F. Cohen for helpful comments and suggestions on the manuscript.

To Carrie Kutney of Wessell Design in Cincinnati for her excellent illustrations.

To Morton R. Startz, Marlene Gross, and Sandra M. Smith, who helped us free up time for writing.

And to Mary Baetz, who started the ball rolling.

Marvin J. Dainoff and Marilyn Hecht Dainoff
Cincinnati and Oxford, Ohio
May, 1986

Preface

Few managers have not been touched in some way by the ever-expanding availability of computer-based office equipment; references to a *revolution* in office technology are commonplace. Computer memory is becoming increasingly inexpensive, computer speeds are becoming faster, software programs are becoming more and more sophisticated, and the video display terminal — the focal point which ultimately links human and computer — has become the ubiquitous component of the modern office. In 1982, in an assessment of the potential impact of office automation, Vincent Giuliano predicted that by 1990, almost half of the total workforce would be using some sort of electronic terminal. In 1986 (the date of this writing), we seem to be well on our way towards the realization of that prediction.

In the rush to take advantage of the truly wondrous capabilities of the computer, it has been easy to lose sight of the fact that this marvelous device is still a *tool*, and that a human being is required to sit (or stand) in front of that terminal, to extract the benefits of its capabilities. Frequently, the needs of that human being have not been considered. Traditional office environments, which have evolved over the years to support people working only with *paper*, are no longer necessarily appropriate for people who must now deal with electronic media. Traditional work practices and training procedures are not likely to be appropriate either.

The result is a series of *mismatches* between the human operator and the things in his or her work environment — mismatches which affect the operator both physically and psychologically, and impair the efficiency of his or her work.

The subject of this book, the applied science of *ergonomics*, deals with the attempts to resolve these mismatches, to improve the *fit* between person and environment. We hope to demonstrate that an intelligent application of ergonomic principles will benefit both the individual employee, in terms of reduced health complaints and increased quality of working life, and the employer, in terms of increased productivity.

Ergonomics, as applied to the electronic office, is still a new field. Accordingly, there are still many areas of disagreement and uncertainty, and advice from experts is sometimes contradictory. So the manager who must make decisions *now* about the working environment may be in a dilemma as to what advice to take or what to do. This book was written with this manager in mind — to attempt to provide a basic understanding of the issues and goals of fitting together the human being and the workplace. This, of necessity, leads to a mixture of both practical and theoretical information, including state-of-the-art *advice* and the *concepts underlying that advice*. To use an automobile analogy, the *advice* in this book will provide you with information similar to knowing that your car needs oil; the *theory* can be compared to understanding the function of oil in the engine. For example, you will not simply find statements such as "Chairs should be adjustable between 40 and 55 cm (16 and 20 inches)." We will also indicate that the goal of chair adjustability is to have the worker's feet flat on the floor and the knees at about a right angle, give reasons why that is important, and note the variability of knee heights among people. These discussions will not always lead to a single ideal solution, since there is frequently not enough research evidence from which to draw clear-cut conclusions.

Our goal is to help the manager to understand the basic underlying issues, in order to make the best decisions with the information at hand, both now and as the field develops further.

Managers in every country face the challenge of competition — worldwide or domestic. In a recent article, economist Robert Reich (1985) argued that American management and labor have two choices in responding to foreign competition. The first choice is to rely on a "cheap, unskilled work force, engaged in routinized tasks, generally angry . . . with no continuing commitment to the enterprise" — that is, to cut labor *costs*. The second choice is to depend on "a highly trained work force that's vitally committed" — that is, to increase labor *value*. Reich argues that the choice we make will determine both the kind of economy and the kind of society we will have.

A highly trained and committed workforce can only result from management's concern for its *people*. An understanding of ergonomics is an essential component of that concern.

Contents

CHAPTER ONE What Is Ergonomics? 1

CHAPTER TWO Ergonomic Decision Making and Results 7
   The VDT Enters the Traditional Office 10
   Decision Making with the New Technology 11
   An Integrated Conceptual Framework for Ergonomics 12
      Fatigue: Grandjean's Bucket 13
      Stress 14
      Resource Allocation 15
      The Integrated Framework 15
   How to Apply the Conceptual Framework 17
   Assessing Scientific Research 18
   The VDT: Helper or Health Hazard? 18
      Some Results of Research 18
      Resolving the Issues 21
      Reframing the Question 22
   The VDT: Health and Comfort Related to Productivity 23
      The NIOSH Experiments 23
      Ong's Workplace Intervention 27
      Springer's Worksite Surveys and Trials 27
      Brill/BOSTI: The Financial Benefits of Ergonomic Improvements 28
   Ergonomic Improvements: The Overall Benefits 30

CHAPTER THREE Seating: The Spine, the Discs, the Aching Back 31
   Seated Posture: Stability vs. Motion 32
   The Spine 35
   Three Postural Options 38
   Anthropometry: The Measurement of Human Beings 41
   Beyond Anthropometry 44
   Does the Theory Work? 46
   Chair, Posture, and Sitting Habits: How They Relate to
      Discomfort Complaints and Performance 47
   Assessing Ergonomic Chairs 49
   Buying a Chair Is Not the Same as Using It: Employee

Education   51
Executive Seating and the Question of Status   52
Elements to Look for in an Ergonomic Chair   53

CHAPTER FOUR   Design of Workstations   57
Workstation Planning: Is It Worth the Time?   57
Applying Standards, Guidelines, and Recommendations:
  Why the Easy Way Out Often Fails   58
The Why of Workstation Recommendations   60
Biomechanical Criteria for Ergonomic Design   62
The Integrated Workstation System   72
Assessing Workstation Components   74
Buying a Workstation Is Not the Same as Using It:
  Employee Education   75
Elements to Look for in Workstation Equipment   75

CHAPTER FIVE   Visual Perception and the Video Display Terminal   77
VDTs: Some History   77
The VDT Debate: What Are the Issues?   79
Eyes and the Terminal: Basic Visual Function   80
  The Act of Visual Perception   80
  The Eye   82
  Vision in the Electronic Office   83
  Potential Sources of Visual Problems   85
The VDT as a Unique Visual Problem   88
Glare and the Vertical Orientation of the Screen   89
  Control of Ambient Light   90
  Control of Glare at the Monitor   90
  Control at the Level of the Workstation   92
Character Formation   92
Direction (Polarity) of Contrast   94
Character Shape: The Language Connection   96
Line Spacing   98
Scrolling and Moving Text   99
The Videotropic Response   100
Visual Defects and the VDT   101
A Summary of Visual Concerns and the VDT   103

CHAPTER SIX   The Physical Work Environment   105
The Dual Office Environment   107
The Proximate Environment   108
  Communication   108
  Privacy   109
  Layout and Workplace Organization   110
The Impact of the Environment on Finances and Behavior:

    The BOSTI Study Revisited   112
    What Is the Cost of a Person Compared with That of a Building?   112
    Is the Open Office a Solution to the Space Squeeze?   113
    Financial Costs or Savings from Ergonomic Changes   115
The Ambient Environment   116
    Noise   117
    Office Music   121
    Ambient Lighting   121
    Thermal Comfort   123
    Air Quality and the Tight Building Syndrome   125
Important Issues in the Physical Work Environment   126

CHAPTER SEVEN   Software Ergonomics   129
    Software in the Electronic Office   130
    The Importance of User Friendliness   131
    Methods for Determining User Friendliness   132
        Technological Characteristics   133
        The Conceptual Approach   134
    How People Work at Computers   136
    The Use of Metaphor in Achieving User Friendliness   137
        Choosing Effective Metaphors   139
        Inventing New Metaphors   141
    Built-in User Friendliness   142
    Ergonomic Design: A Success Story   144
    How Much User Friendliness Is Optimal?   144
        Performance Requirements   144
        The User Population: Expert vs. Novice   145
        Error Recovery   146
        Security   146
    Key Issues in Choosing User-Friendly Software   148

CHAPTER EIGHT   The Quality of Working Life in the Electronic Office   149
    Predicting the Effects of Change   150
    Job Decision Latitude and Job Demand   151
        Regaining Control   152
        Deskilling   153
        Alternatives to Deskilling   154
    Supervision in the Electronic Office   155
        Electronic Performance Monitoring   155
        A Different Approach to Electronic Performance Monitoring   156
        Electronic Supervision and Peformance Appraisal   157
        Using Supervision and Appraisal Effectively   157
    Management in the Electronic Office: A Perspective   159

CHAPTER NINE   New Directions for the Electronic Office   161

APPENDIX I Assessing Research Results   169
APPENDIX II   Anthropometric Data   180
APPENDIX III   Case Study: Putting Together a VDT Workstation   183
GLOSSARY   197
NOTES   209
BIBLIOGRAPHY   215
INDEX   223

What Is Ergonomics?

CHAPTER 1

In its broad sense, ergonomics means the *fit* between the human being and those things with which he or she interacts. Just as you are more aware of your shoes when they don't fit, one is usually more aware of the ergonomic aspects of one's environment when the fit is wrong. Although the focus of this book is on the electronic office, it may be helpful to present some examples from everyday life.

- Can you remember yourself as a child sitting in an adult chair? Your legs stuck straight out in front of you, and it was hard to wriggle on and off the chair. If you were sitting at a table, the chair was too low, so some adult may have given you a telephone book to sit on, which made the height better. But your legs were probably scrunched up against the underside of the table, and the phone book was slippery, so sliding off became a problem if you didn't sit very still. People who were concerned about the ergonomics of the situation made highchairs, or *child-sized furniture*. And if you as an adult have ever had to sit on that child-sized furniture, you will know that the reverse situation is not very comfortable, either.

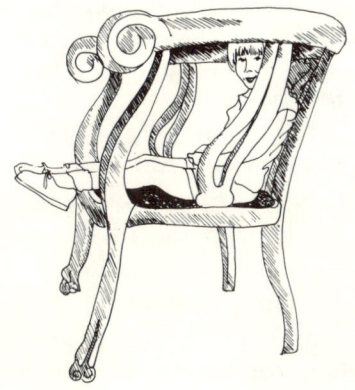

Figure 1-1.
A child in an adult-sized chair.

Figure 1-2.
An adult in a child-sized chair.

- Have you ever been cramped in a car where there was too little headroom and too little legroom, for a long trip? Conversely, if you are short, have you ever been unable to reach the accelerator and lean against the seat back at the same time? The mechanisms that allow a seat to slide forward or back, or sometimes up or down, are examples of ergonomics at work. But some people still need to sit on a cushion or put one behind their backs in order to achieve a comfortable, workable position, because the seat adjustment mechanisms are inadequate.
- Have you ever sat in a booth at a restaurant and found the table was too high for comfort, or so low that you could not cross your legs beneath it — or it crowded you, or was too far away? If the table could be moved to the ergonomic satisfaction of both you and the person sitting opposite you, then all was well. But if not, even for the short period of time that you ate your meal, your comfort level was compromised.

Design *without* humans in mind results in theatre or stadium seats that are so close to the next row that you can't cross your legs and that the people behind you are forever grazing your head or neck. It leads to machines with controls in unlikely positions. And it results in cars with speedometers and other important instruments rendered invisible by the steering wheel, and with horns that are on the sides when the steering wheel is in one position, but up and down when it is in another, instead of reliably in the center.

Design of the total environment with humans in mind is the province of the applied science of ergonomics.

Also referred to as *human factors*, or *human engineering*, ergonomics is concerned with understanding the basic physical and psychological attributes of people as these relate to the things that people use (tools, machines, environments). The goal of ergonomic design is to optimize the person-thing relationship, that is, the *fit*.

We encounter examples of good or bad fit everywhere. Doorways are generally high enough for all but the tallest of us to go through with comfort; chairs with arms are generally wide enough for all but the widest of us. Dining room tables are generally about 66 cm (26 inches) high, desks 73 to 76 cm (29 to 30 inches) high, kitchen counter tops 91 cm (36 inches) high. Typewriter desks have one level for writing and a lower level for the typewriter. All these standard heights have been gauged for the *average* person (although, in point of fact, few of us are average in all our dimensions).

The situation which can make us most aware of ergonomics and which is most analogous to the office workplace is driving an automobile. Let's compare these situations:

- Both driver and office worker are expected to sit in a relatively constrained position, without getting up and moving about, while performing a task (driving to a distant place/performing work) which requires fine motor coordination as well as a certain amount of mental concentration.
- The muscles and bones of the body (the musculoskeletal system) allow us to perform this task better if we are in a comfortable, supported position and if the controls of the machine we are operating are readily differentiated and within easy, unencumbered reach. The accelerator, brake, and clutch are in standardized positions, but the windshield wiper, headlight switch, horn, radio, heating and cooling switches, and other controls are often not. Although the driver's seat is adjustable forward and backward, it is still not always possible to achieve a comfortable position, especially if it must be maintained over a long period of time. The analogous situation in an office is that, although the typewriter keyboard is *fairly* standardized, the controls and commands for computers are not; the furniture is usually not at all adjustable, and is most often not at the proper height; and the functions of typing, reading copy, answering the telephone, and writing must all be accommodated without mutual interference.
- Lighting (in an automobile, outdoor light by day or night, and lighting of the dashboard or dome light by night; in an office, light from windows or ceiling fixtures) is an important factor affecting operator comfort and ability to perform the task. In particular, the presence of glare (on windshield or monitor) causes considerable discomfort, and it also renders difficult the performance of the visual task. This is why dashboards are now made of glare-resistant materials.
- The temperature level of the environment is either appropriate (i.e., it does not cause discomfort) or it becomes a distraction. It is difficult to concentrate if it's so hot and muggy that perspiration is trickling down your brow, or so cold that your fingers are numb.
- The sound level may be quietly soothing (soft background music, muffled conversation) or it may interfere (radio up full blast, loud talking, trucks shifting gears, printer noise). It may even distract you so much that you miss important auditory signals (a horn, a scream, the crunch of metal, or an unusual sound from the car's motor; a beep from an electronic indicator).

- Task design, including the rate at which information must be processed (too many highway signs at once/a software package that is unfriendly or too demanding of immediate response) can increase tension and lead to drainage of energy.
- Rest breaks, whether to provide psychological respite, meals, or bathroom necessities, are an important ergonomic factor, whether the constraint is the necessity of getting to Toronto before nightfall, or getting the report done in time for the 5 o'clock mail.

Thus, ergonomics, in its broadest sense, includes all the physical and psychological variables which contribute to comfort and the ability to carry out a task easily, effectively, safely, and efficiently.

There is always *some* sort of fit between people and the machines/tools they use, whether that fit is for good or for ill. It is like an extra employee, who either works for the organization, contributing to the general well-being in the workplace — or against it, silently sapping the energies of the workers. Making the fit work for you and for your employees is what ergonomics is all about.

Ergonomic issues are important in *all* work environments, and often have not received the attention they deserve. However, the electronic office is where the majority of us today — and even more of us in the future — will spend our time. Consequently, the focus of this book will be on ergonomics in the electronic office. We will show that the office worker's comfort and productivity are as intertwined as a double helix, and that management's attention to these factors can pay dividends in employee morale, reduced absenteeism, fewer health complaints, greater job satisfaction and, ultimately, higher company profits.

Ergonomic improvements, intelligently carried out, present a rare opportunity in the real world: *a no-lose situation*. Employees win because they are more comfortable, they feel better, and they sense that management cares about them as human beings. Managers win because they are able to provide their employees with the best tools with which to work easily and effectively, and because employee morale and productivity improve. And the organization wins because the investment for ergonomic improvements is rapidly paid off by productivity gains — and after that, the increases in productivity are pure profit.

The operative phrase here is "ergonomic improvements, *intelligently carried out*." The word *ergonomic* is becoming something of a buzzword, and not everything that touts itself as ergonomic is, in fact, effective.

In order to assess realistically the value of any changes you institute, or the advice of any consultants you hire, it is important for you to have a basic understanding of what can be accomplished, and a feel for what is and is not known in the field at the present time. By the time you have finished reading this book, you should know enough ergonomics to evaluate progress in the field and to make sound planning and purchasing decisions.

Ergonomic Decision Making and Results

CHAPTER 2

> *... they claim, and I think quite rightly, that ergonomics would be a kind of eternal triangle, among* efficiency, comfort *and* health.
> — P. van Wely (1970)

Elizabeth N. is a 43-year-old mother of four children, aged 11 to 18, who rejoined the workforce three years ago when her husband was laid off from his job. Her husband is now employed, albeit at a lower wage, and although the children do their part by working after school, the family has never really recovered from the financial blow. Thus, it is essential that Elizabeth hold down a full-time job to make ends meet.

Elizabeth was raised on the work ethic: she expects to do a good day's work for a good day's pay. She impressed the people at the Leming Corporation by her enthusiasm and conscientiousness, as well as her excellent typing skills. She was obviously bright enough to adapt those skills to the complicated data entry job for which she had applied.

She, in turn, was extremely impressed by the company. The Leming Corporation was on the leading edge of an expanding growth industry. Their sparkling new office complex, a jewel of steel and glass in the heart of the downtown area, was eloquent testimony to how well they were doing.

The offices themselves were gorgeous. Everything was decorated beautifully; large potted plants graced the floor-to-ceiling windows. Elizabeth's department was located in an airy, sunlit room. The computer terminals were sleek and modern: a single graceful curve bound the monitor and keyboard into a compact, integrated unit. They sat on expensive wooden desks; the desk chairs looked like fine contemporary sculpture. All in all, it looked like a beautiful place to work.

Elizabeth comes in on Monday refreshed from the weekend's rest and change of pace. She pauses a moment to enjoy the sunlight near her workstation and the view of the bustling city, and then begins her work. But she can't seem to get comfortable, and by the end of the morning her shoulders are beginning to ache, her legs have "gone to sleep" a couple of times, and her eyes are tired from squinting at the video display terminal (VDT) monitor. (Definitions for technical terms in this book are given in the Glossary). Lunchtime gives her some respite, but by the end of the afternoon her back feels as if it will never straighten up, her shoulders ache, and her eyes are burning.

Tuesday is rainy and gloomy, and Elizabeth is feeling gloomy as well. Her back, arms, and shoulders begin to hurt earlier in the day, although her eyes are giving her fewer problems. She is under some pressure to get a certain report finished, so she resists taking breaks, but finds herself fidgeting in her chair to try to relieve the back ache. She's not getting as much done as she did yesterday, and she feels this as an added pressure.

Wednesday is bright and sunny again — a real contrast with Elizabeth's mood, for this is a six-aspirin day. She is accomplishing little and making a lot of mistakes. Because her eyes are aching and sitting at her workstation seems physically intolerable, she finds any excuse to go to the rest room, the water fountain, the supply room, etc., and on the way back to her desk she stops to commiserate with her co-workers. When she gets home from work she is grouchy; her back hurts too much for her to do the things around the house that need doing, and she doesn't really enjoy the evening.

By Thursday, she is on the phone to her doctor because of the excruciating pains in her back. She is frustrated because she can't seem to accomplish anything; the boss keeps coming around and asking her for things that are not finished. She feels as if she is in an electronic sweatshop and that there's no way she could be paid enough to put up with this. . . .

Friday is a wash-out as far as productivity is concerned. Much as it goes against her moral grain, Elizabeth spends a lot of time watching the clock. She simply feels too exhausted physically to want anything other than to get *out*.

Elizabeth's unhappiness is typical of the attitude of the majority of her co-workers. Everyone seems to avoid work as much as possible, and getting things *done* is like pushing an unwilling elephant. Management can't understand why everyone is so disgruntled and dissatisfied — after all, they try to be considerate employers, the pay is reasonable, and who could want a lovelier place to work?

Things might be quite different for Elizabeth and for the entire company if management had made ergonomic considerations a priority — if they had stressed ergonomics to their facility planners, architects, and designers. Instead, they ended up with a new building with the latest in architecture and interior design — but a workplace which was not hospitable to the human beings who worked there.

A contrasting case is that of Susan J., who is very much like Elizabeth in terms of devotion to work, personal drive, experience, economic need, and physical health and stature. Susan's employer, Armand-Olympic International, after considering a number of options, decided to remain in its old headquarters, but to invest in adjustable workstations for their employees who spend time at VDTs.

Susan comes to work on Monday mornings to a 40-year-old building located in a less-than-fashionable area of town. She begins work with her characteristic good humor and enthusiasm. After a couple of hours at her VDT, she takes a break. The end of the morning finds her in need of a change, but the lunch hour restores her energy and she is almost as fresh at the beginning of the afternoon as she was first thing in the morning. As her body tires of one position, she is able to make minor adjustments in her workstation to relieve the fatigue, so she is never in a tiring position for longer than it takes her to become aware of it. She is able to readjust her posture, and then devote all her energy to the task at hand. At the end of the day, she is appropriately tired, but not frazzled or worn out.

Susan leaves the office each day with a sense of having done a good day's work. She is able to accomplish the things she wants to do at home, she enjoys the change of pace, and by Tuesday morning, she feels as good as she did on Monday. On each successive workday, she is able to devote all her resources to getting the job done, because each evening she is able to recoup her energies completely.

Susan feels good about herself and the work she is able to do both on and off the job. When her work requires meeting a deadline, or extra concentration, she is able to handle it without undue stress. Susan's coworkers feel much as she does: Armand-Olympic is a pleasant place to work, where management cares about its employees and their health and comfort.

Management is also pleased with the results of its investment in ergonomic workstations. Although it did involve a sizeable up-front investment, productivity and morale have improved within this department. Not only is the actual volume of work produced greater, but turnover and absenteeism — each a financial drain on company profits — have dropped significantly. Consequently, Armand-Olympic's management feels confident that their ergonomic investment has improved the quality of working life, and has also been favorably reflected in the bottom line of the company's annual financial report.

The VDT Enters the Traditional Office

Although they and their companies are fictitious, Elizabeth and Susan are typical of VDT workers all over the world. While there are growing numbers of companies like Armand-Olympic, there are far too many Lemings.

In the mid-1970s, as VDTs were coming into widespread use in the workplace, concerns about health and comfort problems began to surface. By the late 1970s, thousands of men and women who spent their workdays at VDTs were feeling like Elizabeth; trade magazines described their complaints as "epidemic." Were these complaints justified?

Examination of VDT workplaces in operation showed that even the most rudimentary considerations of physical ease and comfort were being ignored. As in Elizabeth's case, VDTs were often placed on standard desk surfaces because the lower typewriter returns were too small for the terminals. This resulted in VDT keyboards being higher than the usual typewriter keyboards. VDTs tended to be *added* to existing office equipment, so if finding desk space was a problem, the terminal ended up on whatever spare table was available. We actually observed one VDT operator who was forced to work sideways, with her legs twisted at 90 degrees, because her terminal was placed on a table with solid sides and no kneehole.

The physical construction of VDTs also posed some problems not encountered before. Glare had not caused a great problem in an office where typewriters and papers were the tools of the day and the major worksurfaces were horizontal. However, the VDT screen was not only vertical: it was made of glass, like a mirror, and the operator could see his or her face and the rows of overhead fluorescent lights reflected on it, right along with the print.

By the early 1980s, studies were showing 50% to 80% rates of visual and musculoskeletal problems among VDT workers — rates which were much higher than for other office workers.

The outcry from VDT workers in Europe, Canada, the United States, Australia, and New Zealand was such that it could hardly be ignored. In some countries in Europe, ergonomic standards were imposed by law. In the United States, Worker's Compensation suits were filed, and legislation regulating conditions of work at video display terminals was introduced in several states.

Yet other workplace surveys showed little or no difference in health complaints between VDT and non-VDT workers. The result was that management was being asked to spend large amounts of money for ergonomic improvements that were considered by some people to be of possibly minor importance. How was the manager to make an informed decision?

Decision Making with the New Technology

Most people would probably agree that, other things being equal, the more uncomfortable and constrained a worker is, the less work he or she is likely to get done. But could 3 or 4 inches in keyboard height really make that much difference? Why would office chairs suddenly be obsolete, just because a VDT has been added to the workplace? Maybe all the hue and cry was just a kind of fear response to a new and unfamiliar technology.

Workers, managers, and legislators began asking research scientists, "Give me the data. Tell me what is true and what isn't, what's important and what isn't." Even today, these questions remain, right at the crossroads of basic science, applied technology, and public policy.

Ideally, the scientific response to these questions would be to provide a set of simple, precise guidelines. An ergonomic handbook could be published, managers could have it implemented, and everyone could go on to other problems. Unfortunately, office ergonomics is barely past its infancy, and the conclusions of one research scientist often cannot be integrated easily with the conclusions of another.

How, then, is a manager to cope when the scientists disagree? The manager needs to be familiar enough with the scientific research to ask informed questions, while not losing sight of the department's or company's objectives. Indeed,

> the art of survival in a technological age is to be able to understand at some level what the scientific issues are, without getting bogged down in technicalities, and to extract the concepts that are applicable to one's own situation.

In any field in flux, it is essential to be able to absorb, evaluate, and integrate new developments in the field. Because so much about office ergonomics is still unknown, today's manager is best advised to gain an understanding of the basic concepts and to become aware of what is and is not known, rather than to blindly accept guidelines or standards which may or may not be based on solid scientific evidence. Two tools commonly used by scientists can help managers to evaluate new ergonomic developments. The first, a *conceptual framework*, is simply a way of looking at ergonomics and work. The second, *assessing the scientific research*, involves asking a few basic questions which help determine whether a given study was conducted according to logical scientific rules. Just as a manager learns some legal principles in order to know when to get legal advice and how to assess it, he or she needs to be familiar enough with scientific principles to make decisions appropriate to the technologically oriented electronic office. The two tools discussed in the following sections can help the manager to make sound ergonomic decisions.

An Integrated Conceptual Framework for Ergonomics

When gathering and describing data, research scientists often find it helpful to work from an explicit theoretical or conceptual framework. This framework — sometimes called a model, or a set of working hypotheses — is based on what is already known, but is always subject to change if new scientific evidence contradicts it. The framework is useful if it provides a reference base from which to view the world, and if it integrates the available information. When a given model can no longer accommodate the available information, it gives rise to a new model. (In the second century, Ptolemy used the conceptual framework that the earth is the center of the universe, and the sun, the planets, and all the heavenly bodies move around it. Using this theory, mathematicians and astronomers plotted the paths of the planets, until the early 16th century when the Polish astronomer Copernicus found that the data fit better if the planets revolve around the sun — that is, he proposed a new conceptual framework.) A conceptual framework helps to make the data understandable, suggests avenues for further research, and perhaps even sheds light on a situation in unexpected ways.

Conceptually, the electronic office is a maze of complex interactions. A physiologist would see it as a place where nerve impulses are translated into motor actions; a psychologist would add perception, cognition, and interpersonal relationships; the eye care specialist, orthopedic specialist, computer scientist, industrial engineer, architect, designer, and facilities manager would each see this world from different, yet overlapping, perspectives. In order to make sense of the whole system, the ergonomist must work from a conceptual framework that borrows from all of these fields. It is this framework that can also help the manager to synthesize, organize, and integrate varied viewpoints, and to understand the issues and conflicts that have arisen since the advent of the electronic office.

This ergonomic conceptual framework encompasses three components: *fatigue, stress,* and *resource allocation*. Each helps to explain further the observed differences between good and bad ergonomic situations, as exemplified by the case studies of Susan and Elizabeth. The framework offers an overview of the *fit* between the worker and his or her environment.

It may at first seem strange that this framework is defined in physiological or psychological terms when ergonomics is commonly described in the more concrete terms of chair size, workstation dimensions, and glare, for instance. In fact, this book will deal at length with the measurements of workplaces and environments which are now considered to be optimal, although better ones may be discovered tomorrow. But *the way it feels* can be described only in subjective terms. If, at the end of a workday, a worker feels exhausted, has aches and pains that were not present at the beginning of the day, or is emotionally drained, it is as if he or she has spent eight hours hiking in an uncomfortable pair of shoes: the fit is wrong. Many factors apart from the physical measurements of the workstation (or the size of the shoes) contribute to bad fit. Details of the task being done, the total demands on the person, the friendliness or inhospitability of the environment (or the terrain) are only some of the variables that determine how the worker (walker) feels. The fatigue-stress-resource allocation framework includes but goes beyond measurement of the physical environment. It encompasses the whole physical and psychological well-being of the person. It describes the quality of working life in its broadest sense.

Fatigue: Grandjean's Bucket

The ability to work effectively generally decreases as a person's fatigue level increases. Swiss ergonomist Etienne Grandjean (1982) visualized fatigue as a fluid which collects in a bucket. This bucket is equipped with a spigot, which can open fully to allow the fatigue to drain off (recuperation), or which can remain partially or completely closed, either keeping the fatigue constant or allowing it to accumulate further. The more nearly full the bucket is, the more fatigued the person is, and the more difficult it is for him or her to work well.

Many factors contribute to filling the bucket: expending physical or mental effort, working under adverse circumstances of physical discomfort, including cold, heat, humidity, and extremes of light, noise, or pollution. Other factors affect the degree to which the spigot is open — that is, how quickly one can recuperate. For example, anxiety about work or private life can be visualized as fatigue remaining in the bucket until that crisis passes. One's state of health is also an important factor in how quickly fatigue mounts and recuperation takes place: after a bout of illness it is as if the spigot had been partially closed, making recovery more difficult.

All the tiring, depleting factors in life fill the bucket of fatigue each day, whereas the more a person is able to relax and enjoy both work and respite from work, the more quickly and completely the bucket can be drained. Chronic inability to drain the bucket leads to decreased effectiveness on and off the job, and to physical and emotional depletion, moodiness, depression, and vulnerability to disease.

Stress

Stress is a *response* that the body makes to the demands placed upon it. Sources of stress (*stressors*) may be physical, such as heat or cold, or they may be mental, such as trouble on the job or change in marital status. Stress may also arise from pleasant circumstances (sometimes called *eustress*), such as getting married or the first day on a new job, or from unpleasant situations (variously called *distress, strain*, or simply *stress*), such as being fired or the death of a loved one.

The stress response, no matter what elicits it, leads to important changes in body chemistry. These changes are part of a physiological response which serves the biological survival mechanism. It enables an animal, when faced with danger, to respond with "fight or flight." Adrenaline and other chemicals are secreted which raise blood pressure and make the heart beat faster. Blood is sent toward the muscles and away from the internal organs so that the animal is more fleet of foot. It sweats and is more alert. Vision is altered so that it sees better at a distance (the better to see the threat). Most of this, however, is less than useful in coping with stressors typically encountered in the modern electronic office!

Although stress can be beneficial, there is evidence that when it is imposed on the body over and over again, it results in excess wear and tear and leads eventually to "stress diseases," including headaches, cardiovascular disease, ulcers, digestive diseases, certain cancers, and even death. The brain also reacts to too much stress: nervous exhaustion, nervous breakdown, and burnout are among the symptoms. Many people under too much stress turn to alcohol or other drugs; a more healthy response is to turn to family, friends, or professional help for support.

The way in which a person appraises a given situation determines how stressful it is to that person. An insurmountable difficulty for one person may be no problem or a welcome challenge for another. However, some kinds of stress have the same general effect on most people. Job stress, for instance, is profoundly influenced by prevailing attitudes in the workplace. Heavy handed, inconsiderate, top down management will be a stressor to almost all workers, whereas management that is perceived by workers to be humane and caring leads to lower stress levels. Poor working conditions are also stressors, and employees will perform better as working conditions improve.

Resource Allocation

Most of the research relating to resource allocation theory has focused on military and aerospace applications, partly because resource allocation is such a crucial issue in these fields. If you have to perform multiple tasks (such as monitoring the altimeter, compass, radar, and landmarks while flying the airplane, keeping track of the enemy, and advising the gunner where the enemy is), can you successfully split your limited resources among them?

Barry Green, the principal bassist of the Cincinnati Symphony Orchestra, performs a solo piece which requires him to perform difficult music on the bass violin while simultaneously telling the audience how hard it is to recite a written script while playing the music. It took him many, many months of concentrated effort to learn to do it. This piece of music, written by Tom Johnson, is aptly called "Failing."

As these two examples suggest, the basic premise of resource allocation theory is that it is nearly impossible to be aware of everything all the time. Sensory cues are all around us. We see, smell, and taste, feel temperature, humidity, and comfort, have a sense of where our limbs are, of whether we are hungry, or of whether we ache somewhere, at the same time that we are working to meet the demands of the specific task we are performing. We could be concentrating on a project, apparently unaware of the surroundings. But if someone were to ask, "Do you smell smoke?" we would turn our attention to the cues that our noses had been receiving all along, although we were too preoccupied to notice.

The same principles apply in an electronic office. Resource allocation theory teaches that all aspects of the task and the total environment, both on and off the job, impinge on the worker's conscious or unconscious being at some level. The worker must cope with all these demands, despite a finite ability to pay attention to them all at the same time. His or her *personal efficiency* consists of the proper allocation of attention and effort to get the work done. To the extent that the worker must battle irrelevant demands, more energy will be used, and fatigue will build up more quickly.

The Integrated Framework

The fatigue concept states that you have only so much energy. The stress concept states that you have only so much tolerance for physical and mental stress and frustration. The resource allocation concept states that you have only so much capacity to devote attention to any event. The three overlap in many ways; yet each adds an important element to understanding ergonomics.

After a few hours at work, Elizabeth's back and shoulders ache and her eyes hurt; this adds fatigue to her bucket. Her poorly designed workstation is also a physical stressor. Her physical discomfort is not just something that makes her tired in a neutral way: it causes physical and psychological stress. Her physical aches and pains and the psychological stress interact and reinforce each other, adding fatigue to the bucket at an even greater rate — and the fatigue itself causes distress.

Elizabeth is also under emotional stress because she knows she is not doing her work in a way that coincides with her moral values; her dissatisfaction with the job only compounds it. Ultimately, her feelings about herself as a capable, moral human being suffer. Her lowered sense of self-esteem aggravates the situation even further, and at some point she will begin her Mondays already tired, already distressed, already defeated.

Susan, on the other hand, is able to offset her fatigue by recuperation each day. She is not always walking around with her fatigue bucket heavy and burdensome, so she is able to tackle more work when that is necessary, simply because she has the energy available. Her ability to cope with her work generates a positive mental attitude, which further reinforces her capability.

The fatigue and stress concepts alone do not give a complete picture of what is taking place, however. Resource allocation theory sheds light on the rational, cognitive, and thought processing activities of the two workers. Consciously or unconsciously, Elizabeth and Susan decide which demands are primary and which are secondary unless, of course, certain demands (such as an aching back) are so overwhelming that they must take precedence. When a worker such as Elizabeth feels at the mercy of the extraneous demands of her environment, she is to some extent out of control, and this in itself is a powerful stressor. Susan's feelings of being in control and able to make rational choices about her work priorities is an equally powerful reinforcer of her sense of capability.

It is important to remember that, from the point of view of this discussion, the only difference between Elizabeth and Susan is a difference in the ergonomic characteristics of their workplaces. Yet the effect on their work and their lives is dramatic.

The value of managers' taking a few seconds to analyze their workers (and themselves) using the fatigue-stress-resource allocation framework is that it gives a good perspective on the impact of ergonomics *in the workplace and beyond,* as well as a sense of the enormous difference between working with an office full of "Susans" and an office full of "Elizabeths."

The ergonomic impact of the workplace is of obvious importance to the manager, from both a humane and a productivity-oriented point of view. The impact of office ergonomics on the worker's life after office hours is also important, and for the same reasons. The contrast between the physical and mental resources with which Elizabeth and Susan arrive at home at the end of a workday is great, and the effects on their families easy to imagine. The resulting tone of the family interaction, in turn, helps to determine the way each comes to work the next morning.

Thus, it is implicit in the fatigue-stress-resource allocation framework that workers (and managers) exist not just from 9 to 5, but also from 5 to 9. What happens in *each* sphere profoundly affects the other. As Elizabeth and Susan illustrate, ergonomic conditions in the workplace can contribute to a downward or upward spiral of employee well-being and work effectiveness (productivity).

If "knowledge . . . is power," managers who know and understand this will have more control over the ergonomic conditions which affect that spiral in one way or another.

How to Apply the Conceptual Framework

At this point, the manager can begin to draw conclusions about many factors affecting his or her workers both on and off the job, simply by applying the conceptual framework tool. This book will describe specific physical and technical aspects of office ergonomics, including good and bad seated positions and keying postures, treatment of light and glare, and so on. This information can be most fruitfully applied by the manager if he or she integrates each set of facts into the fatigue-stress-resource allocation model, even when that is not specifically mentioned. When the manager does this, every awkward, uncomfortable, unhealthy posture, every bit of glare or pollution, will be interpreted as adding fatigue to the bucket, and as a physical stressor. Frustration with unfriendly software, concern about keystrokes being monitored, aching eyes and backs, and lack of privacy will be seen as stressors and as extraneous demands on a worker's resources, competing with the demands of the work itself.

The second tool the manager can use to evaluate new ergonomic developments is critical assessment of scientific research.

Assessing Scientific Research

Not everything in the marketplace which is touted as ergonomic is, in fact, effective — so the manager must be an informed consumer of products and of scientific research. Assessing the research (or a product) is really nothing more than applying critical thinking skills to the evidence presented. Some important questions to ask are these:

- If evidence is presented that one thing or condition is "better," it is essential to know *what it is better than, and whether that is a valid standard of comparison*. This is the concept of the *controlled scientific experiment*. For example, work at typewriters cannot be compared to work at VDTs, for a number of reasons (described in Appendix I and Chapter 5).
- Is there an alternative explanation for the data?
- Does the data fit in with the conceptual framework? Here, the answer must be interpreted with caution. Invalid data may fit the conceptual framework! However, if the data contradicts a logical or established framework, this is reason to re-assess it carefully.
- How were the data collected — from an observation or a controlled experiment (field or laboratory)? How many subjects or workers were included?
- Was the research done in a laboratory or on-site (a field study or a workplace intervention, which involves the introduction of some changes into the workplace)?
- Are the results applicable to the specific situation under consideration?
- Is there an explanation for negative findings (as in finding no increase in health complaints when VDTs are introduced)?

(A fuller discussion of research methods is presented in Appendix I.)

The manager should also be aware that *few studies involving people can be deemed perfect*. No laboratory experiment can duplicate real life, and no field study can be controlled sufficiently to give all the answers. Ergonomic research is rather like describing a mountain by looking at it from different vantage points: it may take several sources and several research methods for a clear pattern to emerge.

The VDT: Helper or Health Hazard?

Some Results of Research

The majority of published work on health problems among VDT workers focuses on *visual and muscular problems*. (A substantial amount of material has also been written on radiation hazards. While discussion of the radiation issue is beyond the scope of this book, most experts agree that radiation levels emitted from VDTs are not large enough to constitute a health hazard.) Neither is it possible or particularly useful to review all of the material on VDT research in this book. Overviews of the major research findings have been published elsewhere (Dainoff, 1982 and 1984).

Instead, three major studies which literally span the globe will be summarized here. These studies, conducted at worksites in San Francisco, Zurich, and throughout New Zealand, are similar to a number of other investigations.

The basic finding in these studies was that the number of health complaints was correlated with (a) use of a VDT, and (b) the nature of the job.

The San Francisco study was carried out in 1980 (Smith et al., 1981) at several newspaper offices and an insurance company by the U.S. National Institute for Occupational Safety and Health (NIOSH). An extensive health questionnaire was given to three identified groups of employees: a control group of clerical workers not using VDTs, "professional VDT operators" (editors, reporters), and clerical VDT operators (data entry, data retrieval). *Eye strain*, at least occasionally, was reported by 60% of the non-VDT control group, 78% of the professional VDT operators (editors and so on), and 91% of the clerical VDT operators. *Neck and shoulder pain* was reported by 81% of the clerical workers using VDTs, but by "only" 55% of clerical workers not using VDTs. The figures for *lower back pain* were 78% and 56%, respectively, for the two groups. No significant differences in muscular problems were noted between the professional VDT operators and the control (non-VDT) group.

Thus, this study found differences in health complaints between VDT operators and employees not using VDTs, and that the kind of job (professional vs. clerical) also influenced the rate at which such complaints were reported.

The Zurich study was conducted by Grandjean and his colleagues (1980) at the Swiss Federal Institute of Technology (in the banking industry). Four groups of operators were identified; two used VDTs and two did not. "Almost daily" *eye fatigue* was reported on questionnaires by 27% of the "conversational" VDT operators (who alternated between looking at the screen and looking at copy), but by only 7% of "transaction clerks," who did essentially the same job, but without VDTs. Yet

17% of both the VDT data entry clerks and (non-VDT) typists reported visual problems.

The extent of *muscular problems*, as revealed on physical examination by a physician, showed a different pattern. Muscle pain was found in 50% of the (VDT) data entry clerks, but in only 23% of the (non-VDT) typists. Conversational (VDT) operators had the same level of muscle pain as the (non-VDT) typists (23%). However, of those people doing essentially the same job (conversational operators and transaction clerks), muscle pain affected 23% of those using VDTs and only 5% of those who did not.

Overall, health complaints (eye plus muscle) were higher for workers usings VDTs: data entry clerks (67%) and conversational workers (50%). Lower totals were found for non-VDT workers: typists (40%) and transactional clerks (12%).

Here again, the type of job affected both the level and the type of symptom reported. Those workers who looked at the screen the most (conversational VDT operators) reported the highest level of visual problems. Those who worked using repetitive movements at high speeds, while looking mainly at copy (data entry clerks) showed the most muscular problems. When people doing essentially the same job were compared, however, those who used VDTs had considerably more health complaints than those who did not.

Finally, a large-scale survey was carried out by the New Zealand Department of Health (Coe et al., 1980) at a number of different worksites. VDT operators were compared to non-VDT operators. The results of the study were basically similar to the previous two studies. *Eye fatigue* was reported by 50% of the VDT operators as a group as compared with only 33% among the non-VDT control operators. Within the VDT group (including programmers, editors, data entry, and conversational workers), programmers reported the least eye fatigue (38%). A particularly interesting finding in this study was the observation that eye fatigue was less (42% vs. 62%) among those VDT operators who were able to take frequent informal breaks (finding something else to do which allowed them to look away from the screen). *Muscle discomfort* while seated affected 37% of the VDT operators, but only 26% of the (non-VDT) controls.

The three studies just described are representative of a vast number of investigations which report similar findings. As a group, they seem to indicate that *something* about working with a VDT, in combination with the job being done, is causing problems.

On the other hand, some studies have failed to find major differences in health complaints between VDT and non-VDT workers.

For example, in studies carried out at AT&T's Bell Laboratories (Starr, 1984; Starr et al., 1982) two different jobs were selected for comparison: directory assistance operators and service representatives. In each job, some workers used VDTs, others did not. For both jobs, the level of complaints was the same between VDT and non-VDT users. A second example is a laboratory study at IBM (Gould & Grischkowsky, 1984), which compared proofreading work on VDTs with proofreading paper copy. The same individuals spent one working day on each task. No differences in health complaints, objective measures of visual performance, or error rates were found. (Overall proofreading speed was faster, however, with paper copy.)

At this point, being faced with a clear contradiction in research results, the manager might well be tempted to throw up his or her hands and accept whatever feels right or is easiest. However, the level of health problems at some worksites suggests (a) a lot of human distress, and (b) that the resources of many workers are probably being allocated to pain rather than the job. Thus, such an attitude might well prove counterproductive.

Alternatively, a thoughtful application of the two tools presented earlier — the conceptual framework and the techniques for assessing scientific research — can be helpful in separating out the issues.

Such an application follows. (A more detailed version of parts of the following analysis is found in Appendix I.)

Resolving the Issues

Consider those studies which have found differences in health complaints between VDT workers and non-VDT workers. *What else*, one might ask, *might have accounted for these findings?* It could be argued that the VDT represents a kind of technological threat to office workers, requiring a major change in work habits and attitudes, and engendering fear of job loss. A worker who feels threatened by the VDT may be more likely to mark down a large number of complaints on a health questionnaire than would a non-VDT worker. Thus, it would be the *symbolic* meaning of the VDT, rather than its physical form and structure, which is responsible for the rash of complaints.

This argument is difficult to refute directly. Most studies find that, even among VDT operators, lower-paid clerical workers — who might be more threatened by VDT technology — report higher levels of complaints than do the more highly paid professionals.

However, can this be the *only* explanation for more than 20 studies from around the world showing VDT/non-VDT differences? It is unlikely that this threat factor would be so potent a psychological force that it could explain away all these observed differences.

Reframing the Question

Is there anything else, then, about the *physical* characteristics of the VDT which could cause visual and muscular problems? The answer, in ergonomic terms, requires looking at the VDT not as an isolated piece of equipment, but as a component in an integrated, interdependent *system*, which includes the physical and mental characteristics of the worker, and the demands put on the worker by the task. If the VDT is only one component of the system, then comparing VDT to non-VDT users is not very useful unless one knows the environmental *context*, both physical and psychological, within which the VDT is used.

The critical point is that *the three studies listed above which found differences in health complaints also reported a number of ergonomic deficiencies at the VDT worksites*. These included disturbing reflections, flickering terminals, lack of adjustability, inappropriate working heights, and inability to rest hands or arms while working. On the other hand, *the two studies which found no differences characterized their worksites (both VDT and non-VDT) as having "good" ergonomic conditions*.

Therefore, it is reasonable to assume that, given equal working conditions (task requirements, rest breaks, management philosophy), a VDT operator working at a good ergonomic workstation with a well-designed terminal should not have significantly more health complaints than his or her non-VDT counterpart. On the other hand, if ergonomic conditions are poor, there are certain physical and operational characteristics of the VDT which would make it more likely that the worker will have visual and muscular complaints than would be the case in a comparable traditional workplace.

This argument is consistent with the bulk of the research evidence, as well as with the ergonomic conceptual framework presented earlier. However, it would be difficult to verify directly, except under stringent and exceptional conditions. The crux of the difficulty lies in the word "comparable." It is not at all clear how one can make a non-VDT task directly comparable to a VDT task. A detailed examination of the skills required, actions performed, and equipment utilized, will inevitably yield a long list of differences between the functions to be performed. (For example, one could simulate VDT glare conditions in a typing task by placing a piece of glass over the typist's copy; however, there would still be differences in the way characters were displayed, errors were corrected, and so on.) Much of the rest of this book will be devoted to explicating the ergonomic implications of these differences.

If comparing VDT and non-VDT work is like comparing apples and oranges, how can one assess the impact of VDT technology and minimize any deleterious effects? The answer is this: by making the comparison directly between *different kinds of VDT worksites*. That is, if operators performing identical tasks alternate between VDT workstations which differ *only* in their ergonomic characteristics, the effect of these characteristics could be directly assessed. Differences in health complaints between good and poor conditions could then reasonably be attributed to *ergonomic* differences alone, since all other factors would remain the same.

In such an experiment, the fatigue-stress-resource allocation framework would predict that if the worker's energy is not being diverted from the task by poor ergonomic conditions, that energy could be used to perform the task. Thus, *performance*, under better ergonomic conditions, should improve.

It should be noted that posing the question in this way changes the focus of attention in subtle but important ways. Concentrating on the VDT/non-VDT comparison tends to have the effect of isolating the VDT as *the* health hazard or potential health hazard. By restructuring the question in this way, the assumption is that VDTs are here to stay, and that our task is to understand the total workplace system, of which the VDT is only one part. Furthermore, through this understanding, we make our workplace not only more humane, but also more efficient.

The VDT: Health and Comfort Related to Productivity

The NIOSH Experiments

Between 1981 and 1983, Marvin J. Dainoff and his colleagues conducted a series of experiments in the United States at the laboratories of the National Institute of Occupational Safety and Health (NIOSH).

The first study, an overall "global" comparison of an "optimal" workstation (circa 1981) as compared to the "suboptimal" conditions commonly found in the workplace, showed greater comfort, fewer health complaints, and enhanced performance up to an average of 24.7% in the optimal workstation. (Figures 2-1 and 2-2 show some characteristics of these workstations.) In a second study, lighting/glare conditions were equalized in the two workstations; performance averaged 17.5% higher in the better workstation. In both experiments, subjects' responses to questionnaires indicated that they preferred the optimal workstation.

Figure 2-1.
Optimal workstation (circa 1981).

Figure 2-2.
A typical workstation frequently found in the field. This kind of workstation — with this forearm-upper arm angle — was simulated in the "suboptimal" workstation in the NIOSH experiments.

The subjects were clerical workers from an agency specializing in temporary help. They established base rates of performance at a data entry/editing task on the first day, and on the four subsequent test days were given incentive pay for performance improvements, with a penalty for errors. They worked for 3 hours each day without a break. On the four test days, each subject alternated between optimal (O) and suboptimal (S) workstations in a counterbalanced manner, either OSSO or SOOS, both to serve as his/her own control, and to control for any psychological, motivational, or time-related variables. This is a summary of the differences between the two workstations in the first experiment:

Experimental (O condition)	Control (S condition)
Lighting	
contrast-enhancing filter	no filter
high character contrast	low contrast
no glare	glare
separate task light	no task light
Furniture	
well-placed copy holder	no copy holder
wrist rest	no wrist rest
adjusted chair with lumbar support	non-adjustable chair; no lumbar support
adjustable workstation, adjusted to give 90-degree forearm-upper arm keying angle	same workstation, but adjusted to give typical 45-degree forearm-upper arm keying angle
Line of sight to monitor	
15 degrees below horizontal	30 degrees or more below horizontal

In the optimal workstation, the experimenter adjusted the furniture to each subject so that each one sat upright with feet flat on the floor, legs and upper arms vertical, thighs and forearms horizontal, and wrists straight. In the suboptimal workstation, furniture was adjusted so that the forearm angle was about 45 degrees from horizontal, and the chair was at "standard office chair" height.

The second experiment was designed to show the effects of ergonomic furniture only.

These were the results of both experiments:

1. *Performance*, in terms of the average incentive pay earned by each worker, was 24.7% greater in the optimal (O) workstation than in the suboptimal (S) workstation in the global comparison (Experiment 1). The difference was 17.5% in Experiment 2. In terms of gross keystrokes per minute (uncorrected for errors), workers in the better workstation typed about 4.8% more keystrokes per minute in both experiments.
2. All subjects expressed preference for the optimal workstation. Aside from some difference of opinion about the lighting levels, not a single positive statement was made about the suboptimal workstation, nor was there a single negative comment about the optimal workstation.
3. Levels of discomfort were assessed by questionnaires. The before-after work differences were significantly higher for back pain and shoulder pain in the suboptimal conditions.

The NIOSH studies were an important step in demonstrating, for the first time in a controlled laboratory experiment, the impact of well-designed VDT workstations on both productivity and health complaints. Because these studies took place in a laboratory setting, rather than an office, it was possible to exert close control over experimental conditions. This advantage, however, must be weighed against the fact that, for the subjects, this was a somewhat artificial experience. Although the subjects worked at a realistic-looking task for a reasonable daily work period, some of the working conditions (the alternating between workstations, the detailed monitoring of performance and health status) would not normally be expected in an office setting. Moreover, the furniture was adjusted for the subjects by the experimenters; this is less than realistic.

These concerns do not invalidate the outcome of the study, but rather, would caution the reader against expecting the same numerical outcome if the study was repeated in the field.

Finally, each of these studies demonstrated that a *combination* of ergonomic components produced changes in performance and health complaints. In the first study, the combination, which included both lighting and furniture components, had a greater impact than did the second study, which included only furniture. However, further research is needed to isolate the effects of specific ergonomic components.

Ong's Workplace Intervention

C.N. Ong (1984), working at the Department of Social Medicine and Public Health at the National University of Singapore, conducted a long-term study and workplace intervention at an airline computer center in Singapore. Ong found that 94% of the data entry workers and 77% of the "conversational" (alternating between copy and screen) VDT workers who took part in his study had visual problems, compared to 44% of the conventional office workers. These figures are comparable to studies done in Europe. Musculoskeletal problems, especially in the neck, arms, and hands, were again most prevalent in VDT workers.

Extensive ergonomic interventions included postural changes, addition of footrests and document holders, and changes in illumination, color scheme, work area dimensions, noise and temperature, as well as further liberalization of an already liberal rest break schedule. As a result, musculoskeletal problems dropped dramatically — in most cases to half their former level or less. Visual fatigue dropped by about one-third, but remained higher than for conventional office workers, indicating remaining visual concerns.

Changes in performance were even more dramatic. The average keying speed increased 37%, and the average error rate dropped 93% in the year following the intervention.

While we do not have access to many of the details of Ong's study, and thus cannot evaluate it completely, it is important in that it represents a long-term study on site, and it shows that ergonomic intervention has positive long-term results both in reduction of health complaints and in increased productivity.

Springer's Worksite Surveys and Trials

T.J. Springer (1982), working at a major insurance company in the United States, documented the dissatisfaction resulting from the introduction of VDTs at suboptimal workstations, and demonstrated that, using a short-term test, the adjustability of the workstation can result in performance gains of 10% to 15%, depending on the task.

Springer conducted surveys of 980 workers, three months before and after the introduction of VDTs, which were placed on standard (nonadjustable) office furniture. Three months after the VDTs were in place, the questionnaires revealed a "marked increase in dissatisfaction." The major complaint was glare; the majority of VDT workers also complained of physical discomfort in the back and neck.

At that point, Springer brought in four new workstations, two of different brands which were easily adjustable, a third, which was less adjustable than the others, and a fourth, which was new but non-adjustable. A group of 110 employees then compared these with the old, standard office set-up (which was used as a control, or comparison), using tests lasting less than an hour. The workers adjusted the adjustable workstations to their own satisfaction prior to beginning the experiment.

The results showed that when performance was statistically corrected for past experience and other factors, the data entry task was performed 15% faster in the adjustable workstations than in the standard office workstations. The fairly adjustable workstation gave intermediate results (but significantly better than the control), and the new, non-adjustable workstation was the same as the old control furniture. This last observation makes it unlikely that employees were responding only to the newness of the furniture.

The Springer studies are excellent examples of well-controlled surveys and worksite trials. The only limitations are the short time of the task (one hour) and the fact that the employees were not instructed as to optimal working postures.

All of the preceding studies provide a basis for asserting that ergonomic design can lead to a significant improvement in productivity. The exact extent of this improvement must depend on a whole host of interacting factors, including how bad things were and how good the ergonomic intervention makes them, and the way in which ergonomic innovations are introduced to the employees.

Brill/BOSTI: The Financial Benefits of Ergonomic Improvements

Estimating a dollar value for the impact of environmental design innovations has been attempted by Michael Brill (1984) and his colleagues at BOSTI (Buffalo Organization for Social and Technological Innovation). Their approach consisted of asking detailed questions before and after some sort of architectural or design intervention occurred in an office. This work is innovative in that it attempts to tie such changes directly to productivity through what Brill calls his "bottom line productivity measures."

For Brill, productivity has two components: *job satisfaction* and *performance*. Human resource accounting techniques made it possible for Brill to make direct dollar estimates of organizational costs and benefits of specific changes in each of these components. Job satisfaction has a direct impact on the costs of turnover and absenteeism, both of which have real and measurable costs. Performance, interestingly, is harder to quantify, but by using statistical techniques, Brill was able to approximate the dollar value to the organization of a given standard increment on a performance rating scale.

Brill's key data was drawn from extensive questionnaire responses from managers, professional/technical workers, and clerical workers, obtained before and after either a move to new facilities or a renovation of existing facilities. Other data was collected on a one-time cross-sectional basis. The questionnaire items included relatively objective details about the workers themselves, their workspaces, and their jobs.

Analysis of the questionnaires for one particular occupational group (professional/technical) showed that *if perceived comfort of chairs/ workstations dropped* as a result of a change to a new environment, this drop was associated with a corresponding drop in job satisfaction. The financial impact of such a drop was estimated to be $701 per employee measured against an annual salary of $31,600. (It is a pure but interesting coincidence that this figure of $701 is close to the current list price of some excellent ergonomic chairs.)

For this same professional/technical group, the major effect of losing *some privacy* as a result of a change, was on job performance, and the dollar value was $1,954 per employee! (Enclosure and privacy will be discussed in Chapter 6.)

Finally, the BOSTI study made use of an interesting exercise to estimate the total benefit of moving the same $31,600 employee from a "bullpen" (desks in the open, no enclosure) to a "systems workstation" (co-ordinated desks, chairs, and privacy panels). It was calculated that the entire cost of the move ($3,500) would be paid back in 16 months through increased productivity, and that, after 5 years, the total return on investment for *one* workstation would be $7,836.

The BOSTI work is interesting and important and it will be discussed in more detail in Chapter 6. However, it has not gone without criticism, largely on the basis that a lengthy user-oriented summary has been published, but not a detailed technical report. These criticisms are summarized in Appendix I.

Two comments are nevertheless appropriate here. First, even if the obtained financial benefits are inaccurate by as much as 50%, the workstation would still be a good investment. Second, at the time that these investigations were being conducted (1979-81), ergonomic furniture as sophisticated as that which we now have was *not* widely available, even at newly constructed sites. Therefore, the positive financial benefits described by Brill and BOSTI may well *underestimate* the potential which could be realized today.

Ergonomic Improvements: The Overall Benefits

In this chapter, the discussion has progressed from the effects of ergonomics on people and productivity, to theoretical concepts, to experiments, to dollars. The evidence presented supports Dutch ergonomist van Wely's (1970) description of ergonomics as "a kind of eternal triangle, among *efficiency, comfort* and *health*."

The evidence is consistent with the conceptual framework in predicting that a tired, stressed, uncomfortable, distracted worker will not be able to get much work done, whereas a more comfortable, healthy worker should be more efficient. It would therefore be reasonable to hypothesize the following long-term results of ergonomic improvements:

- Decreased absenteeism would be a logical expectation because of increased worker satisfaction and fewer health problems. This has been documented with *factory workers* in Norway following ergonomic intervention (Westgaard and Aaras, 1980).
- Decreased turnover due to increased job satisfaction.
- Decreased health costs.
- Better quality of working life.

Each of these outcomes can be viewed as contributing directly to productivity. Productivity can be defined as the ratio of income to cost; thus, by decreasing operating and production costs, the outcomes above will increase overall productivity.

But we have stated that office ergonomics is still in its infancy. Can today's manager afford to wait until all the definitive experiments have been conducted and the ideal ergonomic work environment has been designed in complete detail?

If people were to wait for the ideal computer before purchasing, they would wait for years, as new models with larger memories and faster processing times came into production. If people disdained software until the friendliest, most versatile programs were written, they would also wait for years, because better programs will continue to be available as long as people keep striving and inventing. Similarly, it makes little sense to wait for all the ergonomic data to be gathered before implementing reasonable improvements.

Enough is known *now* to make effective and cost-justifiable ergonomic interventions. The subsequent chapters in this book deal with the current ergonomic issues in the electronic office. These discussions of seating, workstation design, visual perception, software, and quality of working life will be supplemented by suggestions as to how state-of-the-art ergonomic interventions can best be implemented.

Seating: The Spine, the Discs, the Aching Back

CHAPTER 3

Prominently attached to the top of every office chair should be a cardboard tag that says, CAUTION: PROLONGED SITTING MAY BE HAZARDOUS TO YOUR HEALTH. Although the act of sitting is so ordinary that people do not usually even think about it, prolonged sitting is an unwritten requirement in the job description of nearly every office worker.

There is increasing evidence that sitting in a fixed position for long periods of time is responsible for back pain and musculoskeletal problems. Back pain is a frequent complaint of a large and growing segment of the population; estimates are that up to 60% of the adult population suffer from back ailments. Back pain also ranks high on the list of sources of lost work time; a Swedish study (Kilbom, 1983) found that over half of all reported cases of occupational disease related to muscle and back problems.

In the electronic office, more and more information processing and handling functions are being accomplished by people like Elizabeth and Susan sitting at computer terminals for ever-increasing periods of time. Thus, back ache, which already causes a large drain on productivity, threatens to cause an even greater drain. Given estimates that one-half of the entire workforce will be using VDTs by 1990, there is the potential that back pain may become the single largest cause of job-related disability.

The act of sitting, along with the design of the things (chairs, worksurfaces) used to support this act, are not trivial concerns, but, in fact, are at the very focal point of office ergonomics.

Consequently, it is important that the manager be concerned with the technicalities of seating in order to be able to communicate intelligently with vendors, designers, and other experts who are attempting to sell their goods and services. Up-to-date furniture dealers, interior designers, facilities managers, and architects are talking in terms as detailed as those which will be presented in this book. If yours are not presenting such detailed information, it will pay you to be wary.

Seated Posture: Stability vs. Motion

An interesting and important study was conducted by the British ergonomist Branton (1976). He took time-lapse motion pictures of passengers on a long railroad trip. What he observed was a clear pattern: every twenty minutes or so, the chair, in his words, ". . . slowly and repeatedly ejected the sitter." What happened, of course, was that the passenger would start off in an upright position but would gradually slide closer and closer to the edge of the seat. Just before going over the edge he would push himself back up into an upright position, but then the process would start all over again.

This happens because sitting basically puts people in an unstable orientation. If the seated body were stable, people would not collapse when they lose consciousness or faint. Continuous muscle activity is necessary to counter the force of gravity and thus to maintain an upright posture.

Sitting involves a set of fairly complex actions. For one thing, the basic bone structure, the pelvis, is shaped like a pair of inverted pyramids with the points (called the ischial tuberosities, or seat bones) pointed downward. The entire weight of the upper body is thus balanced on these two small bones (see Figure 3-1). This leads to an inherent instability, as would become quite evident if you were to sit on the edge of a high, hard, flat surface (such as a desk or a doctor's examining table) with your feet dangling and without the support of your hands. This posture cannot be maintained for a long time, and to arrest the tendency to rock back and forth, you must use your hands to brace yourself.

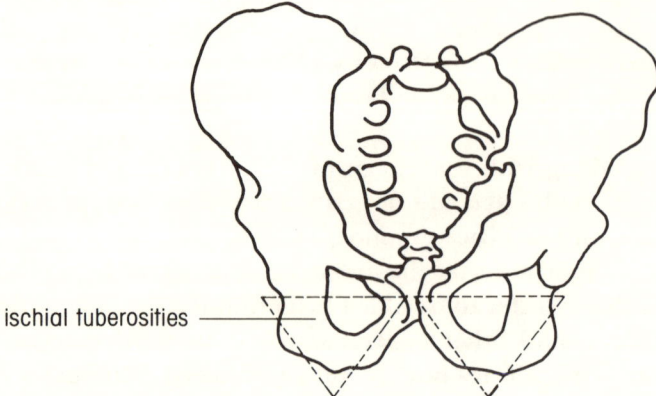

Figure 3-1.
The pelvis. Sitting on the seat bones (ischial tuberosities) is like sitting on two inverted pyramids.

The finer the muscular coordination required, the greater the need for the chair to confer stability. A microsurgeon doing corneal transplants or other tasks requiring extremely fine motor control must have a chair that provides absolute stability, particularly with regard to the arms and hands. Such chairs are massive, finely adjustable machines, sometimes with microscopes attached. Microsurgery is an extreme example, but it dramatizes the need for stability when work requiring fine muscle coordination is being performed.

Working at a VDT is another such task. It requires that a person measuring usually 152 to 183 cm (5 to 6 feet) tall and weighing from about 45 to 90 kg (100 to 200 pounds) must rapidly and accurately press, in precise sequence and usually without looking, one of a series of 100 or more different locations, or various combinations of them, in an area roughly 51 cm (20 inches) wide and 23 cm (9 inches) deep — that is, the keyboard. The eyes are usually fixed on one of two locales, the display screen or the paper copy. Thus the search for stability of the worker's relatively massive frame is paramount, and trying to balance on two inverted pyramids will not do the job.

The first requirement of ergonomic office seating is therefore to confer stability. Support for the buttocks must be provided by the chair's seat (seatpan), the back must be supported against the chair's backrest, the legs must be supported by the floor or a footrest, and the arms and wrists/palms must be anchored.

At the same time, allowance must be made for the continuous muscular action that is necessary to maintain body stability as a person sits on the ischial tuberosities. These muscles work to support the skeleton, and to do this they must have energy. This energy is derived from the chemical metabolism of food or fat stored in the body. If this metabolism takes place in the presence of enough blood-borne oxygen, the end products are carbon dioxide and water. If the blood provides too little oxygen, the end product of metabolism is lactic acid, and lactic acid plays a primary role in the experience of muscle fatigue: when muscles feel tired and sore, it is because of lactic acid buildup.

Under normal conditions, the blood supply to the muscles is adequate to remove the lactic acid and convert it to carbon dioxide and water. Suppose, for example, that you decided to walk to work one morning. It is a beautiful spring day and still quite early, so you stroll at a leisurely pace. The work done by the muscles in moving your body uses up energy, but at a relatively slow rate, and there is sufficient blood flow to keep lactic acid from accumulating. Consequently, if you are in any kind of reasonable physical condition, you can keep walking for a relatively long period of time. Your heart pumps the blood to the muscles at a steady rate, and the blood delivers the oxygen to the muscle tissues. The action of the muscles forces the oxygen-depleted blood back through the veins to the heart, and thence to the lungs for more oxygen.

If, however, you look at your watch and discover that you are about to be late for an appointment at the office, you speed up your walking rate. The increased activity places increased demand on the muscles, but this is offset by an increase in heart rate and breathing rate, resulting in increased blood flow, thus allowing continued removal of lactic acid. This is called *dynamic work*.

On the other hand, if you are seated at a word processor, there is still plenty of muscle activity going on, since the back, leg, and trunk muscles work cooperatively to keep you upright, while your arm and finger muscles operate the keyboard. However, under these *static workload* conditions, the lack of gross body movement keeps the flow of blood at a relatively low level, with the result that lactic acid begins to accumulate. This accumulation is perceived as muscle fatigue or pain, and, if it continues, the affected muscles will eventually cease to function. (Of course, the same thing will eventually happen in dynamic work if you are unable to take in enough oxygen to allow for the removal of the lactic acid being built up by intense muscular activity.)

One of the practical consequences of this biochemistry is that there are limits to how long an individual can hold a fixed body posture. You have doubtless shifted in your seat since the beginning of this chapter, to perform the simple task of reading this book, and you will continue to do so. Even in sleep, the body naturally twists and turns as one part or another becomes fatigued.

The problems of static workload are not trivial. The director of the Swedish Work Environment Laboratory conducted a major survey of Swedish industry in order to determine the most troublesome working conditions from the perspectives of both management and labor (Magnus, 1970). Number 1 on the list was "taxing static muscular workload."

The need to alleviate the stress of static muscular workload and the need for stability are two separate (and sometimes conflicting) seating requirements. The mass of the body must be supported so as to achieve optimum stability while keeping the hands and eyes in proper working orientation. At the same time, there must be opportunities to change position so that adequate blood flow to and from major muscle groups can be maintained.

The popliteal area (behind the knee) is particularly vulnerable to blood circulation problems. In this area are two major veins through which blood is returned to the heart against the force of gravity. In sitting, the weight of the body acts to compress these veins, further slowing down the blood flow. Lactic acid accumulates in the muscles. If pressure on these veins is maintained long enough, the foot and leg "go to sleep"; this is a symptom of too little blood flow (ischemia). Eventually, the veins swell and become inflamed. Because of the mechanics of seated posture, this compression cannot be avoided. However, proper chair design can minimize the effect. If, for example, the front edge of the chair seatpan is gently rounded downward so that it does not reach the back of the knees (a "waterfall" seatpan contour), there will be less underthigh pressure than there would be from a standard cushion with a hard 90 degree corner.

The Spine

The spine consists of a series of small bones called vertebrae. The vertebrae are separated by spinal discs, which are flexible membranes filled with fluid that act as a sort of hydraulic cushion. The whole system is held together by ligaments. Thus, each pair of vertebrae acts as a joint, and the entire spine provides the flexible support which allows the body to bend.

The parts of the spine, labeled from top to bottom, are the cervical (neck area), thoracic (chest area), lumbar (lower back area), and sacral (pelvic area). In a standing posture, the center of gravity of the upper body is located directly over the lumbar portion of the curve, and the whole system is in equilibrium. The forward bend in the curve at this point is called the *lumbar lordosis* (see Figure 3-2). Lumbar lordosis is one of the most important factors to be considered in ergonomic seating.

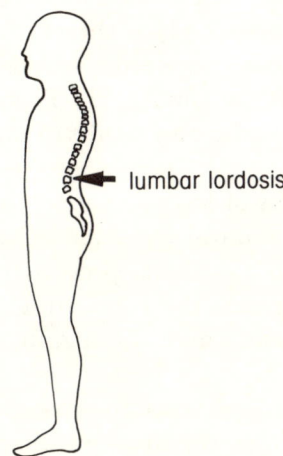

Figure 3-2.
The natural position of the spine during standing.

In moving from a standing to an unsupported seated position, the top of the pelvis, which is normally angled somewhat forward from the vertical, rotates backward. Consequently, the lumbar lordosis begins to disappear, while the curvature of the spine becomes flat or even reverses (kyphosis). This change in the spinal curve is of central importance in ergonomic seating; it can perhaps be best understood through a simple exercise.

First, stand up and stretch your hands as far as you can toward the ceiling, while taking a deep breath. Give a good, satisfying stretch, breathe naturally, keep your shoulders back, and slowly bring your hands backward and down to your sides, and continue standing up straight. Now think about your backbone and how it feels. Hold that posture, and take one of your hands and put it behind your lower back, and trace with that hand the inward curve of your spine just below your waistline, at the small of your back. This forward curve is lordosis. (It is more pronounced in some people than in others.)

Now very carefully maintain that curve as you sit down in a chair. You will still feel as if you are sitting up very straight. Take your hand and make sure that the lordotic curve is still there. Try to keep in your mind how your backbone feels when you sit that way.

Concentrate on how your backbone feels at the small of your back as you now relax and sit the way you would if you were typing or reading papers for a long time at your desk. You will probably feel your spine shift into a different position. Check it with your hand. Usually, as people sit in a regular chair, the spine shifts as they sit down. This new shape of the spine is called kyphosis.

The shift from lordosis to kyphosis has several important implications. First of all, the center of gravity is no longer over the lumbar spine but in front of it. The upper body is therefore no longer in equilibrium. Instead, it tends to rotate forward, and this tendency must be opposed by the large muscles of the lower back. This eventually causes fatigue of the lower back muscles, and also results in increased pressure on the lumbar discs.

Secondly, the loss of lordosis causes the angles between adjacent forward surfaces of vertebral segments to become narrower (see figures 3-3 and 3-4). This puts additional pressure on the flexible discs, displacing them backward against the supporting ligament. Chronic excess pressure on the discs can cause damage to these vital structures. Because discs have no pain fibers, a person does not feel pain in the discs until a disc ruptures. The ligaments do, however, contain pain fibers, and increased pressure from the discs pressing on the ligaments is one likely cause of lower back pain.

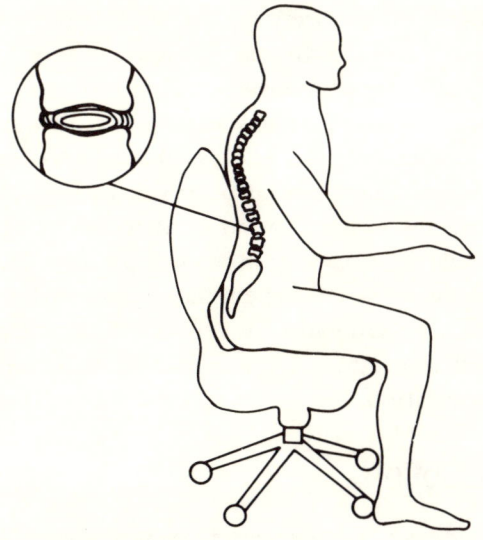

Figure 3-3.
Lumbar lordosis. Insert shows minimal stress imposed by the vertebrae on the spinal discs.

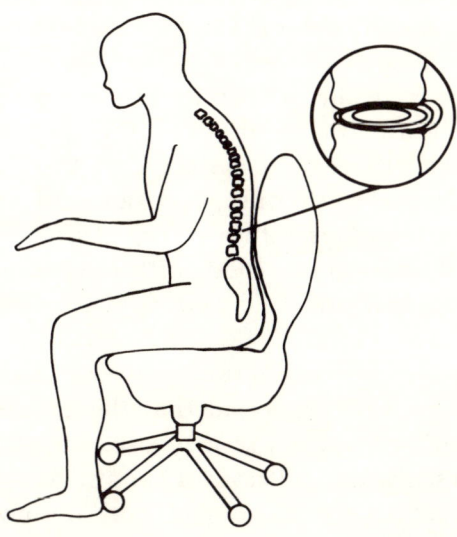

Figure 3-4.
Kyphosis associated with bending forward. Insert shows the resulting pressure imposed by the vertebrae on the spinal discs.

Nachemson and his colleagues in Sweden (1975) have measured disc pressures directly by the insertion of small needles into the spine. These studies indicate that lumbar disc pressure while bending forward in an unsupported seated posture is almost as high as the pressure produced by lifting a 10 kg (22 lb.) weight while bending forward from the waist in a standing position. It has long been known that lifting while bending from the waist is a sure route to back problems. Nachemson's experiments show that an incorrect seated posture can be almost as bad.

If people were always to stand or sit so as to keep disc pressure at its minimum, they would have to stay in a fixed posture. However, there is some evidence that the spine, like the muscles, can suffer from too much stability: the discs may need some movement to meet their own metabolic needs, in much the same way that muscle movement is needed to maintain blood circulation.

Three Postural Options

Given the above evidence, most experts tend to agree that a major goal of ergonomic chair design is somehow to restore lumbar lordosis, and thereby reduce the pressure on lumbar discs. There is disagreement, however, as to how this goal might best be achieved.

A standard solution calls for a backrest which supports the lumbar region by means of a contour or bulge. Sitting against the backrest then tends to promote lumbar lordosis. Chairs with backrests which are vertically adjustable will obviously be able to accommodate varying heights of the lumbar area from the seatpan in different people.

However, this posture also requires that the operator sit straight upright. Unfortunately, it seems to be the case that, given the choice, many people don't like to sit upright. Grandjean and his colleagues (1983) provided VDT workers with a choice of upright posture and an adjustable back tilt mechanism (both with lumbar support), and discovered that the majority preferred to work in a backward inclined posture (see Figure 3-5).

There are benefits to working in this backward tilted posture. Andersson and his colleagues (1979) found that this posture decreased disc pressure as the backrest angle was increased from 80 to 100 degrees, using a horizontal seatpan in all cases. They also found that this shift of backrest angle decreases the amount of work the lower back muscles have to do, as measured by the electrical impulses traveling through the muscles (electromyographic activity). What seems to happen is that the backward tilt allows the surface of the backrest to support more of the total body weight, thereby relieving pressure on the spinal discs and muscles; at the same time, the lumbar support moves the spine toward its natural lordosis.

However, it is important to understand this finding in the context of the VDT workstation as a total system — particularly with regard to the ergonomic requirements for arm and hand orientation and the way they interact with sitting requirements. The traditional recommendation for minimizing muscle strain in upright posture while operating a keyboard has been that the forearm and wrists should be parallel to the floor, and that the elbow should be located at the level of the home row of the keyboard. However, others have argued that an upward inclination of the forearm of 15 to 20 degrees above the horizontal is actually preferable. The issue is still controversial and evidence exists to support both arguments. (This will be discussed further in Chapter 4.)

If an operator is seated in an upright posture with the upper arm vertical and the forearm horizontal and then tilts the backrest backwards, the elbow angle opens up and the forearm is angled at greater than 90 degrees with respect to the torso. This angle is not desirable for keying tasks.

This opening up of the elbow angle did *not* occur in Grandjean's study, because he also provided adjustable split-level VDT desks. When the operator sat with a 104 degree backward tilt of the torso, his forearms were angled upward 13 degrees from the horizontal because he was able to raise the keyboard support surface. In addition, a triangular-shaped wrist/palm support was located in front of the keyboard in order to maintain a flat wrist angle.

Therefore, the benefits of the backward tilt depend on other elements of the workstation, particularly the presence of adjustable worksurfaces. In addition, the backrest must be large enough to support the upper body.

However, backward tilt may involve an appreciable distancing of the head from the screen, amounting, for example, to 17 cm (6.7 inches) for a woman of average height (based on a viewing angle of 15 degrees). If the task requires reading from paper copy, the copy must still be easily read while the operator is leaning backward. Whether this can be accomplished depends on the size of the letters, the operator's visual abilities and/or corrective lenses, location of copy, and mobility of the screen, among other things.

An alternative seating posture has been proposed by Mandal (1981 and 1985). His focus is on the seatpan. He argues that, if the seatpan is tilted forward, the pelvis will rotate forward (more than in upright sitting with lumbar support) and that lordosis will be restored, thereby easing pressure on the discs. At the same time, pressure across the buttocks is equalized and circulation is improved in the thighs and lower legs. An additional advantage is that the upper torso, in response to slight forward tilting of the seatpan, can remain vertical, moving very little if at all. Thus, the hands and arms are still in optimal orientation with the keyboard, while the paper copy and screen are still within clear viewing distance. (Figure 3-6 shows the forward tilt position.)

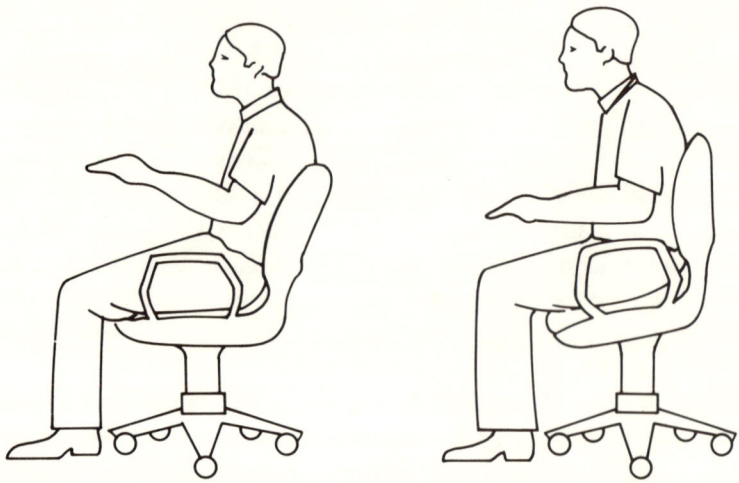

Figure 3-5. (left)
Backward tilt position recommended by Grandjean. The weight of the upper body is largely on the backrest, with its lumbar support.

Figure 3-6. (right)
Forward seatpan tilt recommended by Mandal. By tilting the pelvis forward, lumbar lordosis is restored.

Measurements from several laboratories have confirmed that increased lordosis is associated with forward seatpan tilt. Forward seatpan tilt also has the advantage of relieving disc pressure. However, there is a tendency, depending on tilt angle and texture of seatpan surface, for the operator to slide out of the chair. This tendency can be counteracted by the action of the lower legs, and aided by proper chair upholstery. Research suggests that most people who use forward tilt prefer approximately a 5 degree angle below the horizontal.

It is important here to differentiate between seatpan tilt and backrest tilt, and to determine whether or not one always entails the other (this is something the experts do not always make clear). Experts recommend against ever having a trunk-thigh angle of less than 90 degrees because of the possibility of compression of the internal organs. But they disagree on whether the forward tilt angle of the backrest should be equal to that of the seatpan.

The controversy over the "ideal" configuration of backrest, lumbar support, and seatpan tilt — that is, the multiplicity of theoretical solutions to the problem of lower back pain — brings up two points of prime importance. The first is that *a chair cannot be considered outside the context of the function for which it is intended* — in this case, outside the context of the total VDT workstation and task. The final posture of the worker must enable him or her to carry out all aspects of the task in an ergonomically reasonable way.

The second point is that *even the "simple" requirement of sitting involves many variables* (such as seatpan tilt) *and many givens* (such as the measurements of the human being doing the task, the necessity of keying, etc.), some of which are at odds with others. For instance, what is good for doing the task (stability) may be bad for the muscles (static workload).

There are clear advantages and disadvantages to all three postural options (upright, backward tilted backrest, and forward tilted seatpan). The most reasonable recommendation, given the present state of the art, is to obtain a chair which is adjustable to some degree of forward *or* backward tilt, including the upright position. Thus, the chair might be locked into forward tilt while the worker is keying in material from paper copy, into backward tilt while editing or writing, or into the upright position as a compromise allowing both lumbar support and proper orientation of hands and eyes, or as respite from either of the other positions should they become tiring. This flexibility has the advantage of reducing muscle fatigue, because the worker is spending much less time in any one fixed position.

If flexibility is an important factor in the seating of one person, it is even more significant when one is faced with seating and putting to work a whole office full of people. The next section deals with some of the variables that affect seating for large groups of employees.

Anthropometry: The Measurement of Human Beings

If you think of the tallest person at your place of business — and the shortest and the fattest and the thinnest — you will begin to be aware of the variability of your personnel. The people you have just brought to mind may not even have the most extreme measurements of all the employees who will ever walk through your doors. Trying to think of a chair that would fit all of them ideally will give you some perspective on the issue.

Anthropometry is the measurement of the physical dimensions of human beings which are relevant for designing things people use and wear. Anthropometry documents the range of variability of human size (static anthropometry) and range of motion (dynamic anthropometry), as well as the sometimes considerable variation within and between sexes, ages, and ethnic groups.

There are two widely used sources of anthropometric measurements. One of these is *Humanscale* (Diffrient et al., 1981) which is organized primarily for use by architects and designers. A second, the NASA (United States National Aeronautics and Space Administration) *Anthropometric Source Book*, Volume II (Webb Associates, 1978) is actually a compendium of anthropometric surveys of a large variety of ethnic and racial populations from around the world. Many of these are from military populations. A summary of selected measurements of a North American civilian population has been included in Appendix II.

However, these anthropometric data bases present some problems. The most complete civilian studies of the population of the United States are representative of the adult population *between the years 1958 and 1962*. To apply these figures to present-day United States or North American populations, one would need to ignore the changes in the ethnic (and therefore anthropometric) mix of the population and the workforce which have taken place in the last quarter-century. It might be easier if people were all proportioned in the same way, but they are not: some ethnic groups and individuals tend to have longer limbs, others have longer trunks. In fact, people vary so widely that finding a person who is "average" in all dimensions is a nearly impossible task. Thus, if a chair is built for an average woman, using all average measures for females, any one woman who tries to use it may be significantly different in lower leg length, knee-buttock distance, hip width, height to the lumbar area, trunk length, or any other specific measurement.

The data upon which these averages are based is also old. In countries where nutrition is good, the mean heights and weights of populations are increasing over time. For instance, over a 25-year period, the mean weights of United States Air Force flying personnel increased by 20 pounds, while the mean heights increased 2 cm (¾ inch.) Thus, even without changes in the anthropometric mix of the population, there would still be problems in generalizing from data this old.

The information gleaned from the data bases is thus more problematic than it would seem at first glance. Yet the architect or furniture manufacturer has to start somewhere, and there is a limited number of data bases from which to choose.

The purchaser of ergonomic equipment must therefore bear in mind that the furniture he or she buys for a certain group of office workers was manufactured on the basis of certain anthropometric assumptions which may or may not coincide with the anthropometric variations within his or her specific office. In particular, the data bases in use in North America, simply because of the data which happens to be available — most of it decades old — underrepresents people of shorter stature, such as Asians and Hispanics, and probably other ethnic groups as well. Designer Walter Kleeman (1981) calls these people "the anthropometrically disadvantaged."

Furthermore, many differences in ergonomic recommendations, guidelines, and standards stem from differing *interpretations* of anthropometric measurements. One important example is the decision as to the range of adjustability of the seatpan height. The primary determinant of seatpan height should be *popliteal height*, that is, the height above the floor of the crease behind the knees when the bare feet are flat on the floor and the knee is bent so the thigh and leg are at right angles. Anthropometric tables give values for this dimension, as well as its range of variability. Although it may be too difficult to make a chair fit everyone, one can attempt to fit all but some small percentage of the population. Common decisions are to accommodate all except the smallest 5% of the women and the largest 5% of the men — technically, the 5th percentile woman and the 95th percentile man (see Table 3-1). Some people choose to try to fit all but the first percentile woman and the 99th percentile man.

Table 3-1 U.S. Civilian Body Dimensions, Female/Male, for Ages 20-60 Years

	Percentiles		
	5th	50th	95th
Height in			
inches	58.9/ 63.7	63.2/ 68.3	67.4/ 72.6
centimeters	149.5/161.8	160.5/173.6	171.3/184.4
Popliteal height in			
inches	14.0/ 15.4	15.7/ 17.4	17.4/ 19.2
centimeters	35.5/ 39.2	39.8/ 44.2	44.3/ 48.8

SOURCE: Data extracted from Kroemer & Price (1982). (See also Appendix II.)

Table 3-1 gives the popliteal height of the 5th percentile woman as 35.5 cm (14 inches). Adding 2 cm (3/4 inch) for shoes brings this to 37.5 cm (14.8 inches). This is generally rounded up to 38 cm (15 inches). The same calculation for the 95th percentile male would lead to an upper range of seatpan height of approximately 50.8 cm, or 20 inches.

Therefore, for a North American population, it could be concluded that the seatpan must be adjustable in a range of 37.5 to 50.8 cm, or 15 to 20 inches. But even this degree of adjustability may not suffice: some people recommend that seatpans be adjustable down to 32 cm (12.6 inches), which is approximately the popliteal height of a 5th percentile Asian woman.

Incorporating a range of adjustability from 37.5 to 50.8 cm (15 to 20 inches) in a single chair is technically very difficult in terms of chair manufacture. One solution is to produce one size of chair that accommodates medium to tall people and another that accommodates medium to short people.

Similarly, experts call for different depths of the seatpan. They do agree that the front edge should not wedge up against the leg in the popliteal area. Recommendations range from 33 to 43 cm (13 to 17 inches) deep. It has also been pointed out that seatpan depth should favor shorter people because if chair height adjustment is satisfactory, a few unsupported inches of thigh on a tall person will not be harmful.

There is not even agreement about the precise dimensions of seatpan width. A chair that is too narrow won't accommodate larger people, but if it is too wide, its controls may be harder to reach, it may be too heavy, and even with casters it may not be easily movable by smaller people. Recommendations range from 41 to 48 cm (16 to 19 inches).

Beyond Anthropometry

There are several issues which the anthropometric tables, as generally used in office ergonomics, do not cover.

In the year 1986, flat shoes for women are fashionable, so the 2 cm (3/4 inch) height for shoes added to popliteal height (in the determination of minimum seatpan height) may be a reality for many. However, at different times and in different societies, heel heights, at least for women, may vary by 7.6 cm (3 inches) or more. (This is more than half the span of popliteal heights between a 5th percentile woman and a 95th percentile man.) In addition, as high heels and platform shoes go in and out of style, the crucial dimension, popliteal height plus heel height (or augmented popliteal height), may vary widely on a daily basis. Wearing shoes with high heels can be a real problem for tall women, because it results in their popliteal heights being nearer or above the range for tall men. However, for short women, this can be the nub of a creative solution, because wearing higher heels brings their augmented popliteal height more toward the middle of the range of popliteal heights.

As any manufacturer of denim jeans will testify, there is more to a seated human posterior than is accounted for by seatpan width and depth. These variations in a person's "padding" can change the orientation of the body in the chair. If there is a large, fleshy (either fat or muscle) deposit immediately *below* the pelvis and beneath the ischial tuberosities when the person is in the seated position, accompanied by less fleshiness near the popliteal area, then the orientation of the thigh bone (femur) on a flat seatpan more nearly resembles that of a person in a forward tilted position. Someone with this body build may find a forward tilted seatpan too much, and might even be more comfortable with a backward tilted seatpan, which would bring him or her into an "upright" position in terms of skeletal structure (i.e., the femur would be horizontal).

People who are particularly fleshy *behind* the pelvis have yet another orientation. In certain chairs, the relationship between the chair back/lumbar support and the spinal column may be altered; if there is no room for that person's padding in the chair, leaning against the backrest may even impose a kyphosis. Conversely, people who are extremely thin in this area may find a normal lumbar support too extreme.

Other idiosyncrasies in seated posture, and particularly working (keying) posture, will be influenced by individual variations in both weight and physical fitness of various body parts. It is easier for you to hold this book in one hand close to your body than to hold it at arm's length for a long period of time, because the farther any weight is from its center of gravity, or pivot point, the more muscle power will be required to support it. Thus, heavy arms will be harder to hold outstretched for keying than lighter arms, and they will cause a shift in the center of gravity when held in a keying position, causing a greater stress at the neck and shoulders. Similarly, a woman with large breasts, because of the distribution of weight on her upper body, may well respond differently to various seating postures. The strength and fitness of each person's musculature in counterbalancing these forces will have important effects on the way in which he or she sits.

In research into office ergonomics, these and other individual differences have been largely ignored. However, these differences can help explain why there is variety in personal preference for chairs, as well as why some people might find certain departures from theoretically ideal seated postures more comfortable.

These factors, and perhaps others, may account for the fact that people don't always do what theory says they are supposed to do. There are studies which show that, given adjustable furniture, the positions to which people adjust them vary from what would be predicted. The question of why such deviations occur has at least two reasonable explanations. First, the theories are incomplete. People, at some level of consciousness, "know" what is most comfortable for their own bodies. Second, people are generally unaware of the stressful aspects of prolonged seating in a fixed posture; they rarely know what the "optimal" adjustments are, or the rationale for them. Yet another factor to be kept in mind is that anthropometric recommendations are based on static (fixed) postures, whereas sitting is a task-dependent act which continues and changes over time.

Anthropometric data are not all-inclusive; actual behavior is subject to individual variability because of details of body build, habit, personal preference, and training. Indeed, *physiological* recommendations are sometimes at odds with each other. Postures that are best for maintaining spinal lordosis may not be the most comfortable if they fail to take into account static workload and blood supply requirements. A dynamic equilibrium must be maintained between what is good for one body system and what is good for another, without losing sight of the requirements of the task. The ergonomist must be simultaneously aware of both theory and actual observed sitting behavior, interpreting and correcting each in the light of the other.

Does the Theory Work?

All the material presented so far provides a conceptual framework for seating. Most of these principles originally come from basic science: anatomy, physiology, and biomechanics (the application of the laws of mechanics, physics, and engineering to biological systems). But ergonomics is an *applied science* which leads to theories about different workplace designs (for the purposes of this chapter, chair designs). Looking in the marketplace for ergonomic chairs, one sees the results of a lot of different responses to these basic theories, modified, of course, by both engineering and economic considerations.

Some interpretations of ergonomic theory are better than others. Some are more adaptable to certain types of body builds than others. Some are more adaptable to certain tasks. The interpretations by designers and manufacturers of chairs vary widely. One variation is the chair which moves *dynamically* as the person moves (as opposed to a chair which adjusts to a number of different *static* positions). A potential advantage is freedom of movement, which promotes blood circulation; such a chair may be particularly effective if the job requires a lot of movement. This design concept assumes, however, that the designer can make a single chair which is properly responsive both to heavy, strong people and to relatively light, weak people. For the former, the chair might not give sufficient stability, while the latter might experience stiffness of movement of the chair. The efficacy of these chairs has not been documented; a viable alternative is the chair which allows both static adjustments and dynamic motion.

Other design solutions lock the person into one, fixed, so-called ideal posture. This may solve the stability and lordosis problems, but it ignores the need for movement and flexibility, both in terms of the need for muscle movement to enhance blood flow, and in terms of the different postures required by different task demands.

Many chair designers and manufacturers have thus marketed chairs based on their interpretations of anatomical/biomechanical analyses. Obviously, some of the resulting designs will be better than others. However, prior to making detailed comparisons *among* different ergonomic chair designs, a more basic, crucial question needs to be asked: are ergonomic chairs, *in general*, better than the office chair that's been around for fifty years? It would be a good idea to find that out before several (dozen or thousand) have been purchased.

The answer is found by *testing*: someone is needed to observe real people doing real tasks in ergonomic chairs, to see whether they work, and whether people will use them. The bottom line is validation through analysis of behavior in terms of work performance, gross changes in body movement over time, and subjective reports of comfort/discomfort. Thus, the applied psychologist, who specializes in such behavioral analyses, enters the ergonomic picture.

Chair, Posture, and Sitting Habits: How They Relate to Discomfort Complaints and Performance

Several experiments which support the case for the effectiveness of good ergonomic chairs have appeared in the scientific literature. Two studies were done as extensions of the Dainoff NIOSH studies described in Chapter 2. In the first (Mark, Vogele, & Dainoff, 1985), analysis of videotapes of VDT operators working in the NIOSH optimal and suboptimal workstation conditions clearly showed more shifting of posture, or fidgeting, in the suboptimal workstation. This observation tentatively ties fidgeting to lower performance and increased discomfort complaints. (In the study, fidgeting is interpreted as searching for a more comfortable posture.)

In a companion study (Pustinger, Dainoff, & Smith, 1985) the two workstations were made identical except that in one workstation the operators were instructed as to how to adjust the chair and the workstation surfaces. In the other, the same furniture was used, but it was pre-adjusted to simulate standard office conditions, and operators were instructed not to change the adjustments. The operators did text editing work for one workday in each of the two workstation conditions. The results showed that those operators who fidgeted less performed better in terms of keystrokes per minute. Operators in the fixed condition fidgeted about 10% more than those in the adjustable condition, and also had 23% more discomfort complaints.

In a study conducted at the University of Buffalo (Bhatnager et al., 1985), subjects worked for three hours with rest breaks at a demanding (non-VDT) inspection task. The subjects were in a head-up position viewing a slide projector screen while sitting in an adjustable chair with a level seatpan. The researchers observed a general movement forward of the trunk angle as time went by; at the same time, the error rate increased drastically, as did the complaints of lower back pain — which makes sense, in terms of disc compression. Fidgeting also increased over the course of the experiment. Again, a relationship can be seen between discomfort complaints, poor posture, fidgeting, and decreased performance.

A field study conducted in an Italian telephone company (Cantoni et al., 1984) chronicled the changes in posture which occurred when employees switched from a traditional plug-type switchboard to an ergonomically designed VDT-based switchboard. In the traditional workstation, observed postures were poor (spines were often in kyphosis) and fidgeting was frequent. At the new workstation (with adjustable seat height, backrest, and VDT orientation), postures were dramatically improved, and fidgeting decreased. The investigators found that the calculated biomechanical load on the spine dropped by more than one-third after switching to the ergonomic workstation.

> **These findings clearly indicate that better ergonomic conditions are associated with a pattern of favorable outcomes: less biomechanical load on the back, less fidgeting, fewer discomfort complaints, and better performance.**

Assessing Ergonomic Chairs

The favorable outcomes just described provide a reasonably strong justification for a concerned manager to provide ergonomic chairs for his or her employees. However, a crucial practical question presents itself: which ergonomic chairs should be purchased?

This is an important decision. Ergonomic chairs are expensive and, once purchased, are not likely to be replaced for a long time. (It is usually much more difficult to convince decision makers to replace furniture than it is to convince the same people to replace computer software or even hardware.) The ergonomic principles and advice presented in this chapter should be used as a starting point for decision making. The buying decision should not be made, however, until the final choices are carefully and objectively evaluated on-site under typical working conditions.

Must a manager also become a manager/experimenter? In some sense, yes. No one else has the same anthropometric mix, the same precise combination of job description, physical environment, and organizational climate. At stake are the health and well-being of a lot of Elizabeths, major expenditures of money for equipment to be used over many years, and large potential monetary savings through increased productivity.

Therefore, before managers make any major purchases of ergonomic equipment, they should rate that equipment *over time* on as large and varied a cross-section of workers as possible. Studies indicate that even ergonomists may not be able to tell how comfortable a chair will be from looking at it or examining its specifications. To judge a chair, you must sit in it; there is no substitute for "seat-on" experience.

Additional emphasis for this point comes from an experiment (Daley, Voisard, & Dainoff, 1985) in which a number of subjects worked at an editing (non-VDT) task using three different chairs. After they had worked for 15 minutes in each, they were asked to rate their preferences. Then they were asked to go back and do the task again for an hour in each of the three chairs, and again to rate their preferences. The preferences after one hour were completely different than those after fifteen minutes. The moral is this: a chair that is comfortable initially may not be so after a longer period of time.

No one knows how long it takes for preferences to stabilize. But a workday is the time period during which a chair is ordinarily used, and over a period of several workdays, the "bugs" in the system should be much more reliably evident than they would be over a period of minutes or hours.

It follows, then, that it is not ideal to pick out a chair by seeing it, or even sitting in it, in a showroom, because of the shortness of the testing period. It is also crucial that the chair be tested for comfort *while the task for which it is intended is being performed*. A purchaser talking to a salesperson in a showroom may consider a chair ideal, but once the chair is being used while the prospective buyer is keying in at a VDT for long periods of time, it may appear to be less than the best.

A two-stage decision-making process is suggested. In the first, you might gather some of the basic measurements of the people in your workforce, and then coordinate potential chairs with possible workstations (see Chapter 4). At this point, informal trials, with sample furniture being used for several days in the workplace, are useful for narrowing the range of choices.

In the second stage, when the choices have been narrowed to 2 to 4 chairs and workstations, a more systematic comparison of alternatives may be achieved by using the technique of counterbalanced trials (see Appendix I). In this approach, one operator would alternate between ergonomic chair and workstation A for one workday and ergonomic chair and workstation B for the next workday according to the sequence ABBA (always on successive workdays). A second worker would follow the sequence BAAB. The workers would be assigned to either of these two sequences at random. This process should be repeated until a significant cross-section of workers of various body builds and temperaments are studied, each over four successive workdays.

The reason for this somewhat complex procedure is to guard against the tendencies (seen in many situations involving choices) to prefer either the first thing that comes along or the last thing that is used. Some people naturally tend towards one of these directions, others toward the other. A four-day experiment using A on the first and last days, and B on the second and third, and vice versa, provides a more systematic and accurate assessment.

Before beginning, the manager should be sure that the subjects (employees) know *why* adjusting the furniture is important, and he or she should also make sure that the workers are proficient in making the actual adjustments.

During these trials, operators should be asked to perform their normal work duties. At various points throughout the trials, operator responses to the chairs should be assessed. This assessment can be extensive or brief, depending on resources available. At the very least, operators should be carefully questioned at the end of the four days as to their reactions and preferences. The questioning must be done objectively so that the operator gives an actual opinion, rather than what he or she thinks *the manager* wants to hear. A standardized interview script or questionnaire would be most appropriate.

More elaborate assessment procedures might involve the following: detailed comfort/discomfort questionnaires to be administered at the beginning and end of each work session; observations (direct or videotaped) of postural adjustments and/or movement (fidgeting) during work sessions; measurement of changes of performance under different conditions. Each of these procedures has the potential of providing valuable information, but each involves technical concerns. Advice from someone experienced in research methodology involving human performance (e.g., applied psychologists, ergonomists, industrial engineers) might be useful in specific circumstances.

The manager may end up choosing chairs that are not the most aesthetically pleasing, although some ergonomic chairs have a high-tech beauty that is more than upholstery deep. Different models may also be purchased for different people. An interior designer may not like the choices and the purchasing agent may not appreciate having to order more than one chair style, but the *users* of the chairs will work more comfortably and more efficiently, and will have provided valuable input into the decision.

Basically, you must decide whether you want a showplace or a workplace. In a reception area, where the priority is greeting people and looking good, "showplace" may be the operative word. But where large amounts of VDT work are involved, it pays (quite literally) to have your priorities straight.

Buying a Chair Is Not the Same as Using It: Employee Education

A field study from Finland conducted by Kukkonen and colleagues showed that despite the purchase of ergonomic furniture by a certain company, health complaints remained high among data entry operators. Investigation revealed that the ergonomic furniture was *in place* but that its ergonomic features were not *in use*. The company instituted an intensive campaign of employee education: included were general principles of ergonomics, as well as specific details of how to use the adjustable features. In addition, on-site physical therapy was provided. Subsequently, health complaints and symptoms (as confirmed by physicians) decreased dramatically.

It is impossible to mention too frequently the importance of thorough, ongoing employee education.

> Evidence shows that the employees must be taught not only how their adjustable furniture works, but why adjusting it is important for their health.

We strongly suggest a crash course based on this chapter, with three different levels of employee education: (1) how to use the ergonomic controls; (2) why adjustments are important, the nature of spinal physiology, the benefits of lordosis and pitfalls of kyphosis, the balance between stability and mobility; and (3) the reasons behind the standard upright sitting posture, and the benefits of forward and backward tilt.

The training course is important because the hang tags placed on chairs by the manufacturers are often removed with the packing materials, and are never seen by the users. Even if they are not removed, they vary in their clarity and in their explanations of why adjustments are important. The training course also illustrates management's commitment to ergonomic considerations. It need not last more than an hour or so, but its principles must be stressed over and over again during the ensuing weeks, until the employees use the adjustments routinely. New employees should also be given complete instruction. The friendly interest of a supervisor who observes someone sitting in an unlikely posture and asks, "Are you comfortable with your chair adjusted that way?" would also go a long way toward reminding workers that this is an important aspect of their work.

Executive Seating and the Question of Status

The policy of many companies is that the upholstery on your chair and the height of your backrest is correlated with your job title or rank. Thus, the traditional management chair is massive, expensive, and good for leaning back but probably not very good for intensive work at a desk or VDT.

Status would dictate that the secretary not have a more expensive chair than the executive, but a non-ergonomic executive chair may be less expensive than an ergonomic secretarial chair. Here the problem is confusion between chair as tool and chair as status symbol. It would not make any sense for the president of a trucking company to refuse to allow employees to drive more expensive vehicles than he or she does!

The chair-as-status system also runs into difficulty when the status chair is downright uncomfortable, as with the executive of slight body build (typically a woman but also a smaller man). Some organizations buy expensive secretarial chairs for executives who are not comfortable in the larger traditional executive chairs.

Managers and executives do not usually spend as much time in their chairs as VDT workers do; their overall tasks are not the same, so it is reasonable that their chairs be different. But executives, too, have bad backs. Moreover, many executives, especially at mid-management levels, are spending more and more time using computers, and this leads to special ergonomic needs. At some point, there may be a conflict between status symbol and efficiency, between indicators of rank and the same aching back, neck, and shoulders from which the clerk has been suffering. Whenever possible, every person should have a task-specific ergonomic chair.

It may be naive to suggest that symbols of status be eliminated, although some very effective organizations have moved in that direction. But even in a corporate culture which rewards status with precisely calibrated improvements in the workplace, there are ways to do this which do not conflict with ergonomic principles. Chairs are now available which effectively combine ergonomic and luxury features; adjustability can coexist with fine fabrics and well-tooled fittings. (Smooth black leather, however, may pose a problem with a forward tilt chair, making the user slide forward.)

In any case, since status is fundamentally symbolic, it should be possible for creative management to find better symbols (such as artwork, plants, and the like) which do not subject the top people in the organization to the hazards of prolonged sitting.

Elements to Look for in an Ergonomic Chair

- **Chairs must be considered in the context of the task for which they are chosen. A chair is only one element in a system composed of the worker and the entire workstation. Therefore, the recommendations which follow must be considered within the context of the whole workstation.**
- Designing and engineering chairs to meet wide anthropometric ranges is difficult. It may therefore be necessary to purchase a variety of chairs, or a number of variations on a single chair, to fit different sizes of people.
- *The worker must be able to make all adjustments described below with ease, while he or she is sitting in the chair.* Knobs and buttons should be easy to reach and not strength-dependent.
- Seat height should be adjustable. The low point should be equal to the popliteal height of the smallest individual worker, in his or her lowest-heeled shoes. Depending on the nature of the workstation as a whole, and on the availability of low chairs, it might be advisable to provide a

footrest for short workers. (The use and shape of footrests is, however, the subject of some controversy.)
- Seat width should be adequate for large people, but not so large as to be uncomfortable for smaller workers.
- Seat padding should be soft enough to allow pressure to be distributed, but not so soft that the bones bottom out (i.e., they sink through the padding and end up supported by the hard, rigid chair frame).
- The seat should have a waterfall front — that is, the front edge of the seatpan should be rounded downward, so that it does not cut off circulation at the popliteal area or under the thigh.
- The seat should be capable of tilting forward and backward.
- The backrest should be padded and have a lumbar support which is adjustable in height. The backrest should tilt backward to support the worker if the seatpan is level or tilted backward, and should be tall enough to accomplish this. For forward seatpan tilt, it should be possible to position the backrest at a right angle to the seatpan.
- Dynamic motion (where the chair's movement follows the movements of the user without the user making adjustments) of backrest and/or seatpan is a useful option for some people; however, the chair should also have multiple static posture settings (which lock the chair into any position set by the user).
- Arm rests provide additional comfort and support but should not interfere with the task. Some are adjustable. The texture of arm rests is important. Metal arms may be cold and uncomfortable. A rough surface may be irritating to the skin. Arm rests sometimes interfere with the task because, being located at approximately elbow height, they may get caught under the front edge of the workstation if they are too deep.
- The upholstery fabric should be such that the worker does not slide forward when the seatpan is in the forward tilt position. It should also dissipate moisture and heat.
- Static electricity which can accumulate on people or objects in the office may cause temporary or permanent damage to computer memory, hardware, or software. There are many anti-static computer products available on the market; a chair which is capable of helping to reduce the electrical charge may be part of the solution to this problem.
- The chair should have a 5-pronged base for added stability. (Caution: Having a 5-pronged base does not mean that the rest of the chair is up to par!)
- Casters should provide for enough (but not too much) mobility.

- The chair should be reliable and safe under conditions of hard daily use. Proper use of ergonomic chairs requires many daily adjustments by the worker; the chair may also be used by several workers (especially in workstations used by more than one shift). This requires a workhorse of a chair; fragile models tend to break down frequently and often cannot be repaired.
- Repair service should be quickly available, and repairs should preferably be made on the premises, so that the user does not have to do without the chair for long periods of time. A good ergonomic chair is a sophisticated, complex piece of machinery, and some breakdown is to be expected.

Design of Workstations

CHAPTER 4

Recently, we were attending a meeting in another city and began a casual conversation with the person whose table we happened to share in a crowded fast food restaurant. The conversation turned to ergonomics, and his response to that term was much stronger than one would have expected from a random encounter. He was a departmental supervisor for a large international corporation whose headquarters building had recently been renovated. He described a days-long argument with the designer, who was quite willing to specify good ergonomic chairs, but insisted on a standard set of worksurfaces which matched the overall aesthetic tone of the building interior. Unfortunately, these surfaces were not deep enough for the computer terminal equipment which had been purchased, with the result that the operators, who were highly paid professionals, had to sit with their noses almost up against the screens. The outcome was that the *computer* equipment had to be replaced!

Another horror story we heard recently concerned a designer who decided to specify custom-made built-in furniture in a new facility. Eventually, all of that furniture, thousands and thousands of dollars' worth, had to be ripped out — because the computers did not fit on it.

Unfortunately, stories such as these are all too easy to find. The design of workspaces must include consideration of human functions and technological necessities, as well as aesthetic requirements. In this chapter, the discussion of seating from Chapter 3 will be extended to a consideration of the design of an integrated workstation. "Workstation" will be defined, more or less arbitrarily, as those elements which are in the immediate (reachable) vicinity of the seated operator of a VDT.

Workstation Planning: Is It Worth the Time?

For the busy manager who is concerned about operational efficiency and tight time schedules, the amount of detail and interrelated complexities involved in workstation design may seem overwhelming. However, given the story of our lunchtime acquaintance, the old aphorism, "Decide in Haste, Repent at Leisure," seems appropriate. Conversely, if the same meticulous attention is paid to the details of workstation arrangement that is devoted to other operational and financial concerns, the results should be positive and immediate.

Careful ergonomic design of VDT workstations is much like solving a jigsaw puzzle. It is unrealistic to expect managers and other decision makers to become experts themselves. This is why designers, space planners/behavioral programmers and other consultants are hired. However, it is not useful simply to hire a consultant and tell him or her to go and solve the problem and come back with a solution. The best design solutions are based on a *process* involving a more or less continual dialogue in which specific needs articulated by the informed user are coordinated with a total design recommendation.

Some degree of knowledge and understanding of basic issues is required if the manager is to be an intelligent participant in this dialogue. The goal of this chapter is to enhance the user's ability to participate in a design dialogue so that design professionals can truly *serve* (rather than dictate to) the user/manager/customer.

Applying Standards, Guidelines, and Recommendations: Why the Easy Way Out Often Fails

The electronic office environment has different requirements than a traditional office, and this has given rise to an ever-increasing number of standards, guidelines, and recommendations specifically devoted to VDTs. In theory, the overworked designer/specifier/purchasing agent could simply pull down a list of standards, make sure that the equipment being ordered meets the criteria listed (the seatpan is high enough, wide enough, etc.), and then go on to some other problem. However, there are some serious drawbacks to this strategy.

First of all, there are major differences in intent, structure, degree of detail, and requirements for compliance among such documents. Some standards are established by governmental organizations — usually for health and safety reasons — and compliance is required by law. Other standards are generated through independent standards organizations and are typically based on consensus agreement across major industry groups. At this writing, draft standards on VDT workstation design are being circulated through Canada by the Canadian Standards Association (CSA) and through the United States by the American National Standards Institute (ANSI) in conjunction with the Human Factors

Society. Germany has its own (DIN) standards, as do Sweden and other European countries. Large organizations, both public (e.g., the military) and private, may establish standards in order to simplify procurement, while labor organizations do the same for use in contract negotiations. When using any given standard, guideline, or recommendation for decision making, it is important to be aware of the underlying rationale and approach of that document.

Related to this is the problem of obsolescence. This concern, which applies to fixed standards in any rapidly developing area, is simply that new techniques, approaches, and equipment may become available which accomplish the desired function more effectively and at lower cost than was possible at the time the standards were set. *By virtue of their innovative qualities, however, these new items may not meet the standards.*

The size, shape, and configuration of VDTs, for instance, are far from standard. Yet the interrelationship between the furniture industry and the computer industry on this issue is evident: the current trend toward smaller, lighter computer equipment has already had an impact on furniture design. Some standards and guidelines require specific VDT furniture dimensions which may be inappropriate for the newer VDTs. Moreover, standardizing the configuration of VDTs according to cathode ray tube (CRT) based technology may seriously restrict developments in the newer technologies, such as flat panel displays.

A major problem in VDT ergonomics springs from the fact that the specific contents of many standards simply are not in agreement — and the extent of the disagreement is great. The frustration that this causes is evident in a report of the attempts of Canadian ergonomists Schneider and Martin (1984) to establish a VDT standard for Ontario Hydro. The authors reviewed a number of previous guidelines and recommendations for various dimensions of VDT workstations and found that, in many cases, far from agreeing, proposed dimensional ranges did not even overlap! For example, although most experts recommended that the keyboard supports be adjustable, some specific proposed ranges of adjustment were:

> 56–70 cm (22.0–27.6 inches)
>
> 70–72 cm (27.6–28.3 inches)
>
> 75–78 cm (29.5–30.7 inches)

In these and other guidelines reviewed in that study, one could find justification for keyboard support surface heights ranging from 56 cm (22 inches) through 84 cm (33 inches)!

Similar problems have been found in other guidelines. In his discussion of ergonomic criteria, Galitz (1984) points out that suggestions of experts for seatpan height adjustability range from a low of 32 cm (12.6 inches) to a high of 60.96 cm (24 inches).

The reason for this lack of agreement is that specific design recommendations always involve compromises among different anthropometric and biomechanical assumptions, or different views on what are acceptable solutions. Thus, unless some rationale is given for the decisions which have been made, the end user must, in effect, choose "blindfolded" between two or more sets of numbers.

Furthermore, many recommendations are made on the basis of research in which individual components are studied in isolation. For example, a fair amount of research has been conducted to determine the best keyboard slope. However, the effectiveness of a given keyboard slope is always influenced by interacting variables such as keyboard height, arm angle, chair height and orientation.

The questions then become:

1. To what extent can individual elements of the workstation be considered in isolation, and to what extent are they interdependent?
2. From the point of view of biomechanical stress and efficiency of operation, how important are *deviations* from what appears to be optimal? How much tolerance can be allowed?

At the present time, there is no integrated, empirically based framework that is specific enough to allow such questions to be answered in a systematic way. If there were, there might be more agreement among experts.

In particular, the issue of allowable tolerances tends to be overlooked in many sets of ergonomic recommendations and standards. It would be ideal if optimal stations could be designed for every individual person. However, in the real world, this rarely happens; compromises must be made and priorities established when large numbers of people are being considered.

The Why of Workstation Recommendations

It is instructive to follow a professional carpenter around a hardware store while he or she is looking for a new hammer. Minute details of the tool, its heft, the angle of the handle, its weight, are of crucial importance. The carpenter will spend most of the workday using this tool, so a lot will depend on it. Athletes are often obsessively concerned with the fine details of the tools of their trade. *The same basic principles apply to the tools of the office workers, and they are of no less importance.*

However, there are two major differences between the use of tools by the carpenter and by the typical VDT operator. One is that the VDT worker does not usually choose his or her own tools, and often must share tools with others (employees on another shift, for example). The other lies in the distinction, discussed in the last chapter, between the carpenter's dynamic work and the VDT worker's static muscle work. These differences mean that the tools each uses must be understood in a slightly different way. However, the basic principles remain, protecting the worker's safety and health, and allowing the most work to be done with the least effort and fatigue.

Consider a seated VDT operator. For purposes of analysis, several general areas of interaction between body and environment should be considered: the head and eyes, the arms and hands, the trunk and buttocks, and the feet. Each of these is supported by the worker's muscular and skeletal structures, and by tools in the work environment. The location and form of each affects the others. In the case of the VDT operator, all other systems (muscles, skeleton, chair, worksurfaces) work together to support the fingers, which are doing the major part of the dynamic work, and the eyes, as they scan from copy to screen and back. The entire body, except for the fingers and eyes, must sustain a static workload to enable those two systems to accomplish the task. To be efficient, the VDT worker (like the carpenter) must do the task while minimizing effort and muscle strain.

It is useful to think of the musculoskeletal system of the body (bones, joints, tendons, and muscles) as a series of mechanical levers around pivot points (biomechanics).

As a general rule, the least effort (muscle work) is exerted when the joint is at or near the center of its range of motion, that is, at its equilibrium, or neutral point.

One source of strain occurs when a part of the body moves away from this point. The weight of that body part produces a force (or torque) which must be opposed by static muscle action. One all-too-familiar example of this principle is seen in the VDT operator who wears bifocals. The normal range of head and neck movement goes both backward and forward, with the center of range of movement at about the upright position. In order to view the screen, the worker with bifocals must tilt his or her head backward to look through the bottom part of the glasses. The neck muscles must counteract the considerable weight of the head (3.6 kg (8 lbs.) for a 59.1 kg (130 lb.) person), and the resulting strain reaches conscious awareness rather quickly.

A second general rule is that motion which is repetitive or pushes the limits of the system is potentially harmful.

Thus, a worker who must repeatedly twist or look to one side is likely to have pain in those muscles.

These rules of biomechanics need to be considered in order to design a workstation that protects the worker's safety and health and allows the most work to be done with the least effort and fatigue.

Biomechanical Criteria for Ergonomic Design

The effectiveness of a workstation depends in large measure on the way in which it accommodates specific points of interaction with the body. The relationships among these biomechanical criteria must also be taken into account in the design or assessment of a workstation. An excellent description of the ways in which specific biomechanical aspects of muscle function relate to VDT workplace design is provided by Sauter, Chapman, and Knutson (undated; circa 1985). Eight areas of interaction between body and workstation are important for effective workstation design:

1. Feet and legs
2. Thigh compression
3. Trunk, spine, and pelvis
4. Upper arms and shoulders
5. Forearm and wrists
6. Hands
7. Head and neck
8. Twisting, turning, and smashing

Criterion 1: Feet and Legs

Most recommendations require that the lower legs be vertical and the feet be flat on the floor or footrest; these requirements dictate adjustability of seatpan height to conform with the popliteal height of the sitter. Kleeman's design textbook (1981) describes the physiological effects of a seatpan which is too high: if the feet are dangling, there is excess pressure on the underside of the thigh, the return of blood to the heart through the veins is impaired, and the result can be swollen ankles and lowered temperature in the legs.

On the other hand, many workers adjust their seatpans higher than their popliteal heights. Interpretations of this finding ("What else could account for these results?") are that these workers may be setting their own ergonomic priorities by raising their chairs so as to emphasize proper elbow/arm/hand location at the expense of foot support, which can often be obtained in higher chairs by operators resting their feet on the base of the chair. A possible reason for this trade-off is that the perceptual fatigue/pain signals from the circulatory problems caused by a seatpan that is too high may be overpowered by the stronger pain signals from the arm/shoulder/hand areas which would result if the seatpan was so low that these regions were out of optimal range of operation.

Experts disagree on the use of footrests: some recommend them and describe them quite specifically, while others look on them as an unnecessary nuisance, reasoning that the chair should be adjustable as low as the popliteal height of the worker (allowing for shoes). If this is not possible, however, it is necessary to find some way to augment the worker's popliteal height so that the lower legs are vertical and the feet are supported.

Some footrests are flat, some are angled from 10 to 30 degrees, and others are concave. It is hard for the authors to see the advantage of an angled or concave surface, which would do very different things to the foot and leg depending on whether the worker wears flat shoes or high heels. Furthermore, it is only that part of the footrest nearest to the chair that augments popliteal height; the rest simply supports or raises the toes. It should also be noted that angling the lower legs forward to meet the angle of a footrest can tend to push the chair away if its casters are on a smooth surface.

If the chair in use adjusts down to a seatpan height of 38 cm (15 inches), a sturdy, fixed 6.35 cm (2.5 inch) footrest should suffice to augment a 5th percentile Asian woman's popliteal height from 32 cm (12.6 inches) to the lowest chair adjustment. Any person with a popliteal height between 32 and 38 cm (12.6 and 15 inches) could use the same footrest and still be within the range of adjustability. This assumes, of course, that the table adjustability range allows the elbows to move into their proper working orientation.

The easiest method by which a worker may augment popliteal height is to wear high-heeled or thick-soled (platform) shoes. It is not uncommon for women to wear 5 to 7.6 cm (2 to 3 inch) heels, and wearing shoes with heels of this height may eliminate the need for footrests, depending on the range of adjustability of the chair.

Criterion 2: Thigh Compression

Pressure on the underside of the thighs, which slows blood circulation in the legs, can come from two major sources: improper height, angle, depth, and shape of the seatpan and/or pressure from the top of the thighs being forced against the underside of a table which is too low.

The first source of pressure can be dealt with by the "waterfall" configuration and seatpan tilt discussed in Chapter 3. Dealing with the second source of pressure dictates a careful consideration of the interaction between seatpan height and height of the underside of the table; it generally precludes having desk drawers beneath the keyboard.

Criterion 3: Trunk, Spine, and Pelvis

From the discussion in Chapter 3, it is obvious that the need for support of these areas is a major consideration in designing the workstation. These needs can be met through various chair design approaches to backrests, lumbar supports, and seatpan angles, as discussed in the last chapter.

Criterion 4: Upper Arms and Shoulders

The arms and shoulders contain some of the most powerful muscles in the body. These muscles are used to their maximum potential by athletes or laborers who must lift, push, pull, and twist things, using the dynamic mode of muscle work. Most desk or keyboard tasks involve static muscle work by these powerful arm and shoulder muscles, in order to support their own weight and that of the arm/hand system.

A keying posture in which the upper arm hangs vertically and the forearm extends horizontally, with the weight of the hand and wrist supported near the keyboard, requires the least static load. Consequently, from a design perspective, keyboard height and angle and chair height must be properly adjusted so that the elbow is at the level of the center of the keyboard (the so-called "home row").

Deviations from this posture are troublesome, but in differing degrees. If the elbows are moved sideways away from the body so that the upper arm angle is more than about 30 degrees outward from the vertical, shoulder muscles will be under strain. In industrial settings, production performance has been shown to drop rapidly as this angle is approached. Other studies show rapid onset of pain at about the same (30 degree) angle when the upper arm is moved forward. Both of these cases, however, involved situations in assembly work, where the arm was not supported.

The resulting strain may not be as bad in a keying situation if the keyboard and surrounding worksurface provide some degree of support to the forearm. In fact, studies supporting the backward tilt posture suggest that holding the upper arm about 15 degrees forward of the body is comfortable, as long as (a) the forearm is supported, and (b) the forearm to upper arm angle is between 90 and 100 degrees.

Several new input devices are now in use, such as light pens (devices which allow writing on the screen with a beam of light to which the screen is sensitive) and touch-sensitive screens (where commands are registered by touching certain areas of the monitor screen). These require that the operator keep his or her arms in an elevated position. Non-typists may also employ an input device known as a mouse — a small, wheeled device which controls the cursor by its movement on a table. However, as presently designed, these devices require a rather awkward sideways reach, because they are used in conjunction with (not instead of) the keyboard. Each has important ergonomic implications, but has been neglected in most existing ergonomic guidelines.

Criterion 5: Forearm and Wrists

Much of the controversy in ergonomic standards and recommendations is based on different assumptions as to the optimal posture in the forearm-wrist region.

Initial European standards regarding VDT workstations started with the assumption that the forearm should be horizontal and that the elbow should be at keyboard height. It was then argued that, on anthropometric grounds relating to thigh-to-forearm distance, this posture could not be achieved unless the keyboard was kept very thin (less than 3 cm, or 1.18 inches). The thin, flat keyboard thus became a standard. This had important *economic* repercussions, since most computer keyboards manufactured at the time were much thicker. Several research studies have since appeared which question whether it is crucial that the forearm be exactly horizontal.

The issue of keyboard thickness is important. Its resolution will, in large part, literally determine the shape and adjustability of computer equipment and furniture. The entire constellation of factors pertinent to keyboard thickness includes the inclination of the upper arm and the inclination of the wrist, as jointly determined by the height of table, the thickness and angle of keyboard, and further influenced by seatpan height and angle of the chair (vertical, tilted forward, or tilted backward).

The pace of research activity in this area has been increasing, and some general principles are emerging. For example, it seems that the wrist angle is much more critical than the forearm angle. The wrist is particularly sensitive to bending, because major nerves, tendons, and blood vessels supplying the fingers all pass through a particularly vulnerable passage called the *carpal tunnel*. Bending of the wrist in either direction puts pressure on this tunnel, which is typically smaller, and therefore even more subject to trauma, in women. Any work situation which puts continuous pressure on the carpal tunnel, such as repetitive keying while the wrist is bent, presents the possibility of serious long-term wrist injury.

It follows that a high design priority should be to allow for a wrist angle that is as flat as possible, certainly within 10 degrees. This could be achieved by the combination of horizontal forearm posture and the flat keyboard described above. However, this keyboard would, by virtue of its small height, have a maximum angle of about 5 degrees. This leads to a new problem, since some studies have shown that people tend to prefer keyboard angles in a range from 10 to 25 degrees. If such keyboards are employed, the forearm angle will be inclined upward.

The general conclusion derived from ergonomic principles and user preference is that, in either forward or backward tilt or upright chair position, deviations of about plus or minus 15 degrees from the "ideal" 90 degree orientation between upper and lower arms, are acceptable, so long as the forearm does not dip below horizontal.

Given these facts, a reasonable approach to keeping the wrist flat would be to insure that the forearm, wrist, and surface of the keyboard all lie in approximately the same plane. Thus, some degree of keyboard slope is acceptable as long as bending of the wrist is kept at a minimum.

The use of an adjustable wrist or palm support in front of the keyboard can be a key element. However, this piece of equipment, which is typically the least expensive in the whole system, must be chosen with care. The underside of the wrist is very sensitive, and if the support is hard or sharp, like the edge of the table or desk, it may do more harm than good. The wrist rest should be padded; the parts that come in contact with the wrist should not be cold (and therefore uncomfortable) to the touch. If a proper support is provided for the wrist and the forearm, this will probably overcome any increased load due to the increased forearm angle imposed by larger keyboard angles.

Studies have consistently found that properly designed wrist/palm rests are welcomed by users. It has not been established, however, whether optimal use occurs when the worker's forearms are lowered during pauses, or when they rest continually on the wrist rest.

Criterion 6: The Hands

The hands are the "business end" of the entire system, the point where most of the dynamic work takes place. A 60 word per minute typist who works without stopping for 30 minutes makes about 10,000 keystrokes, each requiring contraction of a forearm muscle. The question is: how can this work be made more efficient?

Key arrangement. It is interesting that a major source of inefficiency was deliberately built into the keyboard. The current key arrangement, dating from before the turn of the 20th century, is the so-called QWERTY keyboard (named for the first six letters in the top row). This was designed after careful analysis of the frequencies of use of letters in English, and the relative differences in strengths among the fingers (the little finger and ring finger are much weaker than the others). However, the purpose of this design was to *slow down* the operator so that the original mechanical key linkages would have time to return to position.

Now that high-speed keyboards are available, proposals have been made to introduce alternative key layouts that favor assignment of high-frequency keys to stronger fingers. The best-known of these is the Dvorak keyboard, named for its designer. There has been a recent flurry of interest in the Dvorak arrangement, but the opposition to its adoption has been substantial. One reason for this is the massive amount of retraining which would be required; another is the cost of replacing the QWERTY keyboards, although the latter is likely to be far less than retraining costs. The obvious mechanical efficiencies to be achieved need to be balanced against the costs, in both financial and psychological terms, of introducing this innovation.

Keyboard shape. The proposals for alternative key *arrangements* have generated a good deal of argument and publicity. However, innovations have also been proposed for the *shape* of the keyboard, which could be achieved much more easily, and which have the potential to achieve significant improvements in efficiency.

Because of its geometric configuration, the conventional keyboard is an inherent source of hand and wrist fatigue. When the hands are at the keyboard in typing/keying position, the longest (middle) fingers are parallel and essentially pointed straight ahead (though curved downward). They are at an angle to the long bones of the forearms, however, and there is a resulting angle at the wrist, known as the *ulnar abduction*. Maintaining this posture for prolonged periods of time will increase the likelihood of cramping and other muscular disorders.

In an extensive series of investigations, Grandjean (1984) has introduced a new modification of an old idea: that of splitting the keyboard, so that it conforms more closely to the natural orientation of the hands. In experimental trials, the keyboard was split down the middle (between the G and H keys), the right side angled off to the right, the left side to the left by 25 degrees, and the whole thing angled 10 degrees from the horizontal. Strain on the wrist was greatly reduced, and subjects reported feeling more comfortable. Grandjean has combined this keyboard with a long forearm support which matches the plane of the keyboard. The resulting combination is very effective when used with a backward tilted backrest.

Keyboard layout. The average typewriter keyboard has about 55 keys; the average computer, well over 100. In some cases, these extra, specialized keys have either been placed in the same locations as the more traditional typewriter keys, or not been sufficiently separated or otherwise distinguished from the more familiar keys. For example, in one popular keyboard, the shift keys are not in their traditional place. The result is that a computer operator must battle long-ingrained habits of working at a keyboard, and often ends up doing things he or she did not intend. Such keyboards can be a major cause of inefficiency, particularly if the operator's work requires an occasional shift between keyboards of different machines.

Key characteristics. All keyboards have a "feel," of which a skilled operator is intimately aware. This feel is determined by the shape and texture of the keysurface, the force required to depress the keys, and how far down the key goes (displacement). The pressure needed on a single key before that character (letter, number, or symbol) is displayed should be great enough that unwanted characters do not result from light, unintentional pressing.

After enough pressure has been applied to print a character, the key should depress farther more easily, in order to give the operator positive feedback through the fingers that the key has actually been depressed. In some computer systems this feedback may be augmented by auditory clicks or beeps through the computer terminal itself.

Given the need for such feedback, the new flat or membrane keyboards present problems for long-term keying. A recent study has shown that tactile feedback for membrane keys can be enhanced by placing domes over the keys and embossing the key surface, and by adding auditory cues. However, it is not clear that even these innovations are effective for more than short periods of time.

Criterion 7: Head and Neck

The head and neck are the other "business end" of the system. The orientation of the head in space is determined by demands on vision, hearing, and speech.

More than 6% of the total weight of the body is concentrated in the head. If the head is bent forward or backward sufficiently to bring the eyes into the required viewing position, the static activity of neck muscles required to hold it in place leads to fatigue and strain. Problems can also arise from repetitive movement, as in the combination of twisting and bending to one side that is required to alternate between a vertical screen and horizontal copy lying on a table next to the keyboard.

Head angle requirements are strongly dependent on the kind of work being done. The customer service operator calling up screen information in response to a telephone message on a headset has a different set of visual demands than does the manuscript typist; one is screen oriented, the other text oriented. Many workers have combinations of screen and text-oriented tasks.

Head angle is determined by distance, height, and orientation of both the screen and the copy. In general, excessive head angles will be minimized if the operator's line of sight is kept between 10 and 20 degrees below the horizontal. However, values ranging from 5 to 30 degrees are found in the literature, and may go lower than 30 for bifocal wearers. Both the eyes and head will move in a cooperative fashion. The goal is to minimize the strain on both.

Preferred viewing distance from the eye to the center of the monitor is likely to be idiosyncratic, and will probably depend on the state of the individual's vision and the size of characters on the screen. Ranges of 40 to 63.5 cm (15.7 to 25 inches) have been recommended, but in practice, larger distances are observed. A rule of thumb that can be used to determine whether the size of characters generated by the computer on the screen will be large enough to be read easily is to divide the size of one character on the screen by the viewing distance from eye to screen (using the same units of measure) and multiply by 3450. If the resulting number — called the *visual angle* — is 16 or more, the print should be readable. This rule is based on the common recommendation that the minimum character size for comfortable reading covers a visual angle of 16 to 18 minutes of arc (there are 360 degrees in a full circle, and 60 minutes of arc per degree).

For ease of focus, paper copy and screen should be at equal viewing distances from the eye. This eliminates the extra work that would be demanded of the eye if it had to focus on objects at different distances. (When one looks at something far away and then at something near, the eye must compensate.) These equal distances can be visualized by imagining half a large sphere, with its center between the eyes and its surface at the screen center. The sphere's surface would include all points that were equidistant from the eye. To minimize the work of re-focusing many times a minute, copyholders can be located on either side of or just below the screen — anywhere on the surface of this imaginary hemisphere. One authority indicates that, under normal office lighting conditions, there is a 10 cm (3.9 inch) tolerance range on either side of this imaginary sphere, where re-focusing is minimized. (This tolerance zone corresponds to depth of focus, or depth of field.)

One difficulty arises from the typically different character sizes found on VDT screens and paper copy. To take a hypothetical case, assume that, for a certain worker, a comfortable viewing distance to the monitor is about 50 cm (19.7 inches) from the eye. The paper copy being used consists of names and numbers from a telephone book, which has much smaller characters — 1.15 mm (0.05 inch) — than those on the screen. The distance at which the phone book is easy to read (based on a 16 min visual angle) is 24.8 cm (9.8 inches). However, the discrepancy between this distance and the viewing distance to the screen (50 cm, or 19.7 inch) is much greater than the 10 cm (3.9 inch) tolerance zone. (That is, 50 cm minus 24.8 cm is 25.2 cm, which is greater than 10 cm, and so the eyes are going to be changing focus as they switch back and forth between copy and screen.) Some researchers believe this is a possible source of eye fatigue.

An obvious solution is to decrease the distance between the viewer and the screen. There are several ways to do this. The viewer could lean forward toward the screen. However, this action is likely to cause the back to assume a kyphotic position, rather than the optimal lordotic posture (see Chapter 3). Depending on the configuration of keyboard and copy, leaning closer, if it is even possible, may also interfere with the optimal position of the arm/hand/elbow system.

Alternatively, it may be possible to move the monitor closer, leaving the back, arm, hand, and elbow in their proper orientations. However, the characters on the screen are made of groups of dots. From a distance, the dots blur together, and the characters look like print. Moving closer, an operator can begin to see spaces between the dots, which can also cause problems for the eyes. (A more detailed discussion of visual problems like these can be found in Chapter 5.)

In practice, optimization may mean making small compromises in meeting each criterion. For example, one could perhaps move a little closer to the screen without jeopardizing other systems very much. With flexible workstation design, a number of such mini-experiments could be attempted, to see which deviations from the ideal are most easily tolerated by the individual worker.

Positioning the copyholder may present a variety of practical problems. Some VDT/workstation configurations allow copy to be placed *between* the keyboard and the screen. This has the advantage that the copy is now at the same distance from the eye as the screen and keyboard, and only slight upward and downward movements of the head and eye would be required to alternate between screen and copy.

However, with the copyholder in this position, the size of the letters on the paper copy would have to be large enough to be viewed comfortably. The phone book, as discussed earlier, could not be used effectively on this kind of copyholder because its characters are too small. (It would probably also be so large that it would block part of the screen.) A free-standing copyholder off to the side would be more appropriate — allowing greater flexibility in changing the viewing distance of the copy. However, it would have to be large enough to support the book. Laying the book flat on the desk is a natural response, assuming there is room to do so, but this solution will also result in the head and neck being bent too far forward.

Some copyholders are now available on the market which "float" — that is, they can be moved up, down, and sideways because they are attached to the workstation by means of an adjustable arm. Some have their own task lights, magnifying line guides, and even a foot pedal that allows the worker to move the line guide electrically. If the task requires that more attention be given to the paper copy than to the screen, it would probably be better to have the *copy holder* directly in front of the worker and the *monitor* off to one side. This is, of course, impossible if the monitor and keyboard are a single integrated unit.

Finally, sufficient lighting must be provided so as to adequately illuminate the paper copy, while at the same time avoiding excessive glare on the display screen. Small "task lights" can be useful for this purpose. These issues will be discussed further in chapters 5 and 6.

Criterion 8: Twisting, Turning, and Smashing

This final criterion is more general, but it applies particularly to the trunk and knees. As previously stated, any static posture results in lactic acid buildup, and motion of some kind is needed to increase circulation for lactic acid removal. However, motion which is repetitive or pushes at the limits of the system is also potentially harmful.

If not carefully assessed, the location, design, and construction of equipment can lead to problems of twisting, turning, and smashing. For example, some adjustable workstations have mechanisms underneath the table so that keyboard heights may be raised or lowered — but if the worker bumps into this mechanism when he or she is moving sideways to reach something or getting out of the chair, a smashed knee may be the result. Sharp corners, knobs, and other structures which interfere with legroom or footroom, or collide with the worker when he or she moves about, sits down, or leaves the workstation, can lead to bruises and/or a lot of annoyance. This is also part of ergonomics!

With the advent of the personal computer, disk drives and disk storage compete for ever more crowded work areas. The manufacturers who place the power switches behind the equipment are not helpful. With one system, for example, a reach much farther than arm's length is required to turn the power switch for the disk drive on or off; thus, an extreme bending and twisting operation is required every time the drive needs to be turned on or off.

Beneficial movement patterns involving general, balanced movements can sometimes be built in through job restructuring. For example, word processing operators could be required to actually deliver finished copy to the originator. This would not only get the operator away from the desk, but would also enhance communication between the word processing operator and those whose copy he or she processes. In other cases, frequent rest breaks and/or exercise breaks may be used as needed respite from static postures.

The Integrated Workstation System

Based on the criteria above, the following ergonomic priorities must be taken into account in order to design or assess an integrated workstation system. (See Figure 4-1.)

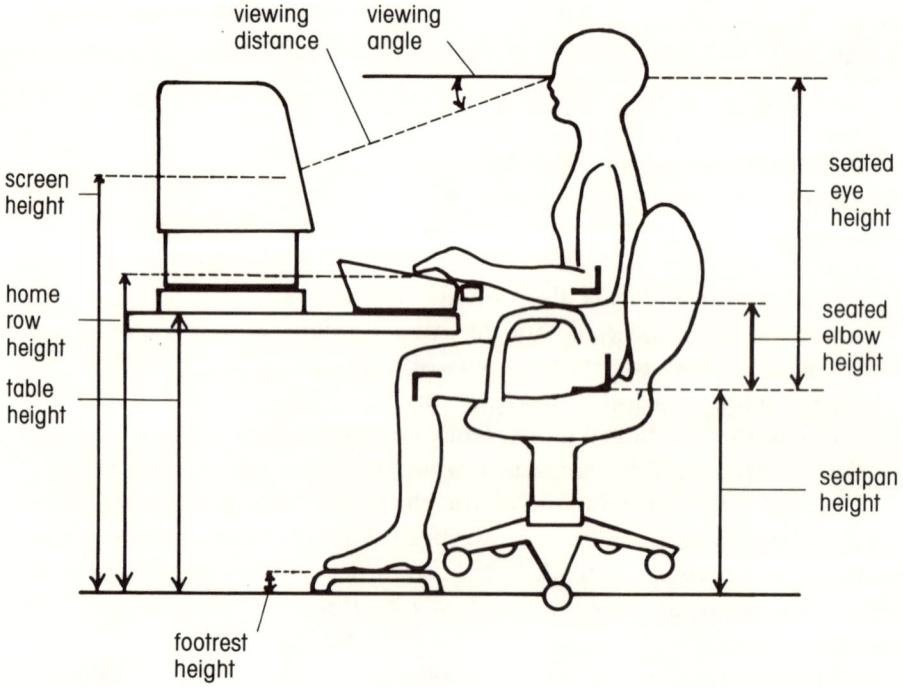

Figure 4-1.
Key measurements for workstation design.

1. The lower legs should be vertical and the feet should be firmly on the floor or on a footrest.
2. Pressure on the popliteal area should be minimized by proper seatpan dimensions, a waterfall front on the seatpan, and sufficient clearance between the top of the thigh and the underside of the worksurface. A footrest may be required to augment the popliteal heights of short workers if they cannot accomplish this by wearing higher heeled or thicker soled shoes.
3. The chair should have an easily adjustable seatpan height while the worker is seated in it, and it should preserve the lumbar curve (see Chapter 3). Optimally, the chair should be adjustable for forward tilt and backward tilt, as well as for standard upright posture.
4. The upper arms should be able to hang vertically, or up to a maximum of 15 degrees forward from the vertical when the worker is in the upright position or the backward tilted position. (With the chair in the forward tilted position they should be vertical.) The forearms should never angle down below the horizontal.
5. The forearm, wrist, and surface of the keyboard should all lie in approximately the same plane. A palm/wrist rest or other support for the wrist is necessary unless the keyboard is flat and there is 4 to 5 cm (1.63 to 2.04 inches) of worksurface available for resting the wrist.
6. Special command or function keys on a computer keyboard are best separated from the alphabet keys by enough space that the worker can avoid mistakes when touch typing. The texture and action of the keys should "feel right" to the worker. Alternate keyboard designs (Grandjean, 1984) can increase comfort and efficiency; alternative arrangements of keys could as well, but would require retraining.
7. The worker's line of sight should be between 10 and 20 degrees below the horizontal, or 30 degrees at most; however, the line may be somewhat lower for bifocal wearers. The top and bottom of the screen should be equidistant from the eyes to minimize character distortion. Copy should be the same distance from the eyes as the screen, plus or minus 10 cm (3.9 inches), and preferably at the same height. A satisfactory viewing distance is highly individual, and depends on character size and composition of both screen and copy, as well as the worker's visual correction. Considerable latitude is advised. Recommendations vary widely, and have ranged from 35 cm (14 inches) to 100 cm (39 inches). (Chapter 5 treats this issue in more detail.)
8. Traumatic twisting, turning, and bumping or smashing of the body into the equipment is to be avoided.

Assessing workstation components against these criteria and integrating them into a fully functional working unit that accommodates a specific workforce is a tedious (but not difficult) process. (It is best carried out initially using pencil and paper.) To help you in the task, a step-by-step case study model is presented in Appendix III of this book. Working through this case study will lead to a better understanding of how all the components should work together, and how the limitations imposed by one piece of equipment affect the whole system. This understanding should, in turn, lead to more enlightened workplace design.

Assessing Workstation Components

Nowhere is "systems thinking" (thinking about how all the parts fit together) more important than in integrating and designing a workstation. Changing any one variable changes most of the others, often in ways that cannot easily be precalculated. In the same way that a builder avoids a lot of trial and error by starting with a blueprint, application of the theory as described above and in Appendix III will save a lot of time and effort.

> **Nevertheless, there is no substitute for lengthy, hands-on, seat-on experience at the actual workstation, doing the actual task.**

Careful thinking about footrests, wrist rests, copyholders and task lights should enable you to decide which of the items now available on the market might be most suitable to your work.

However, neither careful thinking nor brief testing will suffice to make wise choices of chairs, computer hardware/software, and support surfaces. The most prudent course is (1) to *narrow* your choices by careful thinking and brief testing, and (2) to thoroughly test the several best alternative combinations. The testing should be done by a variety of workers who are doing the actual task for a period of several days.

Ideally, this testing should be done systematically and in the counterbalanced manner described for chairs in Chapter 3. The wrist rests, copyholders, and other equipment that have been chosen should also be part of the set-ups, to confirm that the combinations are satisfactory.

Alternately, if the user simply wants to confirm that the final choices will mix, the system can be tested in comparison to old workstations.

If even this is impracticable in a given work situation, several workers should be consulted, and they should be observed using the workstation for a week or more. The purchaser and worker should then assess it together critically and any comments that the worker has about its use should be considered carefully.

This kind of working assessment is critical, because as stated previously, a workstation that feels fine after one hour may not feel fine after eight. An investment in thoroughgoing trials using real tasks should pay off in terms of working the bugs out.

Depending on the nature of your organization, the final equipment decisions may be strictly a managerial decision; yet it is necessary to remember that

> the ultimate authorities on how well a workstation serves as a tool are the people who use that tool day in and day out. If there was ever a time for mutual education and cooperative decision making, this is it. In the final analysis, management cannot be happy with any ergonomic decision unless the workers are happy with it, and workers cannot make an informed decision unless they understand why ergonomics is important, know how ergonomic adjustments are made on their equipment, and test the equipment over an extended period of time in the actual work situation.

Buying a Workstation Is Not the Same as Using It: Employee Education

> The best ergonomic equipment in the world is not useful unless its users know why adjusting the equipment is important, and how to use it — and then in fact do adjust it!

It is imperative that employees know how easy it is to make minor adjustments. They should know that the purpose of the adjustable workstation is not to freeze the worker into an "ideal" sitting posture, but to allow a number of minor variations from that posture which will give fatigued muscles a chance for change.

Workers should be encouraged to set their workstations first thing in the day, and again throughout the day as any one posture becomes tiresome. Friendly emphasis by managers and supervisors on the importance of making the adjustments would remind employees to think about it and do it.

Elements to Look for in Workstation Equipment

- The worksurface(s) must be easily adjustable for both the keyboard and the monitor when all the equipment is in place, while the person is sitting in the keying position. Some tables have indicators that show the height to which they are adjusted. This feature is particularly

helpful in workstations used by more than one worker. Workers can just dial up their favorite heights.
- The table should have no unduly sharp edges. Neither the adjustment mechanism nor the table legs should be something you are likely to bruise your knees or shins on.
- The worksurface should be deep enough to accommodate all hardware, and preferably to allow some extra space.
- The surface on which the monitor sits (whether it is part of a split-level table, an adjustable monitor stand, or a clamp-on support) should allow for some flexibility in the angle of the monitor and viewing distance. This is especially important if the workstation is used by more than one worker.
- There should be sufficient workspace to allow for miscellaneous papers and other items necessary to the task being performed.
- The palm/wrist rest should be sufficiently broad and padded. If a wrist rest is unnecessary because the keyboard is low, about 5 cm (2 inches) of table should be available for resting the palm or wrist.
- The copyholder should either fit between the keyboard and monitor or have flexible positions. Electric line indicators and attached task lights are also useful. If these or other equipment are foot-operated, the footrest (if one is used) must accommodate them.
- A task light may be desirable depending on the lighting environment (see Chapter 5).
- All elements of the workstation should fit together as an integrated, functioning unit which accommodates all the workers for whom it is intended.

Finally, the following guidelines should be followed if wise ergonomic workstation investments are to be made.

- Thorough, long-term testing by *informed* employees performing the actual tasks for which the workstation is intended.
- Participation in decision making by employees who were part of the testing program.
- Thorough education of all employees using ergonomic equipment, including
  a. emphasis on why ergonomics is important,
  b. information on how to adjust the equipment,
  c. follow-up encouragement to use adjustments daily.

Visual Perception and the Video Display Terminal

CHAPTER 5

Let us return to VDT operator Elizabeth, who, as you may remember from Chapter 2, was experiencing burning, aching eyes after a few hours at the terminal. Perversely, the problem seemed to be less severe when the sky outside was dreary and dark than when it was beautifully sunlit. Elizabeth did not recall having such problems when she worked at a typewriter. She had her vision checked by her eye doctor, but didn't mention her VDT work. Elizabeth recalled reading something in the newspaper about radiation problems related to VDTs, which she hadn't taken very seriously at the time, but since she had come to work at the Leming Corporation and her eyes had begun bothering her so much, she started to wonder about it. Finally, she discussed the issue with her supervisor, Jane.

At that particular time, Jane was feeling a bit overwhelmed. She wasn't sure about her ability to understand and properly manage this new and expensive technology that the experts had moved into her department. The last thing she wanted to deal with was the possibility that this thing was a health hazard!

However, Jane also read the newspapers. One day, she noticed an article proclaiming, "Government Study Finds VDTs Not Harmful to Vision." She immediately clipped out the article and showed it to Elizabeth. Elizabeth was somewhat reassured, but her own eye complaints did not go away. She continued to mention them to Jane, but Jane's responses were increasingly less sympathetic. After all, the government itself had given VDTs a clean bill of health — it was probably all in Elizabeth's mind.

VDTs: Some History

The foregoing scenario illustrates many of the major concerns regarding vision and the use of VDTs. Historically, VDTs were first brought to the attention of the public by the visual problems their users were encountering. The integration of the computer into the office environment began to pick up speed in the early and mid-1970s. The keypunch machine was replaced by the VDT as the primary interface between people and computers, and flickering screens began to appear at airline reservation counters and on newspaper reporters' desks. However, increased visual problems seemed to accompany augmented VDT use. Some early field studies reported high levels of vision complaints among VDT workers, and these reports were picked up by the press, along with some additional speculation regarding harmful emission of radiation.

Governmental and scientific agencies around the world became involved. In the United States, the National Institute for Occupational Safety and Health (NIOSH) began the research cited earlier, and, in 1981, initiated a study of the issue by the National Research Council (NRC). The conclusion of this report was, in brief, that radiation levels emitted by VDTs are not hazardous even when measured by the most stringent standards, and that there is no evidence for physical harm, in the sense of permanent physical (anatomical) change to the visual system associated with prolonged work at VDTs. (This was the government study cited in the newspaper article that Jane read.)

The NRC report also emphasized the difficulty in relating the *subjective* sensation that "my eyes feel heavy, burning, etc." to any *objective* changes, either in the immediate functioning of the visual system, or in later permanent changes in that system. This difficulty in understanding the link between eye strain or eye fatigue and visual function or pathology is discussed by virtually every expert in the field, and reflects one of the major frustrations in dealing with this topic. Put bluntly, when VDT users say their eyes are killing them, they may be truly suffering or they may be exaggerating. There is no agreed-upon objective method for determining the validity of such complaints. The best that can be done is to assess the various factors involved. These include visual status (whether glasses or stronger glasses are needed) the visual demands of the job, the lighting environment, age, general health, and even motivational and emotional states.

Consequently, people dealing with VDTs have had to obtain advice about vision problems from many different professional groups. These include the professional eye care specialists (opthalmologists and optometrists), visual scientists who study the function and structure of vision, visual display engineers who are concerned with the techniques of designing and constructing the display itself, and lighting engineers/designers who must be concerned with the overall visual environment into which the terminal must fit. These groups all have different perspectives. The role of the ergonomist is to have a general working knowledge of all of these points of view, to define their interrelationships, and to propose applications to the office.

The VDT Debate: What Are the Issues?

Many different parties have a direct personal and financial interest in the outcome of the debate about VDTs: the operators themselves, the unions which represent or hope to represent them, the manufacturers of computer equipment, the manufacturers of lighting systems, and governmental and quasi-governmental organizations that are concerned with standards and regulations. Finally, and not the least important, there is the manager who must absorb all the recommendations and opinions of professional advisors and interest groups, and then make intelligent purchases and set up good environments and work practices. Yet the lack of consistent scientific advice that is currently available has led to a chaotic situation.

Furthermore, the ability to carry out reflective and judicious dialogue on these issues is certainly not helped by the public attention brought to them by the media. However, one positive result of such attention is that a number of scientists have become interested in the problem, and the amount of research, therefore, has increased markedly. At this writing, the research is still in a stage of ferment. The basic issues are these:

- Many studies have reported higher levels of visual discomfort among VDT operators than among non-VDT control groups.
- A few studies have shown differences in short-term visual function (such as eye movements, changes in focus) between VDT and non-VDT operations. Experts interpret these changes differently.
- Visual discomfort has not been clearly linked to long-term changes ("damage") to the visual system (including cataracts).
- Visual discomfort has not been clearly linked either to changes in operator task performance or to changes in short-term visual function.
- Many terminals on the market at the time of the studies mentioned above did not meet current criteria for the evaluation of visual displays such as VDTs. However, these criteria tend to relate to improved task performance (such as reading more quickly or accurately) rather than visual comfort, although, as just mentioned, task performance and visual comfort are not clearly correlated.
- Based on current criteria for the evaluation of lighting systems, field observations have indicated many lighting system deficiencies, particularly in the area of excessive glare.
- Personal attributes of the worker (including age and/or the type of

eyeglasses required) may be important elements in considering the problem.

In order to understand possible sources of eye problems and evaluate possible solutions, it is necessary to understand some basic concepts about the eye and its associated structures, as well as the kind of visual display generated by the VDT.

Eyes and the Terminal: Basic Visual Function

The human visual system is a marvelously intricate and sensitive mechanism. Visual scientists know a great deal about its *normal* structure and function — several Nobel prizes have been awarded to those who have studied it. Less is known about the *abnormal* function of the visual system.

The Act of Visual Perception

The ultimate purpose of the sense of vision is to pick up the information contained in optical patterns of light. The particular optical pattern under discussion here is the one emitted by the screen of a VDT.

Most VDT monitors, as currently designed, are similar to TV sets. The principal component of both is the cathode ray tube, or CRT. In its typical incarnation, the characters generated on the VDT screen are composed of patterns of dots. A minimally acceptable mode of character generation uses a matrix of dots 7 high by 5 across. For example, to generate the letter "F", an enlarged version of what appears on the screen looks something like this:

Each of these o's represents a dot or spot on the face of the screen. The spots are produced by a narrow beam of electrons which is emitted from an electron "gun" at the far end of the cathode ray tube. This beam sweeps across the face of the screen in a horizontal line starting at the top. At the end of the horizontal line, the beam returns, moves down a line, and starts again. (This pattern made by the beam is called the "raster.") The process is repeated (i.e., the screen is "refreshed") rapidly, typically 30 or 60 times per second. If the beam were constant all the time, there would be no image, but the computer circuitry turns the gun on and off at the appropriate times, leaving the dot pattern on the screen. This "dot matrix" system is essentially the same as that used in many computer printers.

Television sets used in the home work in approximately the same way, although the circuitry is designed for pictures rather than letters. This presents problems for people who purchase home computers that are made for use with standard TV sets. The characters are rarely as satisfactory as those produced on a computer monitor, which is explicitly designed to generate the sharper edges needed for print and graphics.

The fundamental job of the visual system is to detect the presence of each of those individual dots. Once this is done, the eye-brain combination integrates them into a meaningful pattern, the letter "F".

What causes an individual dot to be detected by the eye? Ultimately, it will be detected if the contrast is sufficiently great. That is, the amount of light generated by the dot pattern must be sufficiently greater than the light generated by the background of the screen.

Adequate contrast is an important criterion in evaluating the quality of any visual display.

This holds for print on paper as well, except that the relationships are reversed: the light from the character must be sufficiently *less* (i.e., darker) than the background.

The difference in light levels between dot and background is picked up by the eye and translated first into a pattern of nerve impulses and, ultimately, into the conscious awareness of the letter "F" by the brain. At this point, the higher functions of the brain become involved. The visual information in the light pattern that forms the letter is part of the conceptual information structure called "language." A person's cognitive skills and previous habits and experiences critically determine the way in which the information is processed. In fact, the speed and efficiency with which that pattern of light is perceived as a letter in the English alphabet depends on the fact that the letter "F" already exists as a conceptual structure in the viewer's memory. For example, if the viewer's only language is Japanese, the "F" pattern will have no meaning; it would not be integrated into the ongoing stream of conscious information processing. The viewer's eye would skip over the letter without retaining its information, in the same way that someone who knows no Japanese will skip over the Japanese instructions that accompany many new pieces of equipment.

The Eye

The primary function of the eye (see Figure 5-1) is to bring the light rays from the dots of the letter F to a focus on a layer of light-sensitive cells called the *retina*. (It can be compared to the film of a camera.) The front surface of the eye, the *cornea*, is a part of the lens system which does not change. (Readers familiar with photographic lens systems will know this as fixed focal length.) The eye contains a second structure called the *lens*, which does change its shape in order to bring objects from different distances into focus on the retina. The *iris* is the circular diaphragm in front of the lens which gives the eye its characteristic color; the diameter of its opening can change, thus controlling the amount of light which enters the eye.

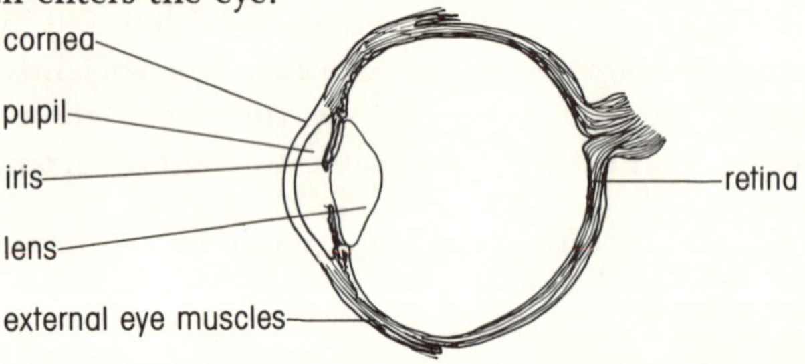

Figure 5-1.
The human eye.

cornea
pupil
iris
lens
external eye muscles
retina

The *pupil* is the name of the opening in the iris (it corresponds to the aperture in a camera lens). As the pupil becomes smaller, which it does in brighter light, objects in front of or more distant than the single object being focused upon are seen more clearly. In effect, there is a tolerance zone of distance within which the image can be in focus. This tolerance zone is called the *depth of focus*. The depth of focus is greater in bright light than in low light. For example, in low light, the pupil will be large, and if the eye is focusing on a screen at arm's length, only those objects slightly in front of or behind the screen will be clearly in focus. However, if the light is made brighter, the pupil will become smaller, and objects somewhat closer to the viewer in front of the screen, and even farther behind it, will be clearly in focus. (For photographers, this corresponds to depth of field.)

Changes in response to different light patterns by both the lens and the iris are controlled by the *internal* muscles of the eye. In addition, three pairs of *external* muscles rotate each eyeball in its socket.

The *retina*, the receiving end of the focused image, contains densely packed arrays of specialized nerve cells called rods and cones. It is the rods and cones that detect light and transform it into nerve signals, which then travel to the brain. The rods, which are more sensitive than the cones, detect very low levels of light, which permits night vision, while the cones are specialized for the fine detail and color of day vision.

An important function of the retina is that of changing its level of sensitivity to light depending on the prevailing light level. When you move from an area of brightness (such as a sunny, snow-covered plaza) to one of relative darkness (a movie theater), or vice versa, *adaptation* occurs. The retina readjusts its sensitivity so that it can function at a lower or higher light level. This adjustment process takes a perceptible amount of time, sometimes several minutes. (Photographers will see in this an analogy to changing film speed; the technically minded will recognize this as a kind of automatic gain control system.)

In most people's daily lives, changes in light levels are usually not this extreme. A second kind of adaptation, which happens much faster, is more relevant to the problems encountered in the office. Assume that you are again outside in the snow, and a small cloud temporarily blocks the sun for a second or so. This event represents two major changes in light intensity with which the retina must rapidly cope. It does this so quickly that you are usually not aware that anything happened. This kind of rapid adaptation occurs when an office worker looks from a brightly lit piece of paper to a dim VDT monitor, and back to the paper in quick succession.

Vision in the Electronic Office

Elizabeth sits in front of her terminal. She calls up a file she has typed before and begins to proofread. An intricate process begins. As she looks at the screen for the first time, three integrated mechanisms work together to bring the dots making up the characters into focus on her retina.

First, both eyes must point toward the same place. To do this, the external muscles rotate each eyeball inward by a precise amount determined by the distance from the screen. This is called *convergence*. At the same time, the muscles of the lens contract, allowing the shape of the lens to assume the appropriate thickness (power) to bring the image into focus. This is called *accommodation*.

Finally, the pupil contracts by reflex. This acts both to provide some control over the amount of light falling on the retina and to maximize the depth of focus at that distance. This decreases the need for precise accommodation to a particular distance. (This reflex contraction is equivalent to stopping down the shutter of a camera.)

Elizabeth is now reading the text on the screen. Her eyes are properly converged and have accommodated to the distance to the screen. Now a different pattern of eye movements takes over, which scans in a horizontal pattern, taking roughly the same path as the raster. The patterns of dots are integrated by the visual portion of the brain into a meaningful set of symbols, which are smoothly perceived as parts of the English language. If she had been scanning lists of numbers, the translation would have been slower because the context provided by the meaning of the words would not be present.

She finds what she thinks is an error. She must move her eyes to the paper copy to check it. But the copy is lying on the desk next to her keyboard. To focus on the copy, she must make a combination eye, head, and neck movement, in which the eyes themselves must first move together to the right and down, and then converge (point toward the same place) to the distance of the paper. Again, the lens must accommodate to the new distance through muscle contraction; the closer the object, the greater the lens power needed, and the greater the muscular effort. Finally, the pupil contracts, thereby increasing the depth of focus and minimizing the need for the final fine tuning of the accommodation system.

One more factor must be taken into account. The paper copy is composed of dark letters on white paper as compared with bright letters on a dark screen. Consequently, the overall level of light reflected from the white paper is higher than the light emitted from the screen, and the retina needs to change its level of adaptation. The pupil diameter will also change in response to the different level of light.

This whole process is reversed a moment later when Elizabeth shifts her attention back to the screen to correct the error she discovered.

The picture can be completed by recalling that Elizabeth sits facing a full wall of window glass (see Figure 5-2) and that behind her are banks of overhead light fixtures. Since it is a bright sunlit day, any time that she raises her eyes even slightly, the image of the bright window falls on her retina. This requires major changes in adaptation.

Figure 5-2.
Elizabeth's office, showing sunlight streaming in the floor-to-ceiling windows and the reflections of the overhead lights on the monitor screen.

In addition, since the face of the screen is glass, it acts as a mirror, reflecting the bright image of the light fixtures behind her and general light from the room (glare). This results in two problems. First, the reflected light and images of the light fixtures interfere with the copy on the screen Elizabeth is reading: as the light of the reflected images is added to the light content of the characters and background, the overall contrast is reduced, making reading from the screen more difficult. Suppose the light intensity of the character F is 10 and the background, 1. The contrast ratio is 10:1, or 10. Now, assume that the light from a reflected overhead lamp falls across the image. Its intensity is 5. Therefore, 5 units of light intensity are added to both the character and background. The resulting contrast ratio is 15:6 or 2.5. This drop in contrast ratio from 10 to 2.5 accounts for the reading difficulty.

Second, since the image of the light fixture is a reflected image of an object several feet away, the accommodative system of the eye tends to change its focus to that distance, at the same time that it tries to keep its focus on the task at hand. Elizabeth's brain is receiving two different visual signals: one from the characters generated by the VDT, and the other from the reflected image of the light fixture. She must choose, at some level of consciousness, which one to focus on. This is, at the very least, a resource allocation problem.

Finally, Elizabeth, who is 43 years of age, wears bifocals. This means that, in order to see the screen clearly, she must tilt her head backward to look through the reading glass portion of the lens. This generates muscle problems in the neck. Because the reading lens of her bifocals was designed for distances closer than the screen, she also has to lean toward the monitor, which results in kyphosis.

Potential Sources of Visual Problems

Each of the elements in the description above reflects the normal operation of the visual system. Even the glare and bifocal problems are hardly unique to the use of VDTs. Why, then, does discussion of VDT work so frequently include reference to visual problems? (Some have suggested that the initials "VD" in VDT stand for "visual discomfort.") To attempt to address this question, it may be helpful to look at the three key categories of potential visual problems to which we have alluded earlier in the chapter. These are:

1. Permanent damage
2. Long-term changes
3. Short-term discomfort

Permanent Damage

Virtually all experts agree that VDT work does *not* present any special hazard to the visual system in terms of tissue damage or disease, such as cataracts. For some occupations (such as welding and working with lasers), such visual hazards are a real possibility. However, in the case of VDT work, there is nothing about the known physical characteristics of the VDT — particularly with respect to the levels of radiant energy it emits — which would make such hazards likely.

Long-Term Changes

Long-term changes may be defined as changes requiring visual correction (i.e., eyeglasses). The possible role of the VDT in long-term changes in visual function is more problematic.

Circumstances that require high levels of visual effort — that is, that require the visual mechanisms to work more than normal — over long periods of time may tend to cause gradual deterioration of visual function, thus leading to the necessity for correction with eyeglasses. If this were the case, and if VDT work required particularly high levels of visual effort, the argument could be made that VDT work leads to long-term visual changes.

Although both of these conditions sound reasonable, they are far from universally accepted by experts in the field. With regard to the first point, some research evidence has suggested that suboptimal visual environments can lead to long-term progressive visual changes in the direction of near-sightedness. However, this evidence is disputed by other experts. Furthermore, it has been argued that work at VDTs is no more visually demanding than many other kinds of tasks in a modern society, such as reading, visual inspection, and microscopy.

There has also been some indication that eye care professionals are consulted more frequently by VDT operators than by other clerical workers. This finding, if supported, could reflect a cause and effect relationship between high visual demand and changes in the visual system. Alternatively, it could indicate a pre-existing visual defect, previously undetected or unnoticed by the individual, but exacerbated by the VDT task.

The current state of evidence does not allow any of these arguments to be either clearly accepted or rejected. One of the complicating factors is the baseline problem: it has been estimated that two-thirds of all people require some kind of optical correction before the age of 40, and that virtually all require correction some time after this age. Furthermore, in any occupational group, the number of people who do not have the *proper* correction is likely to be large. (For example, in a study of relatively well-paid computer professionals, 38% were found to be improperly corrected; this figure agrees with estimates of eye care professionals.) Both of these factors can cause considerable practical difficulties for researchers attempting to identify clear cause and effect relationships between VDT work and incidence of visual corrections required.

Finally, even if such causal relationships were established, it is not clear that the label "health hazard" would be warranted on these grounds alone.

Short-Term Discomfort

There is a large body of evidence suggesting that VDT operators experience elevated levels of visual discomfort following prolonged periods of work at their terminals. However, it has been very difficult for visual scientists to establish direct links between specific reports of visual discomfort and specific changes in the functioning of the focusing and adaptational mechanisms which are presumed to underlie these complaints. Even the labels used are controversial. The common terms "eye strain" or "visual fatigue" imply that excessive demands on eye muscles are the direct cause of the problem. Unlike strain and fatigue in the larger muscle systems (arm, shoulder, back and leg, etc.), these relationships have not been established in relation to the eye muscles. This does not *necessarily* mean that visual discomfort has nothing to do with the muscle systems of the eye: these systems are extraordinarily intricate, and their detailed functioning is not completely understood.

Understanding this system is made even more complicated by the fact that the brain is involved, as well as the eye. For instance, the discomfort experienced at the region of the eyeball may reflect problems existing at higher levels. This can occur in two different ways. One source of these symptoms may be the "mental" effort required to detect, interpret, or otherwise resolve a poor visual environment. Another source may be general psychophysiological stresses in the body as a whole. You can imagine that you may well experience some symptoms of eye discomfort at 2 A.M. while frantically trying to master a lengthy report which you must present at a 9 A.M. meeting. The symptoms will probably occur despite the fact that you are working in a place which is nearly ideal for this kind of visual task. On the other hand, you may feel perfectly comfortable when, two weeks later, you are reading a murder mystery while lying on the beach in direct sunlight — a visual environment with glare and contrast which present appalling reading conditions.

It would be dangerous, however, to leave this discussion with the impression that visual discomfort is somehow "all in your head" and that since it is not understood, it should be ignored. Visual discomfort is a real problem with the potential to affect vast numbers of people. The fatigue-stress-resource allocation model discussed in Chapter 2 would suggest that to the extent that an operator must cope with a perception of discomfort, that operator will have less energy available for the task at hand. Moreover, experts agree *in general* regarding the linkages among poor visual environments, high visual demand, and visual discomfort, even if the precise details of these linkages remain elusive.

Based on what is known, however, some potential sources of problems are fairly obvious. Some studies have linked removal of these problems with decreasing discomfort; others with increased task performance. It is reasonable to infer that conditions which improve visual performance will likewise decrease visual complaints, and vice versa.

The VDT as a Unique Visual Problem

If one assumes that, in general, visual discomfort results from some sort of excess load on the eye-brain system — however poorly defined — there are several potential sources of that load in the VDT workstation. In fact, certain specific elements of the *typical* VDT installation are clearly different from traditional paper-based office environments, and they deserve special consideration.

These distinguishing elements are all present in Elizabeth's office.

1. *Glare*. The display screen is covered with glass, thereby acting as a mirror and reflecting objects and general light behind the operator.
2. *Vertical orientation of the screen*. The display screen is oriented vertically, requiring the operator to work with the head erect, rather than angled downward. This also means that bright sources of light are more likely to be in the operator's field of view beyond the screen.
3. *Character formation*. The characters generated by most VDTs are made up of dots, rather than the solid lines and curves characteristic of print on paper. The dots are regenerated, rather than fixed in time, by a raster scan which is repeated once every 1/30 or 1/60th of a second. This is important with regard to the problem of flicker.
4. *Direction (polarity) of contrast*. These dots are usually bright spots against a dark background, as opposed to dark lines and curves on a light background.
5. *Character shape*. The shape of certain characters may actually differ from conventional shapes. This can affect the ease with which they are "recognized" by the brain.
6. *Line spacing*. The vertical spacing of text on the VDT screen differs from that of text on paper.

7. *Scrolling and moving text.* Text can be moved across the screen in a variety of different ways. It can be "scrolled" (moved line by line) across the screen face. Varying amounts of text can instantly disappear from one place and be inserted somewhere else. A blinking marker or cursor on the screen constantly reminds the operator where to begin keying again. Entire pages can be reformatted instantly.

These characteristics of VDTs are generally thought to place additional demands on the eye-brain system. In the next few pages, we will look at these problem areas — and at some proposed solutions — in more detail.

Glare and the Vertical Orientation of the Screen

The geometry of the VDT display requires the operator to sit with his or her head in a more upright posture than usual. The operator is also sitting in front of a display screen that is covered with glass, the result being that the presence of *glare*, or unwanted light, is more likely to become a serious problem than in the traditional office. Reflections of objects and light sources behind the operator are superimposed on the characters generated by the computer. If the image is of an object at some distance, the focusing system of the eye may be "fooled" into trying to respond to the distant object while at the same time trying to keep the screen in focus. This poses more difficulty for the worker if the reflected image is of a person or object in motion. The reflection of a light source, such as a window or lamp, may also act to veil the characters on the screen lying under the reflection, reducing their contrast in the manner described earlier in this chapter.

However, contrast reduction can occur even if there are no visible reflections. Diffuse reflection of bright surrounding light sources can produce an overall veiling effect across large areas of the screen, and thus wash out character contrast.

The erect posture of the worker also makes it more likely that sources of bright light *beyond* the terminal may fall within the field of view, competing with the dark screen for adaptational control. A bright window, or someone else's desk lamp, or even the overhead lighting system may serve as a source of glare. The extent to which glare is a problem depends on how large and bright the glare source is, how close it is to the operator's field of view, and the extent to which the material on the screen is already difficult to see (either because it is too small, or because its contrast is already low). For workers over the age of 40, normal changes in the structure of the eye make glare an even worse problem than for younger people.

Control of glare and reflection is partly dependent on monitor characteristics, and partly on environmental lighting. So many interrelated variables are involved and so much is unpredictable, even by lighting experts, that it is wise to attempt control at all levels.

Control of Ambient Light

The source of glare, of course, is ambient light, which cannot be eliminated unless people work in the dark. On the other hand, a "more light is better" philosophy is questionable with hard copy, and counterproductive with VDTs. Lower ambient light levels plus individual task lights for hard copy are often the best solution, even though the task light which is placed ideally for one worker may become another worker's source of glare and reflection.

The banks of overhead lights often installed in offices and factories are a common source of reflection, and are often too intense, unusually harsh, and (if fluorescent) prone to flicker. Grid-shaped directional baffles, which direct the light straight downward, can reduce the extent to which these lights are reflected on monitors situated at an angle from them. However, even indirect lighting can sometimes lead to problems with diffuse glare.

Although windows are often a source of glare or reflections, cutting off natural light by draping or screening windows heavily, or eliminating windows (and therefore outside views) altogether, has important negative psychological repercussions. Effective window treatments are not always easy to achieve. However, window glare can be minimized by insuring that windows are neither directly in front of, nor directly behind, the operator. A variety of window treatments — blinds, screens, transparent filters — are available to reduce glare while still allowing visual access to the outside.

Individual desk lights — task lights — may be used, although these take up more space, require additional power cords, and require light bulbs which must be changed. Depending on the office layout, they may still end up as someone else's glare source.

Control of Glare at the Monitor

The curved glass on the monitor acts like a wide-angle mirror, reflecting light that hits it from a wide area behind and above the worker, and even mirroring the worker. Some manufacturers of monitors have tried to alleviate this problem by producing etched screens and chemically coated screens (like coated camera lenses) and even by installing filters during manufacture. These vary in their effectiveness.

Filters may also be purchased separately and placed in front of the screen. Several types are available, which differ in their optical strategies and costs. Neutral density filters, colored filters, and polarized filters are all based on the principle that most ambient light passes through them twice — once on the way to the monitor and once on the way back to the operator's eyes. Therefore, they should affect ambient light twice as much as light coming only from the video screen. Neutral density filters, like smoked glass, simply reduce the amount of light passing through them, thus reducing ambient light twice and light from the monitor only once. Colored filters match the color of the phosphor, and filter out all other colors. (The phosphor is the luminescent substance which coats the inside of the CRT surface, and which "lights up" when bombarded by electrons, thereby generating the image.) Polarizing filters, like polarized sunglasses, filter out light rays going in a certain direction. All these filters present two problems. The first is that light can be reflected from *their* surfaces, especially if they are contoured, like the monitor. (Some filters are treated to reduce these reflections.) A second problem is that all reduce, to a greater or lesser extent, the light of the image coming from the monitor. This can sometimes be counteracted by increasing the brightness of the monitor, but in general, character definition is somewhat degraded.

A different approach is seen in the micromesh filter, which, if magnified, would look like the square grid of an ice-cube tray. The filter acts like a small-scale baffle, cutting off ambient light which hits it at an angle. The mesh itself cuts off some light from the monitor; nevertheless, these screens can be effective.

An often overlooked problem for both screens and filters (whether added on or built in) is that of cleanliness. Dust, greasy fingerprints, and other dirt decrease light and distort images coming from the monitor, and reflect ambient light. Special cleaning agents are often required. Mesh filters are particularly likely to trap dust and dirt.

The effectiveness of filters is a subject of much debate. Perhaps the most conservative position is that of Snyder (1984). Using a sophisticated image quality assessment procedure, he argued that filter technology at the time of his study had not yet progressed to the point where glare could be controlled effectively without also seriously reducing image quality.

According to other studies, however, some users have found certain filters to be effective. If glare problems in the environment cannot be remedied, the difficulties presented by antireflection filters may be offset by their benefits: people may be willing to accept some degree of image quality reduction in exchange for glare reduction. Nevertheless, the best solution is to improve the overall lighting environment. Since all filters have shortcomings, which (if any) will be effective in any given situation is best determined by trial and error at the worksite.

Control at the Level of the Workstation

Physically moving the monitor (and/or the entire workstation) in relation to windows or other light sources may be helpful. In general, the front of the VDT screen should be at a right angle to the windows, and not directly under overhead light fixtures. If there is a line of such light fixtures, the operator's line of sight to the screen should be parallel to that line. Tilting and swiveling the monitor, when that is possible, can eliminate reflections. If the set-up does not lend itself to this, sometimes the monitor can be propped up in the front or the back to accomplish the same end. Shields and hoods can be used like sun visors; they can be either manufactured or makeshift.

Obviously, there are no universally applicable solutions for lighting in electronic offices, because each building is unique in terms of the available external and internal light, as well as office layout. Much depends on the tasks being performed. If work is mostly screen intensive, overall light levels can be lower. On the other hand, tasks such as engineering applications, when workers need to view both high-resolution graphics terminals and detailed engineering drawings, present particularly difficult problems, even for experts. Awareness of the problem will often generate creative solutions in the form of tilted screens, changes in workstation and screen angle so as to reorient the screen away from glare sources, and the use of various forms of baffling, visors, and shields, homemade if need be.

Character Formation

On most VDTs currently in use, the characters (letters and numbers) are constructed of patterns of dots. Some of these characters are easier to read than others. In general, if the spaces between the dots are visible, reading is made more difficult, because the visual system automatically emphasizes and accentuates gaps, breaks, and edges which exist in the visual world. Thus, your brain *expects* to see the letter "F" as three solid connected lines, but your eye tells you that, on the VDT monitor, it is actually a collection of dots. *This perceptual conflict leads to a slow-down in reading speed.* You can verify this simply by noting how long it takes you to read copy printed by a dot-matrix printer as compared with copy from a standard typewriter. (Some newer printers have "near letter quality" modes which produce text more similar to that of a typewriter, in addition to a faster "draft" mode. It is the draft mode which causes the greater perceptual conflict and resulting reading slowdown.) As a general rule, the more dots there are, and the smaller the spaces between them, the more nearly a character will look like print, and the easier it will be to read.

Originally, characters on VDT displays were formed from matrices of dots consisting of 5 columns and 7 rows (as indicated earlier in this chapter). Current VDT display designs allow for larger numbers of dots, so that the spaces between the dots are no longer visible, or actually generate solid characters on the VDT screen. Snyder (1984), who has done much of the basic research in this area, has shown that a dot matrix of 7 × 9 elements or 9 × 11 elements can be easily read, depending on the stylistic characteristics of the typeface that has been used. Snyder demonstrated that a typeface called "Huddleston," which was deliberately designed for dot matrix use, proved to be more legible than alternative typefaces. Unfortunately, most manufacturers have not taken advantage of this kind of information, and seem to have designed their own typefaces without reference to proven legibility studies. However, the 7 × 9 and 9 × 11 matrices are now frequently used.

Paradoxically, the spaces between the dots can be offset in ways that violate normal principles of good vision. Normally, people expect that the sharper (crisper) the edges of an object are, and the closer it is to their eyes (within normal reading distance), the easier it is to read. All of these assumptions are incorrect in the case of dot matrix characters, at least within a certain range. If the character is slightly out of focus, the edges of the dots blur into one another, and the lines and curves look solid. This can be accomplished by moving *away* from the screen until the characters look smooth. On the other hand, if the characters are too blurred, reading time is slowed, and visual discomfort is likely. Thus, an optimal viewing distance must be determined, and this is likely to vary considerably among individual operators. This is one reason for the discrepancies in recommendations for standardized viewing distances.

The strategy of distancing from the screen will not work, of course, if the characters are too small. The minimum character size should be between 16 to 18 minutes of arc, where this can be computed by the ratio of character height to viewing distance multiplied by 3450 (see Chapter 4). (Some VDT screen characters on the market fall below these minimum recommendations at likely viewing distances.)

For reading of text, an *upper* limit of 25 minutes of arc is recommended. Letters larger than this will, in general, slow down reading speed by interfering with the normal pattern of eye movement. Furthermore, if letters are too large, the individual dots may become visible.

Larger letters can be satisfactory as labels or titles, where continuity of text processing is less important.

For ease of reading, the amount of light energy emitted by a character against that of its background should be at least in the ratio of 9 to 1. (Unfortunately, a standardized, accurate technique for making this measurement has yet to be agreed upon; most values presented in the literature are approximations.) If character contrast is less than this, the letters will appear washed out and difficult to read.

Other problems in character legibility may arise from electronic instabilities which cause individual characters to appear to tremble or jitter. In some systems, this may occur when the memory load is near capacity or when the screen is full.

In selecting equipment, managers should ensure that contrast is adequate, that if dot matrix characters are used, at least a 7×9 array is employed, that characters are large enough, but not too large (between 16 and 25 minutes of arc), and that they don't jitter. In effect, the thoughtful manager will develop the same kinds of awareness of visual display quality that a modern lover of music develops towards recorded sound quality.

Direction (Polarity) of Contrast

Elizabeth's work requires her to shift her attention repeatedly from the display screen, which has light characters on a dark background, to the paper copy, which consists of dark letters on a light background. This difference is called the *polarity of contrast*; the display screen with its light letters is considered a *positive contrast* display, while the paper copy has the characteristics of *negative contrast*. Clearly, the focusing mechanisms (accommodation, convergence, and pupillary function) and adaptational mechanisms of the eye must work harder in switching attention between materials which are of different polarities, as opposed to typing in a paper-based office, where changes of polarity do not occur. The issue is whether this extra work is within the normal range of function for the visual system, or whether it is preferable to provide an alternative video display system that has the same polarity as the paper copy.

The relative merits of such a "reverse video display," which, like paper, presents dark characters against a light background, are still in question. It seems unlikely that the extra effort required by the accommodation and pupillary systems to switch from positive to negative contrast is significant enough, in itself, to justify the prescription of reverse video. The jury is still out, however, on the changes in adaptation which are required. Moreover, there are clear advantages to the use of reverse video in that the mirroring effects of reflected light from the face plate are less severe when the background is light.

However, with reverse video displays come a new group of problems. The typical raster scan repeats itself 60 times per second. In the case of positive contrast, the screen background is dark, and these repetitions are not noticed. However, if the change to negative contrast with a 60 cycle per sec (60 Hz) repetition, or refresh rate, is made, the light background appears, to many people, to flicker visibly.

Although people vary in their sensitivity to flicker (older people are less sensitive), it is an annoyance, and can produce nausea and headache in some people. Thus, if a reverse video screen is used, the refresh rate must be increased greatly. Screens with ranges of 85 to 100 Hz are recommended, and are available on the market, but they tend to be more expensive than those with lower refresh rates. This is because standard commercial TV technology uses a 60 Hz refresh rate, and it is less costly to design a monitor using this technology.

People are particularly sensitive to flicker when the monitor is off to one side (either someone else's monitor or a monitor placed to the side when work is more copy intensive). This results from the fact that the human visual system is particularly good at detecting motion out of the corner of the eye — the reason being, of course, to warn of possible sources of danger moving into the peripheral field of view. The perceptual system is set up to interpret any change in the visual field over time as motion (this is the reason that changes over time on a stationary movie screen or a VDT screen are interpreted as movement). When changes occur in the *peripheral* field, they are received by this very sensitive mechanism which warns of something potentially harmful approaching. Flicker, which is also change in the visual field over time, is thus picked up by the same perceptual mechanism, and its impact is difficult to ignore.

Another familiar source of flicker is a malfunctioning fluorescent light tube. This, too, tends to be disturbing, since it is most likely to be seen through peripheral vision.

When selecting computer equipment, it is important for the manager to take a close look at the monitor, observing it under actual operating conditions for indications of disturbing flicker. This is particularly important if reverse video is employed. When choosing software, it is well to remember that it is relatively easy for computer programmers to cause some or all of the screen to "blink" on or off — indicating some operation is in progress — without realizing that this, too, may result in flicker problems. Even the blinking cursor causes problems for some people.

Character Shape: The Language Connection

The principles just discussed are only a set of boundary conditions defining minimum criteria for legibility. However, given current levels of VDT use and the even greater levels predicted for the very near future, electronically generated text is becoming a serious competitor to traditional print on paper. The "paperless office" is not yet here, but some of its effects are already being felt.

If VDT text is gradually supplanting the printed page, its legibility must be assessed against the same standards as hard copy. After centuries of exploration beginning with Gutenberg if not earlier (some by trial and error and some by more scientific methods), the presentation of print on the page has now reached a high level of effectiveness. The VDT text, by comparison, has a long way to go. In point of fact, several studies comparing ordinary reading and proofreading on VDTs and on paper copy, have found paper copy to be superior. These studies agree with our own experience: in preparing this book on a word processor, we found it necessary to print draft copies on paper, because too many errors are missed in screen editing. Informal inquiries indicate that this is a common problem. The reason is that stylistic characteristics of letters and the ways they are spaced greatly influence readability.

The characteristic shapes and forms making up a given set of letters and numbers is known as the *font*, or *typeface*. Typefaces used on diplomas and wedding invitations are used for their aesthetic qualities, but are not very readable; typefaces used in newspapers and books have usually been chosen for function (ease of reading).

Within this century, scientific studies have been conducted on the readability of type, and generally acceptable ergonomic guidelines are available. However, it must be emphasized that these guidelines apply only to traditional print on paper. When the dot matrix video display enters the picture, the old rules are not necessarily applicable: the limitations of the matrix size, particularly when there are fewer elements, exert considerable constraints on the capability to form characters.

Consequently, special fonts have been developed for use with dot matrix displays. The better ones have been designed carefully with regard to insuring that characters which normally look very similar (such as "O" and "Q", "I" and "T") be differentiated as much as possible. An important research study by Snyder (1984) indicated large differences in the number of errors made in reading characters formed from different dot-matrix fonts, even though these fonts were of the same size and number of dots. He also showed that, within certain limits, performance improved as the number of dots in the matrix increased and the size of the letters decreased, both changes having the effect of decreasing the spaces between the dots.

In designing dot matrix characters, it is sometimes necessary to distort some aspects of character shape deliberately in order to make the characters more easily distinguishable within the constraints of the dot matrix. One example is the crossing of zeros, to distinguish them from the letter "O". Another is that in the font called "Huddleston," which Snyder showed resulted in the fewest character recognition errors, the diagonal crossbar of the letter "N" is three times thicker than the two upright bars, and the width of the top portion of the number "8" is 55% less than that of the bottom portion. Both of those characters run into a conflict between *identifiability* (whether they have clear, sharp details which differentiate them from other characters) and *acceptability* (how closely they resemble the general notion of what they should look like) (Bouma, 1980). Many characters in Huddleston and other fonts which are deliberately designed to be identified easily in a dot matrix format do not look much like the letters and numbers generally used in print. (Another example of designing a typeface to meet a technological requirement is the font called "Computer," which is used for the bank numbers seen at the bottoms of checks. However, these are meant to be read primarily by computers, not humans.)

Even if they are not being deliberately distorted, many dot matrix characters differ in subtle but important ways from print characters. In lower case printed characters, for example, the lower portions (called *descenders*) of the letters "p" and "q" extend well below the baseline of the text. However, in some dot matrix fonts the "p's" and "q's" are simply shrunk and pushed upward so that the total letter occupies exactly the same height as other lower case letters, with the bottom of the descender resting on the same baseline as the letters that do not have descenders.

It is known that the form and shape of *words* as well as letters can be important determinants of the speed and ease of reading extended passages of text. In the basic dot matrix configuration, the matrices are equally spaced within a given word. Accordingly, all characters (even "i" and "m") have the same width; this is also true of most typewriter characters. However, in *typeset* materials (such as this book) and in material produced by some typewriters and printers, some characters occupy more space than the others — an "m" generally occupies three times as much space as an "i", for instance. This is called *proportional spacing*, and has been shown to be easier to read than equal spacing (Beldie, Pastoor, & Schwarz, 1983).

As VDT hardware and software sophistication develops, better fonts are becoming available. Advertisements have begun to mention "true descenders" and "proportional spacing." As VDT text comes to resemble traditional typeset copy more, readability will improve. The potential buyer of terminals, software, and printers should be aware of the time (and money) that is saved when copy is easily legible, and make purchase decisions accordingly.

Line Spacing

Line spacing also has an important effect on legibility. In the complex perceptual processes by which text is read, specific eye movement patterns occur. Typically, three types of patterns are seen (Bouma, 1980). *Reading movements* scan left to right (in languages like English), picking up about ten letters per scan. When the end of the line of text is detected, a *line movement* is programmed by the brain, and the eye moves down and toward the beginning of the next line. Usually there is error in this movement, with the point of focus landing some small distance to the right of the beginning of the line. Thus, a third kind of movement, a *correction movement*, from right to left, is required. Correction movements also occur when there is some difficulty in reading, in either content or form.

The vertical spacing between lines helps to determine the accuracy of eye movement from one line to the next. A rule of thumb states that line spacing should be at least 1/30 of the line length. If the spacing is less, the downward part of the eye movement may be too great, and one or more lines may be skipped. If the text that is being read has some degree of meaningful continuity, the reader will notice that suddenly the text does not make sense, and will go back and search for the beginning of the proper line. If, on the other hand, non-contextual materials (such as rows of numbers) are being read, the error may not be detected. In either case, speed and accuracy of processing have been impaired.

This rule also explains why, in newspapers, where a goal is to get as much print on a page as possible, text is presented in narrow columns. Because the line length is short, less space is needed between lines for accurate reading, and so the print can be made more dense.

Unfortunately, the television-based origins of VDT technology may make meeting this vertical spacing criterion difficult. Most VDT screens, like television screens, have horizontal dimensions that are greater than their vertical dimensions, while with most paper copy the reverse is true. Accordingly, depending upon the spacing parameters built into the raster patterns, the spacing may be less than optimal.

It is reasonable to assume that subtle but important differences between conventional printed text and electronic text can result in less efficient use of basic reading skills and habits. Observed symptoms of visual discomfort may reflect excessive demands on the brain's visual and interpretive functions. Both comfort and performance may be related to the extent to which electronically generated text is similar to print.

Scrolling and Moving Text

In contrast to the subtle character generation distinctions described above, perhaps the most obvious difference between text on paper and that on VDT is in the method by which large or small chunks of text may be moved. In a typical text-editing or word-processing program, the entire display can be moved up or down one line at a time (scrolling), or the entire screen can be replaced (paging). Within a given screen display, whole blocks of material may be moved instantly from one place to another (inserting). Letters, words, lines, paragraphs, even entire pages may be deleted by a single key stroke. In an already filled screen, new material can be inserted at any point, and the remaining text will automatically make way like a row of obedient soldiers. Recent advances allow the creation of "windows" or screen partitions through which different passages of text can be moved independently.

These characteristics, of course, are what give such systems their remarkable flexibility. People who spend large amounts of time preparing written materials will, after having learned to use such a system, tend to feel seriously cheated if forced to return to a typewriter. However, the fact remains that, for people who have spent most of their lives dealing with stable paper copy, such changes are different than anything their visual systems have previously experienced. Eye movement patterns, learned over years of experience, are developed in the context of a stable visual field. Inherent differences in perception take place when the text itself moves.

It might be argued that humans have always experienced the movement of text in the course of reading. One might pick up a letter, read it, and then turn it over. However, in this case, there is a precise linkage between eye, brain, and hand. The amount and direction of muscle activity in the hand turning the paper is precisely correlated with the perception of the angle of the turned paper. In a sense, the brain knows exactly what to expect.

In the case of the page movement command in a computer text editor, the linkage between muscle action and perception is essentially arbitrary. The muscle action used to execute the command which moves the page has no direct physical relationship to the direction and extent of "movement." Furthermore, these acts — typically pressing one or a pair of keys — will differ with each new word-processing program.

Much research has been done in experimental psychology to determine what happens when the correlation between motor feedback and visual input is disrupted. In a typical experiment of this kind, found in most introductory psychology textbooks, a person wears reversing prisms, which make the visual world appear upside down. (A much milder version of the experiment occurs for anyone who changes to a new prescription for eyeglasses.) If a person wearing such prisms starts walking through a normal environment, or even observes his or her own hand in motion, there is a severe discrepancy between visual and muscular information, and this discrepancy is typically accompanied by feelings of eye strain and nausea.

The similarity between the prism experiments, in which the visual-motor discrepancy is significant, and the examples of paging and scrolling, where the discrepancies are relatively minor, is strictly suggestive and hypothetical at this point. Furthermore, in the prism experiments, subjects are eventually able to achieve some degree of adaptation to the distortion. Nevertheless, the possibility that these new modes of textual manipulation add to the visual/cognitive demand on the brain, and that such demand is reflected in added discomfort, cannot be rejected out of hand. For some people who have had both experiences, the discomfort of wearing the prism seems very much like that experienced in using the scroll control for the first time.

The Videotropic Response

Informal observation seems to support the presence of what we call *the videotropic response*. The videotropic response is defined as the sheer unwillingness or inability of an individual to remove himself or herself from a video display. This response is acknowledged in the common lore that refers to people "welded" to TV sets; to children (of all ages) lured to videogames or mesmerized by the images on the screen; and to computer fanatics ("hackers") who will not even leave a VDT to eat. It also appears, to some extent, in many ordinary people who spend all or part of their workday in front of a VDT. It is somehow easier to put down a book or paper, or move away from a typewriter, than it is to move away from a VDT.

To the extent that this is true, it would provide yet another explanation or potential cause of visual discomfort, because it is a general rule of thumb that, when all else fails, sufficient rest breaks can be useful in alleviating eye strain problems. It follows from the Grandjean bucket theory that properly spaced rest breaks would allow dissipation of the fatigue associated with visual demand from any source. Such breaks do not always have to be formally legislated rest breaks; on the contrary, research has shown that short, informal rest breaks, as needed, are more effective than scheduled rest breaks.

Rest breaks, accompanied by enough physical movement or exercise to increase circulation, are of great importance because of the fixed viewing distance, fixed posture, and high visual demand conditions of typical VDT work. However, to the extent that the videotropic response occurs, the worker may not want to take such breaks even if they are feasible. Thus, the fascination with the medium (or whatever is responsible for the videotropic response) can cause a worker to ignore symptoms of fatigue or eye strain longer, compounding any stresses imposed by the special characteristics of the VDT.

Visual Defects and the VDT

The discussion so far has been based on the assumption that the worker's visual system itself was functioning satisfactorily. However, as mentioned earlier, there are estimates that at least one-third of the population have uncorrected vision problems. New VDT users might first notice such problems if their VDT work imposed higher visual demand than the work to which they had previously been accustomed.

Farsightedness (hypermetropia) results from a weakness in ability to focus the lens (accommodation). Attempting to focus on close objects requires extra muscular effort, and farsighted people must expend this extra effort at all viewing distances. If their vision is uncorrected, these individuals may be particularly susceptible to discomfort. The opposite is true for *nearsighted* (myopic) people, whose lenses are too powerful. Objects in the distance are blurred, and no amount of effort will correct this; objects which are close will require less effort than in a normal person.

The astute observer can pick up clues relating to possible visual dysfunction from the worker's posture. A nearsighted worker is likely to either bring the monitor and hard copy closer, or bend closer (resulting in kyphosis) to see them. The reverse may be true for the farsighted worker, who may tend to stay in the backward tilted posture. As a result, workers with uncorrected visual problems may also complain of musculoskeletal problems.

Another common problem is that of the person with *astigmatism*, in which the lens system is distorted. Unlike the case for nearsightedness and farsightedness, no action by the individual can completely rectify this situation, although the person may try by angling the head. Workers with astigmatism are particularly susceptible to headaches if corrective lenses are not obtained.

Presbyopia, also known as old-age farsightedness, hits people universally in late youth (about age 40). The presbyopic worker often already has bifocals or half-lenses for close work in general, and will attempt to look at the monitor through the bottom of the glasses, which again leads to musculoskeletal problems arising from angling the head backward. Even if this posture could be maintained, the correction in the lower lens is for reading well within arm's length, whereas the VDT is usually farther away. As a result, the operator may still have difficulty focusing.

If the external muscles of the eyeball are not in balance, and the angle of convergence is not correct, the result is known as *muscle phoria*. Temporary muscle phoria has been observed after intense periods of close work, and may lead to complaints about eye problems. Some people have proposed eye exercises to correct temporary phoria, and that would seem to be reasonable.

The simplest way to deal with all these problems is for the worker to get eyeglasses. In all cases, the person prescribing the lenses should be aware that VDT work is involved, and should be told the actual range of distance of the worker's eyes from the screen. He or she should also be aware of whether other task demands impose additional visual needs (such as looking at distant objects, greeting people, etc.), so that the glasses can be made to minimize strain in holding the head at awkward angles for long periods of time. If VDT work is the primary task, the VDT viewing area of the lens should be placed so that the head angle will not be affected during long hours at the VDT, and so the top or bottom portion of the lens can be used for other visual tasks.

In many cases, the lens prescribed for VDT work may not be satisfactory for general wear. Often, monofocal lenses corrected only for the proper VDT viewing distance will be the most satisfactory. Again, placing hard copy at that same viewing distance, or within the range of depth of focus, is important.

It seems only reasonable that, in an occupation where vision is so important, efforts should be made to insure that it receives proper care. However, there is always a fine balance between putting responsibility on the individual and putting responsibility on management. One issue is whether management or the individual should bear the cost if specialized eyeglasses are required for VDT work. An even more basic issue centers around the extent to which already existing visual defects contribute to eye problems at VDTs.

Many authorities on the subject assume that individuals whose vision is not properly corrected are more likely to encounter VDT-related eye problems. One logical response to this assumption would be the establishment of stringent visual requirements for VDT operators, not allowing individuals to work at a terminal unless they have passed a screening examination.

However, one recent study (Bellucci & Mauli, 1984) found that levels of complaints were more closely related to ergonomic adequacy of the work environment (with respect to location of glare sources, etc.) than to individual visual performance as assessed by opthalmological examination. Moreover, visual complaints decreased after workers were shifted to more ergonomically adequate workstations. These investigators also cited a correlation between more ocular symptoms and worse *general* ergonomics (i.e., work organization, relations with management, air conditioning, posture, etc.), although it is difficult to separate the effects of visual and general ergonomics. This study suggests that at least as much, if not more, attention should be paid to the visual environment as to the visual status of the operators.

It might be fitting to close this chapter with the advice given by the physician Ramazzini, the father of industrial medicine, circa 1700, to printers, sedentary workers, learned men, and those who do fine work: "It would help such workers very much if besides wearing spectacles they would give up the habit of keeping the head constantly bent and the eyes fixed on what they are making; if they would now and again drop their work and turn their eyes elsewhere or snatch a respite from their task and rest the eyes by looking at a number of different things; and we know what Plautus says: 'Sitting hurts your loins, staring your eyes.' "

A Summary of Visual Concerns and the VDT

- Higher levels of discomfort are reported among VDT workers than among non-VDT workers. These complaints are legitimate and must be addressed.
- It is unlikely that damage or permanent visual changes result from prolonged work at VDTs.
- Visual discomfort is thought to be caused by excess demand on the visual (eye-brain) system; certain physical characteristics of VDT work are likely sources of this excess demand.

- Glare presents a greater problem in the electronic office than in the traditional office as a result of both the reflective characteristics of the screen and the upright orientation of the operator's head and neck.
- Glare control should be attempted in the ambient environment (lighting systems and window treatments), and at the terminal itself.
- The dot matrix mode of character formation makes letters and numbers more difficult to read. The less space there is between dot elements, the better the visual quality of the character. Characters should be large enough, and the font should be readable.
- Most characters are displayed as light on a dark background; switching to reverse polarity may aid in glare control, but may also introduce flicker problems.
- Displays should not flicker.
- Reading and manipulating text on a video display terminal requires a different set of muscle/brain functions than reading traditional text.
- The vision of individual operators will vary; some may need glasses to work at a VDT and some may not; some may be more tolerant of ergonomic design problems than others. Visual ergonomics probably plays a greater role than individual visual defects in discomfort.
- Special eyeglasses for VDTs may be required, and these will not have the same prescription as those normally used for reading.

The Physical Work Environment

CHAPTER 6

Five stories above Elizabeth's floor is the Corporate Analysis Department, staffed by teams of M.B.A.s, financial analysts, and other technically trained professionals. Miriam, who has just joined the Leming Corporation with a recent Ph.D. in economics, is in the process of reporting to Eiji, the group chief, who originally hired her. Eiji, however, is in the middle of a crisis and is somewhat distracted.

"We're really delighted to have you aboard, but we'll have to wait until tomorrow for me to welcome you properly," he tells her. "We're very tight on office space, but I'm pretty sure that there's a desk in Room 1232. Everyone's friendly here; why don't you just introduce yourself? I'll get back with you tomorrow."

Carrying her new book of corporate procedures, Miriam looks for Room 1232. She finally finds it, and peers through the glass door to see a standard office, about the size of Eiji's, but with three desks and assorted file cabinets. One desk is, in fact, empty; sitting at the others are two people, a man and a woman. Miriam can see from the name plates that they are both analysts. The woman is named Rose, the man, Kelly.

Miriam walks in and introduces herself as their new office mate. The response is not what she expected.

"Damn it, Kelly, I told you we should have had that desk moved out while it was empty!" shrieks Rose. Then, in a somewhat softer tone to Miriam, "Nothing against you personally, of course. They hire two new useless supervisors, give them huge offices, and everyone else has to double and triple up."

A week later, Miriam has been given her first project, a large chunk of which consists of making sense of a four-foot-thick stack of oversized computer printouts. Her office mates somewhat grudgingly manage to clear out two file cabinet drawers for her, but the file cabinet is across the room, and the printouts won't fit in it. When she first received the printouts, she had planned to leave them in their cardboard boxes on the floor next to her desk. However, Rose told her about a friend who did that, and who subsequently had to spend a frantic three hours searching through the trash in the basement, because the janitors had carted them off! Miriam's printouts end up stacked on her desk.

Miriam has laid out the four sets of numbers she needs, and is starting to work out the best method of comparative analysis, when the phone on Kelly's desk rings. He starts talking in low, anguished, but perfectly audible tones (he is only five feet away) and within 30 seconds, Miriam deduces that he is in the process of breaking up with his wife. For 45 minutes, she tries to concentrate on her analysis and to block out the talk of shame, blame, and retribution.

Some time later, Miriam hears a tap on the door, and Lee, a statistician, comes in. Miriam has been told that part of her project overlaps with work that Lee is doing and she is looking forward to collaborating with him, since he is known to have an excellent conceptual grasp of complex problems. Miriam is ready to launch into her current analyses, but Lee suggests that they get a cup of coffee in the cafeteria. As they wait for the elevator which will take them from the 12th floor to the cafeteria on 2, Lee explains that Kelly and he are in competition for a senior analyst position in another department, and he would prefer that Kelly find out as little as possible about the work he is doing. Because his office doesn't even have an extra chair, and the one conference room is tightly scheduled, he suggests that they meet regularly in the cafeteria.

As they get into the elevator, they are joined by Lucy, a friend of Lee's. Lucy, it turns out, has a private office of sorts: a converted equipment room in an out-of-the-way corner of the corridor. She appears to be starved for human contact and keeps up a steady stream of talk all the way to the cafeteria. It is natural for her to join Lee and Miriam at a table, and soon they are joined by yet another friend, Mark. Even though it is the middle of summer, Mark is carrying a sweater. He explains that he works in the computer room, which is heavily air conditioned. He takes out his contact lenses and Miriam notices that his eyes are red and puffy. She comments on this sympathetically, but Mark replies that he always has this problem. Lee adds that he has had sinus problems ever since he started working in this building; Mark and Lucy report the same thing.

After about half an hour, Mark and Lucy leave, and Lee and Miriam are finally able to start discussing the project. But Miriam begins to feel a little uncomfortable about the level of discussion: she is a precise, careful worker who doesn't like to make a statement, particularly one with quantitative implications, without double checking. But all of her printouts and notes are 10 floors away. She begins to worry about how she'll carry out her end of this collaboration if they keep meeting in the cafeteria.

Now it's 4:45 P.M. Miriam has spent the afternoon trying to concentrate on her work, but it seems that one of her office mates was always talking on the phone. She reviews what she has accomplished and is appalled at how little she has done. She decides that instead of exploring her new city, as she had intended, she had better take some work home. As she gets up, she feels pressure behind her nose, and remembers what she heard at lunch about sinus problems in the building. This job looked wonderful when she was interviewing, she thinks, but maybe it wasn't such a great choice after all. . . .

The Dual Office Environment

The multiple problems encountered by Miriam and her co-workers fall into one of two categories: defects in the *proximate* (or immediate) environment and defects in the *ambient* (or surrounding) environment. The proximate environment is essentially the individual's workspace, or "workspace envelope." Its characteristics include the layout of the office equipment and furniture and the relationships between workspaces. The extent to which the layout enhances communication and insures privacy also determines the nature of the proximate environment. The ambient environment, on the other hand, is characterized by sound (or noise), lighting, temperature, and air quality.

Both environments can be analyzed in terms of the conceptual framework introduced in Chapter 2. Both impose greater or lesser degrees of fatigue and stress on the individual worker, and both affect the worker's ability to concentrate on the task to be performed. Both thus profoundly influence the worker's physical and mental health and therefore his or her productivity, either directly or indirectly.

At the Leming Corporation, as in real life, problems in the proximate and ambient environments tend to overlap. However, the crowded office conditions, the small amount of storage space, and insufficient privacy for most workers suggest problems in the proximate environment. (Lucy's out-of-the-way office, which provided privacy at the expense of opportunity for communication, falls into the same category.) Mark's irritated eyes and the sinus problems experienced by most of the workers point to poor air quality and circulation, a deficiency in the ambient environment. Suboptimal conditions such as these act as sources of fatigue, adding to Grandjean's bucket. They also act as sources of stress, and as distractions leading to poor allocation of resources from an already limited pool. This chapter will be devoted to a closer examination of the workplace as a dual environment that can be analyzed and controlled to prevent or to alleviate these problems.

The Proximate Environment

Communication

The fundamental reason for the existence of the office, automated, electronic, or otherwise, is the *processing of information*. Data (facts, numbers, ideas) are received, stored, organized, and analyzed. Decisions based on this data and its transformations are made and transmitted. Although an increasing number of these functions are being accomplished automatically by machine, it is the exchange of information between *people* in offices which is crucial in determining the effectiveness of organizations. This process of information exchange (*communication*) between people is a mutual act, requiring reception of the message as well as transmission. If the boss writes a beautiful letter to the employees, but it is only posted on the bulletin board, where it may be buried under a host of other material, effective communication has not occurred.

The oldest, and still the basic, mode of communication is face-to-face verbal communication, that is, talking. This can be accompanied by a parallel nonverbal channel of information, sometimes called body language. The president of your company or another superior may say to you, "Your work here is going well," but if he or she avoids eye contact, shows a slight facial expression of distaste, has a flat voice intonation, and is turning away from you, the verbal content of his or her message is being contradicted by these nonverbal signals, and you should quite rightly conclude that things are *not* going so well. If, on the other hand, the speaker faces you directly, looks you in the eye, emphasizes the word "well," and smiles, verbal and nonverbal messages are congruent, and you can believe what is being said.

As the products of technology were introduced, the face-to-face mode of communication became less common, and there was a corresponding loss of the information contained in the nonverbal channel. The first such technological product was writing. Writing extended the ability to communicate over large expanses of space and time, at the cost of both immediacy of contact and nonverbal communication. Many centuries later, the electrical transmission of voice messages brought back both the sense of immediacy and some degree of nonverbal content, in the form of voice intonation.

Today, a dazzling array of technological mechanisms is available to allow people to communicate with one another. The capability now exists to simultaneously record electronically what people say, what they look like when they are saying it, what they write, and the pictures (diagrams, graphs) they produce. Within limits which are rapidly diminishing, this information can then be delivered to whomever the speaker wishes, at whatever time and place he or she wishes.

The decision maker now has the opportunity — and responsibility — to select the best mode of communication from among several options ("Shall I telephone, write, or wait until I see him in person?"). He or she must decide which kinds of transactions are likely to require nonverbal content to be effective (e.g., telling people they've done/not done a good job), and which do not require nonverbal content (e.g., listing stock market quotations). Only then can the proper physical environment and equipment be provided to support whatever kinds of communication methods are selected. The role of ergonomics in communication is to focus on how the physical environment can be structured to make communication as easy and effective as possible.

Privacy

The other side of the communication coin relates to privacy. Although it is important to facilitate office communication, it is equally crucial to insure that privacy is not jeopardized as a result.

In the office, there are two principal kinds of privacy which can be either sacrificed or preserved. These are *visual privacy* and *auditory privacy*. Visual privacy relates to the sense of visual awareness of other people. You lack visual privacy to the extent that your actions can be seen by others or that you can see theirs. Similarly, you lack auditory privacy to the extent that others can hear what you say or you can hear extraneous sounds. (In Chapter 8, a different kind of privacy will be considered: that involved in computer monitoring of work performance.)

Lack of privacy has a direct impact on your work if the realization that you are being observed or listened to inhibits or makes more difficult the things you are doing. In the opening scenario of this chapter, Miriam and Lee were forced to spend significant amounts of their workdays in the cafeteria, which prevented them from doing continuous, concentrated work, and from exchanging essential, confidential information. (In this case, insufficient privacy also made communication ineffective.) Lack of privacy can also lead to job dissatisfaction, which gives rise to organizational costs in terms of increased turnover and absenteeism.

Privacy also has a perceptual component, which occurs in the form of distraction caused by other people moving within the field of vision, by other people talking, by telephones ringing, by printers making noises, and by other noises within range of hearing. It is known that the human visual system is particularly well adapted to detect movement even at locations 90 degrees from where the eyes are pointing. As for hearing, one does not need to consult the research (although research in this area is plentiful) to comprehend the resource allocation problems involved in concentrating on a complex mental task while trying to ignore a clearly audible conversation.

An important qualifier to the above discussion relates to the ability to *control* visual and auditory access. The disturbances caused by visual and auditory stimuli have much less impact if they can be eliminated at will — by closing a door or muffling the sound of a printer, for instance. Unfortunately, this option is often not available in work situations.

On the other hand, there can be too much privacy, or too little sound. Lucy, who joined Lee and Miriam at the elevator, was "starved for human contact." The isolation that occurs in such instances presents difficulties for most people. The isolated person feels left out of the networks that are an important part of the informal structure of the organization.

Layout and Workplace Organization

Both privacy and ease of communication are greatly influenced by the overall organization and layout of the workplace components. The workplace layout may be the result of anything from haphazardly sticking things in wherever they fit, to carefully arranging things into an organized workflow.

Whatever systems of organization or organizational planning are employed, management will face challenges from the simultaneous pressures of wanting to introduce new office technology while also needing to cut costs by decreasing the amount of space allocated per employee. The transitional nature of current office technology implies that people are, at present, mostly *adding* things to the office. Secretaries are not yet entirely willing to give up their typewriters (indeed, sales of electronic memory typewriters seem to be having a growth spurt). So competition for space is even greater.

The VDT is not the only item that requires extra space. Printers, disk drives, central processing units, modems, diskette holders, and operating manuals, among other things, must sometimes be added as well. Even the power cords and cables associated with all this equipment are so bulky that specialized means of handling and storing them must often be found.

Presumably, one of the benefits of office automation will be the reduction in storage space needed for *paper*. In the ultimate paperless office, all work and communication, whether to other people or to files, will occur via VDTs. Each employee will have at least one terminal. In theory, paper storage will then pose a less serious problem. However, only a few specialized jobs, such as some directory assistance and reservation systems, are currently fully computerized. Files and cabinets for paper storage are still a crucial part of the office.

Managers faced with the task of reconciling conflicting demands on space can take an analytic approach to the problem. For example, on the basis of common sense, past experience, and job analysis, one might measure both the frequency of use of each item and its relative importance to the typical daily work pattern. The frequency and importance ratings for each item could then be combined in some reasonable way: they could be added, multiplied, or simply assessed. This would then give some sense of priority as to which item should be placed within the immediate workspace envelope of the individual, and which could be farther away. As an example, the novice computer operator might want to place the instruction manual right on the desk. It might not be needed very frequently, but it would be frustrating and time consuming to have to go to a file drawer or to a bookshelf several feet away each time it is needed. On the other hand, an experienced worker might need the manual only once or twice a year, so filing it in a nearby drawer makes better sense than cluttering up the desk. Similarly, if a secretary is using the typewriter primarily as a backup for the terminal, it could be moved from its traditional "place of honor" on the return to a surface farther away, such as a movable stand. Well-designed storage space that allows the worker to group together all items needed for one task, and that is properly located, would help to solve many of these problems.

The same analytic approach can be used equally effectively on a larger scale where several individual workers must engage in cooperative work. Would it have made more sense for Miriam to have had her office close to Lee's, because they shared projects, rather than with people of like rank and job function, with whom she did not work cooperatively? Is it more efficient for a secretary to deal with a specific department, and specific people, and to have her desk and files near their workspace, or for all secretaries to be together in a secretarial pool, and all files in a file room? The placement of shared equipment (such as a copying machine) may be determined by finding out who is using it, how frequently they are using it, and by assessing the importance of the tasks for which it is needed.

In this case, it may also be useful to do what is called a *link analysis*: looking at the relative frequency with which each individual task component is linked to each other component. This type of analysis may be applied to the action of one person using *different components* in sequence, or work itself moving between *different people*. Obviously, as the number of components increases, the analysis becomes more complex.

These techniques may be helpful if they are viewed within the context of a total environment. Work procedures change, equipment changes, and an environment which is well designed for one task may suddenly become obsolete. As with chairs and worksurfaces, designed-in flexibility, while initially more expensive, may later prove to be a good investment. Finally, it is important not to let what appears to be pure functional efficiency override the concerns about privacy and communication described earlier.

The Impact of the Environment on Finances and Behavior: The BOSTI Study Revisited

The work of Brill and the BOSTI group introduced in Chapter 2 provides an interesting perspective on the effect of office layout on worker behavior and company finances. As stated earlier, Brill collected his key data from extensive questionnaire responses from managers, professional/technical workers, and clerical workers, both before and after a move to new facilities or a renovation of existing facilities. We will look at the outcome of some selected analyses in terms of a *change* (an improvement or drop) in either job satisfaction or job performance scores before and after moves to new quarters.

What Is the Cost of a Person Compared with That of a Building?

Office space is expensive. In the face of cost-cutting pressures from many directions, the temptation is great to make more "efficient" use of existing floor space by cutting down the amount of space allocated to each individual. This reduction, unfortunately, often occurs at the same time that new automated office equipment is introduced.

Space reduction is apparently a frequent occurrence. During the period of their study, Brill and his BOSTI colleagues found that a result of moving to new quarters was a net loss in working space for 30% of managers, 60% of professional/technical workers, and 80% of clerical workers. For those employees for whom the size of the loss exceeded 25% of their previous office space, job satisfaction also dropped. Thus, the direct short-term financial advantage to an organization of reducing space must be evaluated against the indirect, but nevertheless real, costs of absenteeism and turnover which have been statistically linked to decreases in job satisfaction.

A longer-term context within which to view such space-versus-people decisions is based on the BOSTI view of an office with its personnel as a *tool* for accomplishing a particular set of tasks. A proper *economic* analysis must apportion the total cost for the use of that tool into appropriate components. In the case of the office, such costs can be divided into two components: cost of physical plant and cost of people. Here is one of the analyses Brill used to determine these relative costs.

As a target location, the authors deliberately selected a site (New York City) that was characterized by extremely expensive construction costs. They then calculated the cost for constructing and maintaining an office building — including workstations, VDTs, and all supporting equipment. In New York, that cost, over a 10-year period, would be $35,000 per person.

Next, using industry publications as a source, a reasonable salary for a senior systems analyst was estimated to be $35,000 per year. (This position was more highly paid than that of a clerical worker but lower than that of a manager.)

Extrapolating salary and fringes over a comparable 10-year period for this sample person yielded a figure of $483,572. Thus, the costs of hiring a *person* were estimated to be more than 13 times the costs of constructing and equipping the office he or she worked in. (In the case of leasing a building, the ratio would be "only" 5:1.) Obviously, the exact ratios will differ depending on location, salary levels, and related variables.

In general, however, the bulk of the office system investment is in people, not physical plant.

To that extent, relatively small investments in physical plant, properly made, may have significant long-term benefits if they facilitate the work of people by improving working conditions. On the other hand, as will be seen, not all apparent "improvements" will actually make working conditions better.

Is the Open Office a Solution to the Space Squeeze?

Many pressures, including the need to economize by allotting less space per person, led to the open office concept. The open office is one in which the removal of walls and their replacement by potted plants and file cabinets, for instance, would theoretically lead to feelings of openness and spaciousness, along with enhanced interpersonal communication. With this type of office layout the manager is moved out of a private office right down to the floor, accessible to everyone and able to supervise everyone. The supporters of the open office suggested that the reduction in privacy that would occur by taking away walls, or, more technically, reducing the degree of enclosure, would be offset by an increase in ease of communication.

The data from the BOSTI study and from other sources suggest that very few of these theoretical assumptions were borne out in practice. It appears that not only did the open office limit people's privacy, but it made communication more difficult, rather than easier. Moreover, these effects were greatest for the highly paid managers.

BOSTI defined *enclosure* in terms of a graded series of steps reflecting the height and numbers of enclosing elements, that is, walls and panels. Enclosing elements on each side of a workspace were assigned to one of the following categories: wall (floor to ceiling); high panel (workspace not visually accessible to a standing person); low panel (workspace visually accessible to a standing person); and element absent.

Based on questionnaire responses from people who worked in various degrees of enclosure, a series of behaviorally meaningful enclosure steps were defined. The lowest level of enclosure, implying virtually no privacy, was found to be equivalent for each of the following: a "bullpen" (no walls or panels); one or two panels of either height; and three low panels. Adding a fourth low panel to a group of three resulted in some visual privacy and comprised the second level of enclosure. A major increase in privacy was achieved by the use of three *high* panels, and adding a fourth had little effect. Finally, as might be expected, the most privacy, and greatest level of enclosure, resulted from a private office (with four walls and a door).

Changes in an employee's degree of enclosure as a result of a move resulted in a specific impact on job performance. Those whose new offices represented an increase in enclosure of at least two steps (implying the new office had high partitions on at least three sides) showed an overall increase in job performance. When the move to a new office represented a two-step or greater drop in enclosure (as in the case of a manager going from a private office to a low-panel open office system), there was a drop in job performance.

Unfortunately for the organizations involved, most of the moves studied were in the direction of less-enclosed workspaces: 47% of the managers, 43% of the professionals, and 38% of the clericals reported losses in enclosure. The comparable percentages for gains in enclosure were 11%, 13%, and 21%. Moreover, the losses in enclosure were accompanied by decreased ease of communication (as in holding a private conversation), increased distractions (by other people's telephone conversations, telephones ringing, etc.), decreased ability to control access of others into their workspace (and consequently more intrusions into personal workspace by others).

An interesting negative finding was related to the question of visual supervision of clerical workers. A presumed benefit of open offices is that lower level clerical workers are directly under the eye of the supervisor. However, the data show no differences in either job performance or job satisfaction between those under constant visual supervision and those not under constant visual supervision.

When a move to a new office did not mean a shift toward less enclosure, people were more likely to be satisfied. In general, people who described the overall layout as improved at the new site were also those who showed improved job performance. Improved layout included having a single entrance in front of the workstation (controlled access, enhancing privacy), not having people working directly in front of them (avoidance of visual distractions), not having a side of the workstation open to an aisle, and sufficient enclosure and working space.

Financial Costs or Savings from Ergonomic Changes

The BOSTI group developed an integrated financial analysis of the dollar value of various environmental improvements. These values were estimated from the financial value of reported increased job performance and satisfaction which accompanied such improvements.

In the case of managers, an average salary of $41,500 was estimated. The total annual dollar value, in terms of improved *job performance* was computed to be $5,085. Of this, $2,943 was attributed to improved enclosure (for those managers who were lucky enough to move from a more open to a more enclosed office) and the remaining $2,142 from a generally improved layout. The total benefit of improved *job satisfaction* was $1,231. However, these figures came from a variety of sources, the bulk being in improvements in light, glare, and noise (these aspects of the ambient environment will be discussed later in this chapter). As a sidelight, $405 of the job satisfaction total came from a reduction in frequency of relocations. While not exactly in the purview of ergonomics, this cost might be considered by those organizations which seem to delight in "churning" offices within buildings.

For one manager, the total dollar value of all observed environmental benefits was $6,316 per year, or 15.2% of annual salary, excluding fringe benefits. Comparable total figures were $4,650 (14.7%) for a $31,600 per year professional, and $3,042 (17.5%) for a $17,400 per year clerical worker. In each case, between 25% and 30% of the total value was attributable to job satisfaction, the rest to job performance. Brill estimated that the total cost of moving a programmer from a bullpen to an enclosed system furniture workstation ($3,500) could be paid off within 16 months.

The BOSTI study represents an enormous effort to provide a solid research-based link between *ergonomics* and *economics*. Their approach is reasonable, and is based on accepted methods. However, although their published report is 400 pages long, with many tables and charts, it is only a user summary, and more specific detail on procedure and analysis is needed to make it completely open to scientific analysis, critique, and verification. (For a more complete discussion, see Appendix I.) Nevertheless, the BOSTI data is in agreement with many other findings in the literature which suggest that positive benefits, financial and otherwise, can result from proper ergonomic improvements.

The manager must be cautious in applying either precise dollar gains/losses or percentages of productivity increases to any specific place of business, based on *any* experimental data or the experience of any other business. This is extremely difficult, because workplace ergonomics embraces many complex interrelated factors, from physical layout to emotional/organizational ambience.

The usefulness of quantitative experimental data, including all the experiments described in this book, is in predicting the general size and direction (good or bad) of ergonomic changes. In any given case, the benefit can be less, or it can be more.

The dollar amounts predicted by BOSTI, for example, may as likely be an underestimate of potential benefits as an overestimate, for a variety of reasons. For instance, in computing the dollar value of environmental improvements on work performance, BOSTI deliberately underestimated the value of such performance, and that underestimate was more pronounced for highly paid professionals than for clerical workers. Furthermore, as stated earlier the furniture and other equipment which was available at the time the BOSTI studies were carried out (pre-1984) was likely far less effective ergonomically than state-of-the-art equipment today, so today's improvements may make more of a difference.

Although these precise dollar values can, for the reasons cited previously, be used only as estimates, it is unlikely that their accuracy is much worse than the accuracy of more traditional cost/benefit approaches used by management to justify even larger expenditures for equipment.

The Ambient Environment

The ambient environment — sounds, light, temperature, and air quality — can pose a particularly frustrating problem to the manager. An ambient environment which is "pleasant" is, almost by definition, one which is unnoticed in daily life. Only if people are asked (by a researcher, for instance) are they likely to notice that, yes, the air is fine and it's not too drafty. However, when something goes wrong (when it's too hot or too cold, when the temperature fluctuates, when there is too much glare, or when the room smells strange), the environment suddenly enters conscious awareness and cognitive resources need to be devoted to it. That is, people complain, and if the manager is at all responsive, the technical experts are called in, and the workers' subjective feelings and perceptions are analytically mapped onto mathematical charts of decibels, footcandles, BTUs, and parts per million. In the next several pages we will look at some of the circumstances in which workers can become unpleasantly aware of the ambient environment. Some facts about sounds, light, temperature, and air quality will then be explored, along with recommended solutions to problems.

Noise

For the human being, hearing and vision are key channels of communication with the world. From an ergonomic perspective, three different issues with regard to hearing and noise are important. Each reflects a different concern about noise, as illustrated in the following examples.

> Case 1. *Sam, who is now 40, has worked in the computer room for 12 years next to two constantly chattering high-speed printers and a card reader. At a physical examination, it is found that he has a permanent hearing loss of 10 decibels. Sound level measurement at his workstation yields a value of 90 decibels.*

Excessive sound levels over time, like those to which Sam was exposed, will cause *predictable permanent damage* to the sound receptors in the inner ear. Consequently, governmental agencies prescribe noise exposure standards which are designed to protect the hearing of its citizens. If people are expected to work in environments where the noise levels are greater than the number of decibels specified in these standards, laws require that specific precautions be taken. Technicians and baggage handlers at airports, for instance, all wear ear protectors.

The physical measurement of sound takes into account both intensity and pitch (or frequency). Humans are most sensitive to frequencies produced by the sounds of human speech (200 to 5000 cycles per sec, or 200 to 5000 Hz), and less sensitive to very high and very low frequencies. This means that a very low or very high frequency sound would have to be much more intense to be heard than would a sound in the mid-range.

Any environmental source of noise is composed of a mixture of frequencies and intensities. A sensitive meter could separate out and measure the intensity level at each frequency band, but this process is cumbersome and expensive. The "A-weighted decibel," or dB(A), is a measure of sound *intensity* which is weighted according to the human sensitivity across various frequencies. The term dB(A) is frequently used by experts on noise.

The noise level in Sam's work environment was measured at 90 dB(A). A quiet office typically gives a measurement of 50 dB(A). A chain saw, measured at the ear of the operator, yields about 105 dB(A), and the noise measured 61 m (200 ft.) from a jet plane at takeoff is about 125 dB(A).

In the United States, the Occupational Safety and Health Administration established an 8 hour per day exposure to 90 dB(A) as the lowest point at which hearing damage becomes a concern. Others have argued that the limit should be 85 dB(A). From the point of view of actual damage to the ear there is little likelihood that there are any sound sources in the modern office environment that are of concern, with the notable exception of the computer room. Typewriters may operate at a level of 65 dB(A); office printers — and the human voice — may go as high as 80.

Sam's case does point to the need to assess noise levels in the computer room, however. If a worker at a desk located between a high-speed printer and a card reader is subject to sound levels of 85 dB(A), permanent hearing damage may result.

> Case 2. *Renee is sitting at her desk reading the first draft of the annual report and looking carefully for typos and mathematical mistakes. Her open plan workstation is peaceful and quiet. Six feet away, behind a non-acoustical partition, someone turns on a radio at high volume to the local rock station. Renee feels a rush of anger. Her blood boils. She throws the report on the table, gets up, and paces back and forth in front of her desk. (She does not, however, complain or ask the people to turn down the radio.) She then tries to calm herself down and continue with her work, but she overlooks a serious error in the manuscript.*

In this case, the person who turned on the radio was looking for some eustress. To Renee, however, it was distress. Her annoyance at the intrusion of the noise into her personal space caused the same type of stress reaction that was discussed in Chapter 2. The *psychological* impact of the sound was what made it a stressor for Renee; the actual sound level was well below that which would cause physical damage to her ears.

It is interesting that the stress Renee felt may have been due more to the intermittency of the noise and her inability to control it than to the level of the noise itself. Evidence for this comes from two experiments by

Glass and colleagues (1977). In the first, they used, as noise, a recording of a mixture of sounds of two people speaking Spanish, one person speaking Armenian, a mimeograph machine, and a desk calculator. The subjects were asked to do a proofreading task during either constant noise or intermittent noise. The results were that the unpredictability of noise (intermittency) produced more errors than the noise level. These findings were more pronounced for complex tasks than simple ones, and are consonant with the general finding that unpredictable stressors are worse than predictable ones.

Furthermore, the effects did not end when the noise ended. After that part of the experiment was over, Glass and colleagues gave the subjects two tracing puzzles to do as a measurement of their tolerance for frustration. Unbeknownst to the subjects, one of the puzzles could be solved and the other could not. Those subjects who had been exposed to unpredictable noise were much less willing to continue trying to solve the puzzles than were those who had been exposed to steady state noise. (These aftereffects are also consistent with the general observation that feelings of frustration or satisfaction carry over from one aspect of the day to the next, or from one's day at the office into one's after-office activities, and vice versa. They can also be related to Grandjean's bucket: the increased fatigue and stress caused by the intermittent noise leaves the worker more fatigued and less able to cope with additional tasks.)

In a second study, these researchers gave the subjects a switch, with which the subject could stop the noise and end the experiment. Although few subjects used the switch, the frustration tolerance of those who had switches (as measured by willingness to continue trying to solve the puzzles) was greater than for those who were helpless to stop the noise.

Exposure to unpredictable stressors makes people feel that they are not in control of their environment, and their reaction to stressors is therefore much more intense than if they felt they were in control. These reactions are clearly dependent on the individual's psychological makeup: if the noise is not assessed as a stressor, it doesn't stress.

> Case 3. *Miriam, who is sharing the office with Rose and Kelly, is desperately trying to do her work while Kelly is discussing divorce strategy with his lawyer on the telephone. Right in the middle of Kelly's property settlement, her own phone rings. It is Lee, wanting to check out some data with her. She tries hard to concentrate on what Lee is saying as Kelly gets hotter under the collar and begins yelling over the phone. Finally, in an effort not to hear Kelly, she puts her right forefinger in her right ear; however, because her left hand is holding the phone receiver to her left ear, this makes it rather difficult for her to look through her papers.*

This case is somewhat similar to the last, but it focuses on the very specific, but unfortunately common, situation in which environmental noise actually interferes with the sounds of speech. This interference is at least as much due to the *content* of the speech as to its loudness.

When Miriam begins to talk to Lee, Kelly's conversation acts as a powerful source of interference with her own conversation. This, of course, works in two ways. Not only does the sound of Kelly's voice distract her in her attempts to hear Lee, but, to the extent that Lee can hear Kelly, this same sound pattern makes it difficult for Lee to hear Miriam's voice.

For any given level of sound intensity, the sound which most interferes with the ability to hear speech is some other speech. Communications engineers have devised a series of standardized techniques to measure noise levels of this type. One common technique, called the Speech Interference Level (SIL), is an average of the sound intensities measured at three different frequencies within the normal human speech range. The SIL is approximately 10 less than the number of dB(A) (i.e., dB(A) − 10 = SIL). In a private or semi-private office or conference room, acceptable noise levels are between 38 and 47 dB(A). Using a telephone becomes difficult at more than 60 SIL, or 70 dB(A). Above 80 SIL, or 90 dB(A), it is impossible. Given that a person talking very loudly may reach a level of 86 dB(A), the nature of the problem is clear.

In addition to the effect measured by SIL, the *content* of the speech along with its unpredictability may produce varying degrees of task interference. If Kelly had been discussing the vicissitudes of the local bowling league, it may be assumed that, unless Miriam was an avid bowler, the interference with her conversation would probably have been considerably less. The reason is that the content of a conversation about divorce is likely to be more compelling; by its nature it demands more attentional resources than would the bowling discussion. Further, if Kelly suddenly switched to speaking in a language Miriam does not know, both the content and its internal unpredictability would, in effect, disappear, and the interference would be even less. Thus, when the speech of others acts as a source of noise, the interference effect measured by SIL is only a baseline, to which the cognitive impact of its content and its predictability must be added.

From the BOSTI study, the three most bothersome noise problems reported were phones ringing, people talking face to face, and people talking on telephones. Perceived increases in noise level were associated with lowered levels of job satisfaction. These decreases in turn translated into costs of $102 per year for a clerical worker, $254 per year for a professional/technical worker, and $344 per year for a manager.

Given these figures, it is reasonable to postulate that, like other ergonomic improvements discussed so far, introduction of noise abatement treatments would be a fruitful investment. For the majority of office environments, careful selection of sound-absorbing paneling systems would simultaneously ameliorate the problems of visual and acoustic privacy/interference.

Office Music

Two different kinds of music are generally used in the workplace. *Industrial music* is specifically programmed music which attempts to give people a boost, or increase their arousal levels, at times when their ordinary arousal level would be dropping. This kind of music often includes recent hits and vocal music. By contrast, *background music*, the kind often played in grocery stores and shopping malls, is bland, seldom varies in volume, and never uses vocals.

Industrial music seems to be primarily useful in assembly situations and is not considered appropriate for office tasks requiring primarily cognitive activities. However, studies have shown an increase in productivity following the introduction of background music into the office. With a boring task, background music may help. However, other studies show that it interferes with mental concentration. Here, again, there are wide individual differences. A potential trend for the future is the very light-weight earphones which are attached either to individual radios or to a central music source. Workers could have a choice of what they wanted to listen to, if anything, as do passengers on many commercial airlines.

Ambient Lighting

The introduction of VDTs into the office has thrown a confounding factor into previously accepted guidelines and standards for ambient lighting, because, as mentioned in Chapter 5, the contrast requirements for most pre-VDT workplaces were defined in terms of dark objects against lighter backgrounds on relatively nonreflective surfaces. Therefore, the "more light is better" philosophy prevailed. Now, however, it is apparent that too much light may be as problematical as insufficient light.

The dilemma of simultaneously lighting the hard copy, avoiding glare and reflections on the screen, and taking aesthetics into account has generated some real conflicts. These are not made easier by the technical concerns that need to be addressed. The various systems and nomenclatures by which light is measured are perhaps the most complicated of all sets of physical measurements. The following discussion will be restricted to the inch-pound (English) and metric versions of the two most basic practical units. If other source materials use other units, those units can be converted into one of the two types mentioned here.

Illuminance is a measure of the total amount of light *falling on* the surface of an object. In the inch-pound system, illuminance is measured in *footcandles*; in the metric system, in *lux* (lx). One footcandle is approximately 10.8 lx. A desk located directly below a fluorescent light fixture containing four bulbs receives approximately 594 lx (55 footcandles). A well-lit workstation for a watchmaker would require between 10,800 and 21,600 lx (1000 and 2000 footcandles). Illuminance drops off as the light source moves away. For example, if the desk is moved away from its place directly below the lights, it will receive less light. (The governing principle in this case is the inverse square law: the light decreases as the inverse of the square of the distance from the source.)

Luminance is the opposite of illuminance. It is a measure of the amount of light *coming from* the surface of an object in a specific direction. This light can be emitted from the surface directly (the sun, a light bulb, a VDT screen) or reflected from some other source onto the surface (the moon, the table surface, the paper copy, the glass face plate of the VDT.) Luminance is measured in *footlamberts* (fL) in the inch-pound system, or in *candellas per square meter* in the metric. One footlambert is approximately 3.4 candellas per square meter (cd/m^2).

One interesting property of measured luminance is that it does *not* change as you move away from the surface. This physical characteristic of light intensity parallels the human perception of light intensity: just as the perceived brightness of the lighted surface does not change as the person moves away from it, so the measured brightness does not change as the meter is moved away, as long as the meter is reading only that object. (Some people may refer to the reading from the meter as the measured "brightness" of the source, but most researchers reserve the term "brightness" for the psychological impression rather than the physical measurement.)

If, however, instead of measuring with the eye or the luminance meter, a meter measuring illuminance is used, the reading will drop as the meter is moved away. The illuminometer is registering the amount of light falling on its own surface.

Thus, of the two ways of measuring intensity of light energy, luminance more closely resembles the perceptual characteristics of the eye. Unfortunately, lighting standards are almost always given in terms of *illuminance*.

Another property of surfaces can be determined by measuring how much of the light falling on the surface (illuminance) is reflected (luminance), that is, the ratio of reflected to received light. This is called the relative *reflectance* of a surface. Typically, it is measured simply as a percentage of the incoming light. A mirror would have a 100% reflectance in a given direction (this is called "specular reflectance"). Matte finished surfaces have lower reflectances than shiny ones.

In the workplace, the lighting has to provide enough light to allow the worker to see the paper copy clearly and has to avoid creating sources of glare for VDT work, preferably without jeopardizing the attractiveness of the office setting. There are no easy, definitive solutions to this problem at the present time. However, a reasonable recommendation is that paper documents should be illuminated at levels between 540 and 810 lx (50 and 75 footcandles), but that 216 to 324 lx (20 to 30 footcandles) is more appropriate for VDT viewing. This suggests task lighting for paper copy and a general low level of ambient illumination. In addition, highly reflective worksurfaces should be avoided; reflective values should be kept below 50%.

The placement and type of lighting fixtures and the orientation of workstations with respect to windows must also be examined carefully (see Chapter 5). The trend toward predominately glass buildings and greater dependence on natural lighting, as in Elizabeth's case, presents problems for the VDT worker in terms of (a) reflections, (b) glare, and, (c) on sunny days, a bright light source, sometimes within the field of vision.

The BOSTI study showed that 20% of workers surveyed had difficulty seeing properly; half of these felt they had too much light. When glare was present, job satisfaction decreased. Glare was a problem especially for people sitting near windows, and was even worse for people working at VDTs. The dollar value of glare reduction was $195/year for a manager, $132/year for a professional, and $70/year for a secretary.

Thermal Comfort

Most of the issues just discussed with respect to noise have their counterparts in the discussion of thermal comfort. At the extremes of heat and cold, the thermal environment acts as a physiological stressor, evoking sweating or shivering as compensatory reactions of the body. Extreme levels of cold and heat are unlikely to be encountered in the modern office unless the heating or air conditioning system breaks down; however, large computer rooms are still kept very cool, requiring workers like Mark, at the beginning of this chapter, to wear sweaters or other warm clothing, even in summer.

The brain interprets temperature signals from the skin in a complex manner, and this process results in the person feeling comfort or discomfort. Sensations of being too cold or too warm are highly individual and variable: many people feel uncomfortably cold when they are indoors at 15°C (60°F) on a cold winter day, but feel wonderful when they are outside on a lovely spring day at 15°C.

As in the case of noise, the perception of control has a great deal to do with subjective feelings of thermal comfort. Kantowitz and Sorkin (1983) report the case of an indoor tennis court where the customers complained of lack of heat. The management installed thermostats (which were non-functional, although the customers did not know that), and the complaints decreased. Kantowitz and Sorkin quite rightly comment on the ethical implications of this strategy; however, it does point out the importance of feelings of control. Except in private offices, it would be difficult to give each worker a thermostat; however, workers will have more control and feel more comfortable if there are at least vents and windows which they can use at will.

Although the individual's perception of thermal comfort is quite subjective, it is possible to establish some general guidelines. Perception of thermal comfort is jointly determined by air temperature, temperature of adjacent surfaces, humidity, and air movement. Industry guidelines state that the human comfort zone is roughly defined by a range of 20% to 70% relative humidity and a temperature of 22 to 27°C (71 to 80°F). However, practical problems may arise when humidity is at the lower end of the scale. During the winter, heating without proper humidification may result in relative humidities dropping below 30%. In this range, the ability of the mucus membrane of the throat to clear itself of dust particles is impaired, and the mucus membranes of the nose and throat can become irritated. At very low humidity wearers of contact lenses may experience irritation of the eyes. Interestingly, equipment may be less tolerant of extremes of humidity than humans: mold starts to grow on paper when the relative humidity is above 67% and magnetic tapes begin to deteriorate at humidities below 37%.

Air movement is typically measured in meters per second. Cold drafts are more uncomfortable than warm; drafts of greater than 0.5 m/sec (0.54 yards/sec) are unpleasant, even with warm air; and air currents from behind are more uncomfortable, especially in the sensitive zones of the neck and feet. Drafts of 0.1 to 0.2 m/sec (0.1 to 0.2 yards/sec) are found in the workplace; but even 0.1 m/sec (0.1 yard/sec) can be perceived as unpleasant for a person seated in a fixed position. Yet, a room where the air is too still is perceived as stuffy.

Brill suggests that energy conservation measures have resulted in greater temperature fluctuations inside buildings in response to outdoor temperatures. He cites studies showing performance decrements from both overheating and overcooling. The BOSTI results showed that 25% of the workers reported offices being generally too cool, while another 25% reported that they were generally too hot. However, 33% of his sample reported being disturbed by the extreme *fluctuation* of temperature. It was this response, not the complaints regarding temperature extremes per se, which were correlated with either increases or decreases in job satisfaction. Dollar values assigned to this component were $344/year per manager, $141/year per professional, and $70/year per clerical worker.

Air Quality and the Tight Building Syndrome

Even if the air circulating within an office is of the right temperature and humidity, it may bring with it a wide variety of chemicals which cause unpleasant sensations, irritation, or even illness. The sources of these chemicals are various.

Outside air is not always fresh and pure; depending on where the fresh air intake is located, the air may be laden with exhaust fumes, fumes from other places within the same building, exhaust from other buildings, material from bird roosts, and pollen.

The ventilation system itself may be a source of impurities; humidifiers and cooling systems are potentially responsible for circulating bacteria and fungi which can cause illness.

Pollution is even more likely to arise from within, sometimes from sources that are not generally suspect. When new, building materials often give off fumes, particularly fumes containing formaldehyde. New office partitions and furniture, especially those made from particleboard and other manufactured wood products, contain high concentrations of formaldehyde; formaldehyde can also be released from rugs, drapes, and other textiles. Paints, solvents, wood preservatives, asbestos, glass fibers, cleaning agents, correction fluid, and pesticides are all sources of airborne pollution which can cause irritation or disease. In addition, some of the chemicals used in office copiers and spirit duplicators can contaminate the air, especially if they are not used in well-ventilated places. (Many other office products, such as carbonless copy papers and toners, cause skin rashes — contact dermatitis — even though they may not become airborne.)

Another major source of pollution is tobacco smoke; its presence can be extremely irritating to many people, especially to those with respiratory diseases, heart disease, and asthma, as well as to wearers of contact lenses.

In recent years, *tight building syndrome, sealed building syndrome,* or even *sick building syndrome*, has been used to describe the health complaints of office workers in a number of new office buildings or recently remodeled buildings where windows do not open. Irritation of the eyes, nose, throat or skin, headaches, and sometimes nausea or dizziness are the principal complaints; these arise inside the workplace ("Monday morning sickness"), and decrease or gradually disappear when workers leave the building. The reason symptoms occur in these buildings is that the inside air is mechanically recirculated, keeping inside the building whatever airborne pollutants happen to be there. Especially in newly constructed buildings, or those with new furniture, rugs, or other chemical-releasing products, the effect can be quite pronounced. When energy conservation efforts limit the intake of fresh, unheated/uncooled air, matters can be made even worse. At the Leming Corporation Lee, Mark, Lucy, and finally Miriam suffered from sinus problems attributable to tight building syndrome.

Analysis of airborne pollutants sometimes shows that buildings in which these symptoms occur have levels of pollution below those currently thought to be hazardous. However, many people are far more sensitive to circulating pollutants than others (hay fever sufferers are one example). Even if this syndrome has a considerable psychological component, as some have suggested, it makes good sense to remedy the situation, if only for the sake of employee morale and increased working efficiency.

In any building, symptoms of irritation will often be more pronounced in certain areas, and workers will have some idea of the source of the offending odors. Some pollutants, however, such as carbon monoxide, have no odor.

Measures to insure adequate air quality include providing for adequate intake of clean, fresh air, and keeping all ventilators, humidifiers, and filters well maintained and clean. Smokers can be put in a room separate from non-smokers, or smoking can be prohibited except in certain places at certain times. Copying machines, addressing machines, and other machinery which uses solvents that vaporize easily or give off fumes can be used in separate rooms with exhaust fans, or in well-ventilated areas. Care should be taken in handling any chemicals, including cleaning products and pest control products.

Important Issues in the Physical Work Environment

- A balance must be struck between communication needs and the need for privacy.

- Important items and items that are used frequently should be placed close to the worker. Unimportant or infrequently used items should be stored in a convenient but more remote place.
- Several alternative logical layouts of equipment and furniture should be examined, to take into account patterns of workflow and functions of various personnel.
- For each employee, salaries and fringes cost more than physical plant, so relatively small investments in workplace improvement will pay off if they improve working conditions.
- Significant increases in enclosure result in increases in job satisfaction and performance. Gains of enclosure are also accompanied by greater ease of communication, fewer distractions, more control of access by others, and therefore fewer intrusions by others.
- Good noise abatement devices are generally a good investment.
- Noise can cause physical damage, but in the office context, it is more likely to be a psychological stressor or to interfere with speech communication.
- Reasonable recommendations for illuminating paper documents are levels between 540 and 810 lx (50 and 75 footcandles) but 216 to 324 lx (20 to 30 footcandles) is recommended for VDT viewing.
- Shiny, highly reflective worksurfaces (with reflectance greater than 50%) should be avoided.
- Glare should be reduced whenever possible.
- Recommended temperatures for thermal comfort are 22 to 27°C (71 to 80°F) and recommended relative humidity is 37% to 67%.
- Air that is too still makes a room stuffy; yet even warm drafts of 0.1 yard/sec (0.1 m/sec) can be unpleasant for a seated person.
- Adequate intake of clean, fresh air should be provided. Ventilators, humidifiers, and filters should be clean and well maintained.
- Any equipment which uses or gives off airborne solvents or pollutants should be used in a well-ventilated area, preferably with an exhaust fan.
- Smoking, if bothersome to personnel, should be prohibited except where smoke can be removed by exhaust fans or open windows.
- All chemicals should be handled with care, in accordance with precautions on their labels.
- Ergonomic improvements in these areas can be expected to pay dividends in terms of employee morale and job satisfaction, health, and improved job performance. Many are directly linked to bottom line financial savings, although the amounts of these savings are highly idiosyncratic.

Software Ergonomics

CHAPTER 7

Elizabeth has been using a new word-processing package for about a week. Having just finished a long document, she shifts into the "Command" mode in order to store what she has written. However, she recalls that there is one more thing to add, so she needs to get back into "Edit" mode. She momentarily blanks on the command sequence needed to return to Edit (CLEAR then F1) and, without thinking, reverts to the program she was using last week and types in the word EDIT. Unfortunately, in this system, the initials EDIT stand for three separate commands: the first causes the system to assign Everything that she has typed to a single file; the second Deletes that file; the third letter Inserts whatever follows it (the letter "T") in the file. Thus, she has just wiped out everything she has done, and has nothing but a T left. Angry and humiliated, she reaches for the aspirin bottle, and after a break to try to collect herself, starts over again.

Her word-processing equipment uses shared logic, which means that it works through a central computer, and there is only one printer for a group of users. By mistake, she hits CONTROL E in her typing, which assigns the printer to her control. Unfortunately, the system gives no indication that this has happened, so she is not aware of it. Meanwhile, five workstations down the aisle, Anne is trying to print a file that her supervisor wants right now, and she can't figure out why she can't get command of the printer.

An angry wail is heard in the next office. Sean has hit CONTROL Z, and discovered that he has permanently deleted all his files.

Ricardo, in the main office, has a meeting in 10 minutes with the divisional vice-president, and he has to present a budget. He is at his personal computer working on a spreadsheet, just getting the last figures in order. He heaves a sigh of relief, reaches to enter the SUM command, which will give the final total, and the building lights blink. To his absolute horror, the screen goes blank, and only the blinking cursor is left to tell him that everything has been wiped out.

Meanwhile, Kelly, the analyst, sits down in front of his terminal, enters his special password, and requests a confidential market survey file. The file appears on his screen, but after scanning it for a few seconds, he begins to swear softly but emphatically. Key summary statements — representing months of hard work — are gone. In their place is a series of obscene statements. Someone who is very intelligent . . . and very malicious . . . has managed to break into the system. Kelly can't even begin to estimate the extent of the damage.*

Software in the Electronic Office

Software is the focal point of the electronic office. The components which have been described up to now — the chair, the worksurface, the workspace and surrounding environment, even the screen and keyboard — could be called the background of the electronic office system. Although these components can exert strong effects on operator *behavior*, these effects are rarely in the forefront of the operator's conscious attention (unless the chair is really uncomfortable or the noise is really distracting). They should be, for all intents and purposes, unnoticed.

It is the content, form, and structure of the material seen on the screen — the software — which occupies the bulk of an operator's attention. It is through the *active* manipulation of the software that the actual work of the electronic office is carried out. This work differs in major ways from anything that has ever gone on before and it gives office workers more power than ever before to accomplish tasks efficiently.

Unfortunately, software use can also lead to problems like those experienced by Elizabeth, Anne, Sean, Ricardo, and Kelly. The enormous speed and capacity of the modern computer has a down side: mistakes can be equally fast and equally large. In the pre-electronic office, nothing short of a fire in a filing cabinet could have caused as much trouble as quickly as can a computer.

From the operator's point of view, the possibility of these occurrences represents a serious stressor. As the cases at the beginning of this chapter indicate, software which allows the deletion of vast amounts of data without warning at the touch of a single key, which does not show changes in the status of the system on the screen, and which is wide open to tampering, can be a user's nightmare — as are temporary blackouts of the electrical system.

---

* (The first three examples were adapted from Card, Moran and Newell (1983) and the fourth from personal experience.)

This kind of stressor cannot be dealt with physically, as one would adjust a chair or change the lighting level, but it is just as real, and the general principles of ergonomics still apply: the fit between the user and the tool (the software) can be maximized.

The *computer-human interface* (sometimes abbreviated CHI) refers to the components of software systems by which the human interacts directly with the computer. Although software systems include many operations invisible to the operator, which allow him or her to communicate indirectly with the computer, it is the CHI which determines the *fit* — good or bad — between person and machine. (CHI will be used in this book to refer only to the software interface; the term is sometimes used more broadly. See glossary.)

It is quite feasible to design computer-human interfaces which take into account human responses and human errors, which make simple, frequent, nondestructive manipulations easy and destructive ones more difficult, which keep the user informed of important changes in status and give warnings about pitfalls. Software which has these characteristics has come to be called "friendly" to the user. Software ergonomics is basically about user friendliness.

The Importance of User Friendliness

Until fairly recently, the primary concern of software designers was to get the program working efficiently. The assumption was that if you wanted to use it, you would sit down and learn all the quirks and complexities, and eventually become part of the brotherhood or sisterhood who dealt with such technical complexities and spoke in so much jargon that they could only communicate with each other. There was an implicit assumption that the essential fascination over what computers could do, once properly programmed, would produce such high levels of motivation that mundane concerns like awkward command syntax (the "grammatical" rules for computer commands) and terse, unintelligible error messages were really not worth bothering about. However, enormous technical advances simultaneously increased the power of the computer and reduced the size of its components. Then the computer itself escaped its glass-enclosed air-conditioned fortress and moved into the office proper. A generation of users arose for whom the computer was only another tool and, for many, a not-always-welcome addition. Consequently, the concept of user friendliness became so important that it rapidly became an international buzzword.

At present, it seems that virtually everyone, vendor and user alike, agrees *in principle* on the need for user friendliness. Research activity in software ergonomics, a field which has only very recently come into existence, has increased enormously. By now, hundreds of research articles and analytic papers on the subject have appeared. However, given the newness of the field and the rapid rate of change of computer technology itself, it is difficult to draw general conclusions from all of this information. The question is how best to give the interested nonspecialist the kind of practical advice needed, particularly when almost every vendor is claiming that his or her product is user friendly.

Methods for Determining User Friendliness

Before examining the characteristics of software in general or the specific attributes of a given software package, the buyer concerned about fit should follow the recommendation that organizational development professional Mary Baetz made with regard to the introduction of any new technology. In *Planning for People in the Electronic Office* (part of this Converging Technology series), Baetz (1985) points out that the first step an organization should take when introducing new technology is to state clearly its *philosophy* and *goals*. The organization should first decide what the total *system*, human plus machine, should accomplish. Whatever innovations are being proposed should be able to meet organizational goals better than existing methods do. The potential buyer will have prepared the way for user friendliness if these analyses are done thoughtfully, if some consideration is given to the capabilities and limitations of the users, to the training requirements and to methods of introducing the new equipment. (These issues are discussed extensively by Baetz.)

Once the system goals have been defined, specific functional goals can be outlined and arrangements made to purchase the hardware and software. Knowing what functions are needed, it is a relatively straightforward procedure to determine in a general way whether or not the equipment and software under consideration can do the job.

For any specific set of requirements, it is likely that several software packages will be capable of doing the job. Yet they may differ appreciably in emotional tone or in propensity to cause error and frustration. Some software packages, although designed (or even custom-designed) to do a certain job, can work counter to the organization's goals (see the example of Zuboff in Chapter 8). Thus, consideration of the overall thrust of the software program is vital.

For a specific evaluation of software characteristics, a more detailed analysis is required. Two approaches to this problem are possible. The first is to assess the software as one would assess the *functioning* of any complex machine (called the *technological* point of view). The second is to evaluate the *principles* that contributed to its design (called the *conceptual* approach). First, let's examine the technological approach.

Technological Characteristics

The technological approach to determining user friendliness typically entails collecting specific studies from diverse sources and organizing them into sets of desirable software system characteristics. For the manager who is not a specialist in computers, a recent book by Galitz (1984), *Humanizing Office Automation*, provides an excellent overview of the system characteristics that contribute most to user friendliness. The following is a list of the attributes delineated by Galitz, which may be used by managers as a starting point from which to make a more detailed analysis of the software characteristics necessary to his or her operation. Galitz argues that a system should be

1. *Adaptive*. It should be capable of meeting the needs of a wide variety of users.
2. *Transparent*. It should allow the user to focus his or her energies on the work itself rather than on the details of the interface.
3. *Comprehendible*. Users should be able to "comprehend" or "group" easily how and why specific actions should be taken.
4. *Natural*. Actions required to operate the system should be similar to those with which the user is familiar.
5. *Predictable*. Responses by the system should be those that might normally be expected.
6. *Responsive*. Feedback about what the system is doing should be provided every time the user takes action.
7. *Self-explanatory*. Actions should follow logically, and be clearly explained.
8. *Forgiving*. Users should be able to make and correct mistakes and still return quickly to the point from which they can continue the job.
9. *Efficient*. Wasted effort by the user should be avoided.
10. *Flexible*. A system should be accessible to a novice, while at the same providing sufficient capabilities for an experienced user.
11. *Available*. None of the rest of these criteria will be of any benefit if the system is always out of order ("down") because of some malfunction.

In his discussion of these criteria, Galitz includes specific advice about such characteristics as proper display format, command language formats, error message structure, and use of function keys. This advice is based on specific studies relating to each of these topics, along with his own considerable experience with software. The result is, in effect, a detailed checklist for software evaluation.

However, there is a practical difficulty inherent in this approach, which Galitz himself raises, concerning the question of priority. If all items on a checklist have equal importance, making a comparative assessment of two software offerings is straightforward: the one which meets the greater number of checklist criteria is better. The problem is that not all items are of equal importance. For example, a checklist may include these items:

1. HELP is available. This means that pressing a certain key will display some sort of instructional aid regarding the operator's problems.
2. Important commands may be canceled. That is, if a potentially disastrous command, such as erasing a file, is issued by mistake, the operator should have a second chance to cancel it.

Are these two items of equal importance? A software package missing a HELP display will still have some sort of manual available. Thus, the primary result of not having a HELP display is a loss of time while the operator reaches for the manual. On the other hand, if the ability to cancel a command is lacking (item 2), the potential for difficulty is much greater. Obviously, software which contained a HELP facility but no CANCEL commands would be less desirable than a second package with the opposite characteristics.

Not all decisions are this easy to make. Without a more integrated view of the task as a whole, it may indeed be impossible to assess software characteristics effectively. To see how the individual task components relate to software characteristics, and to fit them together into some kind of overall pattern, it is necessary to be aware of the principles (the conceptual approach) that have been or should have been taken into account by the designer of the system.

The Conceptual Approach

Proponents of this point of view argue that user friendliness will be achieved when software designers can draw explicitly upon a scientifically based theory of human operator behavior in designing the form of the computer-human interface. Some concept of human behavior is implicit in every program. If Sam is designing a management information system, and decides to use a "mouse" rather than a typewriter keyboard for input, he has a clear theory of human behavior in his mind, which includes the concept of managers not being willing or able to cope with keyboards.

Those who recommend the conceptual approach note that the primary scientific basis for design of user-friendly software actually rests in the data and theory of cognitive psychology. Cognitive psychology is the study of the ways in which people pick up information in the outside world, the ways in which they store that information (either briefly or for long periods of time), how they integrate it into existing memory structures, use it to make a decision, and then act on that decision by executing some more or less complex pattern of motor activity (pressing a sequence of keys, talking, running away).

Conversely, researchers in cognitive psychology have typically been more interested in advancing knowledge than in making it useful to the software design community. Thus, designers have essentially had to make do with their own intuition-based cognitive theories, perhaps supplemented by individual studies devoted to solving specific problems (such as efficient keyboard layout) as they arose.

However, we are now at the point where the scientific knowledge derived from cognitive psychology can be assembled in a form directly usable by the software designer interested in user friendliness. This knowledge will also be useful to the manager who is interested in gaining the competitive edge in operational effectiveness by purchasing and using software that is truly user friendly.

Just as "ergonomic" has become a buzzword in the furniture industry, so "user friendly" has become the buzzword for software. However, the simple assertion that "my program is easy to use," if taken seriously, directly implies an underlying cognitive psychological basis. It is our contention that a software vendor should be able to document the *process* by which a product was made user friendly and that such documentation should be, at least at some level, understandable to those affected (user, manager, purchaser). This concept is not new. Publishers of psychological tests routinely supply a technical manual documenting the way the test was constructed and its statistical characteristics.

The need for user-friendly software is now so great (and such a strong selling point) that it seems reasonable for software vendors to make an effort to communicate just what user friendliness means to them by documenting how they have achieved it. Managers and others in purchasing positions also need to know how to assess that documentation. The ensuing discussion should provide managers with an overview of the cognitive theory of user-friendly design that can help to evaluate software currently on the market. It should give the potential buyer sufficient background to ask knowledgeable questions and to appraise the vendor's approach.

How People Work at Computers

If you look at the letter Q, it takes 0.1 seconds for the image of that letter to get to your brain.

If you are asked whether the two letters AB are the same or different, it takes you 0.07 seconds to make that decision.

If you are shown two very brief flashes of light, one of which follows the other by less than 0.1 seconds, you will see only one.

If you are asked to make a note of the 7-digit number 9530284, it will take you about 4.9 seconds to write it in longhand; or, if you are experienced at entering numbers on a computer or typewriter, recording the number will take you less than one second. If you have not recorded the number within 7 seconds of seeing it, you will have forgotten it unless you were "rehearsing" it in the meantime. In fact, unless you have glanced back at it again, you have probably forgotten it by now. The same would be true if you were asked to remember RHPKZWL.

On the other hand, if you were given an even larger number or string of letters, but they had some meaningful context, such as 98765432 or CHOCOLATE, you would probably remember them all several pages hence, despite the fact that you are busy reading this text. The reason is that meaningful characters are processed differently — as a single element ("chunked") — by the brain.

This information is typical of that studied in the field of cognitive psychology, and its importance for using and designing computer hardware and software is significant.

For example, when designing a flicker-free display screen, it is important to know that two light flashes are perceived as one if the time between them (the perceptual processing time) is less than 0.1 seconds. The time it takes to make certain decisions or to execute certain motor movements, the difficulty or ease of remembering certain commands or combinations, the speed with which certain signals are read and comprehended, are all pieces of information which have a practical impact on the way the human being interacts with the machine.

A major step in the application of this kind of information has been accomplished by Card, Moran, and Newell, a group from Xerox and Carnegie-Mellon University, with the recent publication of their book, *The Psychology of Human-Computer Interaction* (1983).

By combining the individual elements, such as cognitive processing time (in the example above, are A and B the same?), perceptual processing time (one flash of light or two?), memory characteristics (long-term, short-term, and working memory), reaction times, and motor processing times (writing vs. typing), these investigators were able to construct a hypothetical model of how a person interacts with a computer. They called it the Model Human Processor. From the data available on the Model Human Processor, predictions were made about how long it takes (in seconds) to perform functions such as moving a paragraph, locating a phrase, and deleting a line in any specific word processing package. This model was able to predict which of two word processing systems would be more efficient, with 75% to 85% accuracy.

The designer/planner can incorporate data from the model directly into the design concept, rather than trusting to intuition, or just ignoring these issues. Furthermore, Card, Moran, and Newell have organized the data as a kind of cognitive handbook to which a system designer can refer when making decisions.

These investigators give a hypothetical example in which a system designer in the process of setting up design specifications for a given software package must decide between using menus (lists of possible computer manipulations which appear on the screen, like a restaurant menu) or keyboard commands (which require that the operator look up in a written manual or memorize how to do the manipulations). Extra computer memory and display are required for the menu system, and the additional costs for this are known. However, in looking at the increased training times predicted by the Model Human Processor, the designer quickly sees that the additional cost of training an inexperienced user to operate his specific keyboard command system would be greater than the total cost of the computer itself. This hypothetical example illustrates how applying data from the Model Human Processor to the design of software can minimize costs and increase efficiency.

The Use of Metaphor in Achieving User Friendliness

In introducing people to computers for the first time, it is common to give explanations in terms of something with which people are already familiar. Thus, a novice is told that the new word processor is "really a typewriter with a screen." The typewriter, a familiar object, has just been used as a *metaphor* to explain the word processor — something which is unfamiliar. John Carroll, of IBM's Watson Research Laboratories, has written extensively about the importance of metaphor as a major component of software ergonomics.

There are two major reasons why metaphor, and its links to cognitive psychology, are of such practical importance. First, *any* new concept or idea is typically learned by use of some sort of metaphor linking it to something already familiar. (Earlier in the book, the structure of the eye was explained in terms of a camera.) Second, virtually all software designers make use of some sort of (usually implicit) cognitive theory of human behavior in making decisions about the form of their computer-human interface, and, for the most part, these theories rely heavily on metaphor. Perhaps the best-known example of metaphor in software at the present time is the Apple Macintosh. The Macintosh display uses pictures of familiar objects (file folders, scissors, wastebaskets) to suggest particular software functions (create a file, move text, delete). However, this kind of approach can be made more powerful and more systematic by a deliberate use of the tools provided by cognitive psychology.

Like the Macintosh, many other software systems use some version of a *desk* (with or without a typewriter) as a basic metaphor. From the perspective of cognitive psychology, the question can be asked: *What is a desk?*

Scientists believe that the brain stores the concept of "desk" as a structured network or collection of attributes in long-term memory. It looks something like this:

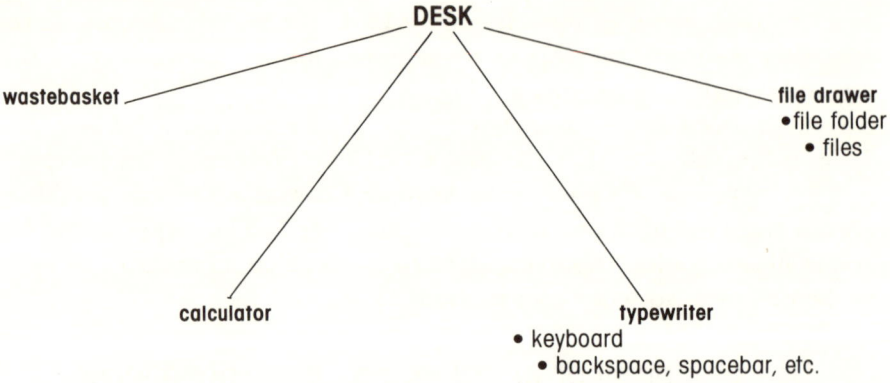

Of course, one person's memory structure will look different than another's. Nevertheless, it can be assumed that, for a group of people who share similar backgrounds, their structures will have more similarities than differences. Some theorists call these structures *schemas*; they represent little packets of knowledge about the world.

Schemas which already exist in the brain are used as frameworks for the development of new schemas. In other words, what you already know forms the foundation for absorbing things you want to know. The mechanics of this process are thought to be approximately as follows.

> *James is learning how to use a word-processing program. He reads in the manual: "The first step is to create a file."*
>
> *The information from this sentence is temporarily stored in Working Memory (as in the Model Human Processor of Card, Moran, and Newell)*

while a search through Long-Term Memory is carried out in order to find some schema to which the key word "file" can be related. After some obviously inappropriate schemas are rejected (e.g., a file is a steel tool for grinding edges), the key word is located in the "desk" schema, and some portion of this structure is "downloaded" into Working Memory. At some level of consciousness, James is aware that the manual is probably talking about something like a file folder.

The next sentence in the manual is this: "To create a file, you must assign a filename."

The information from this sentence now joins the first sentence and the file-folder-related components of the desk schema in working memory. At this point, things are getting crowded, since working memory has a limited capacity. A decision must be reached as to whether the file folder schema is still appropriate. The decision is positive; the concepts "file" and "filename" now become linked to the "desk" schema, which has become accepted as the memory structure through which other information will be interpreted. James imagines writing a name on the tab of a file folder.

It is important to point out that, in this example, James did not have the "desk" metaphor available ahead of time; it was arrived at spontaneously. Carroll points out that a novice exposed to a new system will quickly come up with *some* metaphor to help understand what is going on, and once chosen, it is unlikely to be easily discarded.

Choosing Effective Metaphors

Not all metaphors are equal in their effectiveness, and there is no guarantee that the metaphor first selected by an individual will continue to work effectively. The solution, of course, is for the software designer to provide an already-existing metaphor ahead of time. If this metaphor has been carefully thought through, the learning process will be much faster, since the novice operator will not be expending mental effort in the search of his or her own metaphor.

On the other hand, selection of an inappropriate metaphor may actually hinder later use of the system. Suppose, for instance, that James takes the file-folder metaphor literally. Entering information into a word-processing file is, he thinks, like taking a piece of paper out of a file folder and sticking it in his typewriter. He then calls up a word-processing file, and makes some entries through his keyboard. Still thinking about the typewriter, he notices that it is lunch time, and turns off the computer, intending to finish the file after lunch. Of course, he has forgotten to SAVE the file, and when he returns, it has vanished forever: the typewriter metaphor does not include files vanishing when the machine is turned off. This error is extremely common, and happens to virtually everyone who works with computers. Professional programmers with years of experience forget to save files on which they have spent hours working. The metaphor of the paper file is so dominant that even experienced operators forget that computer files no longer exist once the computer is turned off, or a new file is brought in. These problems have software solutions: "autosave" options are now available which automatically save files while they are being worked on. Also, friendly word-processing programs will not let the operator read a new file into memory without first giving warning that the old one is about to be wiped out.

The problem is, of course, that no metaphor is exact. There are always elements in the new object which are different from the metaphor being applied. This, according to Carroll, can present problems, but may also have positive benefits. Learning based on an explicit metaphor can be *active* learning, as compared with more traditional passive instruction in which the characteristics of the system are simply described in detail. The operator, in effect, acts like a scientific explorer examining a new territory. "Let's see now, if this program is really like a desk, if I throw something into the wastebasket (DELETE FILE), I should be able to pick it out again (RECOVER FROM DELETE) unless the janitor has cleaned out the wastebasket (overloaded the recovery file or turned off the machine)." This process of active exploration is known to be a more effective way of learning a new system.

However, the metaphor must be presented in a way that makes it clear both that there are explicit limits to the metaphor and that the metaphor itself can be used to push beyond itself. For example:

> "I now know that a file has something like the characteristics of a paper file but it is also different, since it takes on different physical characteristics, depending on where it is located. If it is in the memory of the computer, I can see it on my screen, but it's very fragile. If the power fails, or if I read in another file by mistake, it will vanish. I can transform my file into a more permanent form by putting it in another place (saving it to disk), but even here, strange things can happen to it to make it disappear. (Files can mistakenly be erased from disks; disks can fail or be damaged.) To be absolutely sure, I can actually print my file on paper. However, I can then no longer make changes in it."

The desk metaphor has been extended to a more general spatial metaphor in which files exist in different places in different states. The metaphor is now *mixed* so as to better account for the larger set of properties, and life is getting complicated. There is a fine line between providing an oversimplified metaphor which leads to trouble, and giving an overcomplicated mix of metaphors which just confuses.

Inventing New Metaphors

Providing a novice operator with an explicit metaphor seems to be an excellent way to make the software more accessible and usable more quickly, so long as the limitations of the metaphor are explicitly pointed out, and additional metaphors introduced at appropriate points. One stumbling block is that the most common, *fundamental* metaphor for a computer is that of a complicated *machine*. Most programming is conceptualized in terms of "making the machine work," and this engineering metaphor extends to the computer-human interface. The machine is given "commands" which it "executes," and if *you* give the wrong command, then a terse message will inform you that you have given an "illegal command" or that perhaps you have made a "IOF 33 error." This is perfectly reasonable to those users who enjoy working within and mastering a tightly structured logical system. However, there are many other people who want and need to be effective users but may be intimidated or repelled by the technical jargon.

At least one successful programmer, Paul Heckel, feels that the engineering metaphor is wrong, and that software development is, in effect, an art form akin to creating movies.

In his short and readable book, *The Elements of Friendly Software Design*, Heckel asserts that the main problem of creating user-friendly software is that of *communication* with the user. Therefore, one should look for advice to those who make their livings practicing the craft of communication: filmmakers, artists, writers, salespeople, and even magicians. Many of the attributes of *artistic* quality, he says, can be translated directly into *software* quality.

Heckel also offers useful specific advice, covering somewhat the same ground as Galitz and Carroll, but his greatest contribution may well be the very act of suggesting a new metaphor: software as a work of art (film) rather than software as a machine. Following the basic principles of cognitive psychology as we have described them, thinking of software from an artistic/communication perspective allows a new set of memory structures (schemas) to be brought to bear on the problem of user friendliness.

Some may balk at the film metaphor, assuming that Heckel's points may be relevant to computer *games*, but pointing out that software in the office is used for *work*. However, it is important to note that for some people, the challenge of mastering a complex system and using it to do their bidding provides a degree of satisfaction and enjoyment beyond that of financial reward. For these people, challenge itself provides intrinsic motivation — it is fun — and the entertainment/work distinction is blurred. Obviously, such people will be an asset to the company.

However, it should be possible to tap some of this kind of enthusiasm in other workers by making the software more inherently enjoyable to use. This means programming qualities of fun and challenge into everyday working software systems. The hope is to try to incorporate into office software some of the attributes which have attracted millions to computer games.

These points have been made explicit by Galitz and Carroll, among others. Carroll discusses the popular computer game "Adventure," in which the player, given a minimum amount of initial information and a few simple ground rules for communication, can spend months exploring a fantasy world (in words, not in graphics) of secret caves, evil dwarves, magic spells, and buried treasure. He then compares this game with a typical word-processing system, arguing that both systems present the user with a series of problems to be overcome. However, the exploration-based environment of the Adventure game makes the very act of overcoming problems intrinsically rewarding, whereas the usually passive learning environment, in which the operator is told, "Here is what the system does; now learn it" is more likely to generate frustration. Carroll argues directly that word-processor software should simply be made more game-like.

At least two other implicit factors contribute to the usual difference in attitude between the user friendliness of games like Adventure and that of typical office software. Once you are interested in it, the game leads you on out of curiosity and a sense of wonder and fascination. In contrast, common office software packages come accompanied by weighty, obscurely written instruction manuals. With such intimidation, what happens to wonder and fascination? Yet the machine *is* wonderful, and exploring its capabilities and those of a good software package can be an adventure. Well-written software and simple, clear, good-humored manuals could go a long way toward decreasing intimidation and increasing the comfort and delight that should accompany the use of such a powerful, versatile tool. Software designers may succeed in creating more user-friendly systems by working from the software-as-work-of-art, software-as-game, or other positive metaphor. Managers purchasing software may find it useful to take note of the metaphor used when assessing a system's effectiveness.

Built-in User Friendliness

The resources from which designers may draw to create more user-friendly software are extensive. Cognitive psychologists are able to quantify behavior patterns of operators, and to provide insights into the way people learn to work with software by creating and changing metaphors. If these observations were combined with the kinds of specific technological guidelines found in Galitz, and the whole applied systematically, the user friendliness of software would take a quantum leap forward. However, such application rarely occurs at the product development stage.

Unfortunately, the typical role of the ergonomist/human factors specialist has been to evaluate the product (system) *after* it was designed or at the final production stage, when changes are difficult to make. Design improvements were made as a result of learning from past mistakes, or when feedback and pressure from the marketplace made it financially attractive. Any ergonomic gains that have been achieved have been determined largely by the experience and the personal perspective of the individual systems designer.

Principles for insuring the user friendliness of software might be better applied if the ergonomic input were incorporated as an integral part of the design process, right from the beginning. A conceptual framework for accomplishing just this was proposed by IBM-Watson Labs researchers Gould and Lewis (1985). They defined three important criteria to be followed in the design of user-friendly software.

The first step calls for *early focus on the user*. Potential users are involved in setting design goals early on, and in developing a specific understanding of the human skills and capabilities required by the job. "Know thy user" is a phrase used frequently by software ergonomists. This means that potential users, as well as ergonomic experts, become members of the design team.

A second requirement is *early and continual measurement of user responses to the system*. Prototypes — simplified versions of the program — are continually developed and evaluated by the users. This prevents an entire program from being built on a set of assumptions which turn out to be tenuous, or even false.

Finally, *iterative design* is crucial to this method of software development. This means going back to the drawing boards over and over again to incorporate the results of user testing.

At the present time, the average software does not have the earmarks of having gone through this design process. In many cases, it has not been technically feasible to find points that are both early enough in the program development cycle to allow for major changes without considerable effort and expense, and far enough along for program components to be complete enough for users to test them.

To alleviate the problem of intermediate testing, a number of new techniques are under development which will allow the designer to simulate a variety of possible display and keyboard formats and procedures *before* programmers begin to prepare the computer sequences needed to execute these procedures. In this way, the designer can conceptually specify a way to accomplish some procedure, and the method can be tried out ahead of time.

One of the most important points for a designer to keep in mind is to know how the user responds to the system so that interfacing problems do not become an integral part of the design. With complicated designs, it is impossible to check out all the decisions; thus, many must be made arbitrarily. However, if difficulties are caught early enough through intermediate testing, changes can be made more easily. The result should be truly user-friendly software.

Ergonomic Design: A Success Story

It is important to point out that these principles of user friendliness are not simply a set of "wouldn't it be nice" guidelines proposed by academics but not really practical in the real world. One of the co-authors of these guidelines, John Gould, was a member of a small design team at IBM which, in six months, put together the computerized voice message system used at the 1984 Summer Olympics in Los Angeles.

Using these principles of early focus on the user, early and continual measurement of user response, and iterative design, the team put together a successful system which made it possible for any of 10,000 Olympic athletes to either receive a recorded voice message from anywhere in the world by telephone, or to send and receive voice messages among themselves. Operating the system required no formal training, and the system functioned in 12 languages.

Gould and his colleagues (Boies, Gould et al., 1985) stated that this achievement could not have been accomplished without explicit reliance on the principles outlined above. In this case at least, user friendliness was indistinguishable from operational effectiveness.

How Much User Friendliness Is Optimal?

Performance Requirements

The manager, armed with knowledge about the approaches to user-friendly design described in the preceding sections, is in a better position to understand its implications. Those purchasing hardware and software will of course first consider issues of computer system functionality — that is, can the system do what is needed in terms of its functions and memory storage capacity? However, systems with similar functionality may differ widely in other performance characteristics, such as ease of training and speed of execution, and those who purchase software should have enough information to be able to make decisions as to which of these characteristics is to be given priority. "Know thy user" applies as much in this situation as it does to the program designer.

The User Population: Expert vs. Novice

User friendliness of software involves certain trade-offs. The manager must consider who is expected to use the program — experts or novices — and under what conditions. The first area where the interests of these two groups diverge is that of training manuals. Although manuals are supposedly for novices, many are so full of technical and obscure language that they themselves are "unfriendly." In a practical office setting, this means that a person who is expert in that program is called away from his or her own work to instruct the novice. Thus, an important issue in assessing software is whether or not there will be a need (or opportunity, especially for new employees), for formal classroom training, as opposed to self-instruction with a manual, or even no manual at all. The quality of the manual, if one is required, is an important consideration.

It is difficult to strike a balance in the software program itself between choosing one too difficult for the novice and choosing one too cumbersome for the expert. Some applications, such as automatic bank tellers, are aimed only at novices. However, most systems are aimed at both the novice and the expert user. Here, the differences in performance requirements become quite striking. A complex data base or word-processing system can be made friendly for a novice through the use of an elaborate system of menus (display screens listing possible options which can be carried out) through which the user is led step by step. However, an expert user to whom intermediate steps come naturally might become frustrated rather quickly.

A major challenge for software designers is to provide simultaneously, ease of use for the novice and speed of execution plus increased capabilities for the expert. A futher consideration is the worker's *transition* from novice to expert. A very promising approach to this problem is described by Carroll and Carrithers (1984) as a "training wheels" system (as in learning to ride a bicycle). This approach allows the novice to be exposed initially to just the minimum number of functions required to run the system at its lowest level of capability. As experience builds, other components can be introduced. For a word processing system, the initial instructions allow the operator to learn very quickly how to type text, make simple insertions and deletions, save the text to a file, and print the text. Later on, the more complex moves such as screen formating and paragraph moves are introduced. However, the system has sufficient flexibility that, eventually, as the users become experts, they can choose more sophisticated options for accomplishing the same tasks.

Although it is important to insure that new users will have sufficient on-screen help, in addition to clear instruction manuals, the manager should not *underestimate* the potential abilities of a user population and build in too many aids and menus for the novice, at the expense of the expert's efficiency. It may be better to purchase a system with an effective training program than one overloaded with "user-friendly" on-screen advice. A recent software review, for example, comments that a popular word-processing program was so loaded with built-in training materials that the speed of operation was severely reduced. Furthermore, a badly written set of instructions does not automatically become better because it can be accessed by pressing a key on the terminal rather than turning the page of an instruction manual.

Error Recovery

As the introductory examples in this chapter pointed out, electronic information processing allows for the possibility of errors on a truly magnificent scale. No matter how simple and straightforward the command structure or menu system is, someone will discover a way to make an error! The potential buyer of software should be aware of this, and consider packages that have some protection against time-consuming errors. In text editing, for example, if the command to move the cursor up a line is similar to that for moving to the top of the page, making an error by choosing the latter when the former is intended is annoying and hinders efficiency. The user must scan back down the copy, trying to find the relevant line.

A more serious problem would occur if the operator inadvertently pressed the DELETE key. Such potential disasters are guarded against in systems that give the user a second chance (by asking, ARE YOU SURE? or DELETE WHAT?, for instance, when such a command is issued.) In addition, it may be important to investigate a system that "fails gently": in the case of power failure, many large systems have emergency power supplies which keep the system operating long enough for crucial files to be transferred to temporary storage on disk or tape. Other systems are now available which automatically save materials at frequent intervals.

Security

The issue of system security is not usually thought of as a component of user friendliness. As demonstrated by Kelly's experience in the opening scenario, however, systems that are easily tampered with can wreak havoc with the organization's confidential information. This can also make them serious stressors to the operators. However, because the goal of security measures is to make it difficult for the *unauthorized* users to gain access to the system, they must inevitably have an aspect of *user unfriendliness* — that is, they can also hinder the *authorized* user.

Furthermore, the presence of built-in security measures in a program will not, of itself, guard against unauthorized access to files. For security to be effective, the available security measures need to be used properly. The problems of security vary, of course, with the kind of computer system in use. In situations with large numbers of terminals connected to a centralized system, the focus is on access by unauthorized persons, and the major approach to security is through proper use of passwords. Many organizations have not, apparently, realized the importance of frequently changing passwords in order to maintain the security of central files. Unfortunate results abound when single letters or easily guessed sequences of characters (such as the user's name or birthday) are used as passwords to protect confidential files.

In a personal computer environment, a major security application has to do with control over the large number of diskettes that are generated. The problems are compounded by the fact that many employees using personal computers at work have similar machines at home, and very often take work home. Security, in this situation, is much more difficult. Physical accountability and control of diskettes by supervisors might seem to be a reasonable solution, but in practice, it is virtually unenforceable. A better solution seems to be the more obvious one of orientation and training. Many users are simply not aware of the vulnerability and confidentiality of the files they are creating, and the need to use reasonable safeguards.

Technological solutions are becoming available to deal with these problems. Software systems are now available which will electronically scramble (encrypt) stored versions of confidential files. The user would, after creating such a file, call up an encryption program which would, in turn, take a series of unique words provided by the user, and use these words to scramble the material on the original file. The original file would be erased.

Such a system might be effective, but the worker must be willing to make the extra effort to use it. Clearly, the encryption software itself would have to be exceptionally reliable and user friendly. One would need to have a particularly strong degree of trust in a software package which systematically makes unintelligible one's only copy of one's work.

A final method of insuring security for both centralized and decentralized systems is currently being developed. The "smart card" is, in effect, a plastic credit card containing a microchip. The microchip will contain password and encryption instructions that will allow the holder to access a network, or scramble/unscramble a file simply by placing the card into a card reader.

Security, error recovery, expertise and developing expertise of the user, and hardware-software performance requirements are all factors that the manager needs to consider before investing in a given software package. By correctly identifying areas of priority in his or her own operation, the manager will be able to acquire a system that meets the company's needs and improves the "fit" between worker and software.

Key Issues in Choosing User-Friendly Software

- User-friendly software should be adaptive, transparent, comprehendible, natural, predictable, responsive, self-explanatory, forgiving, efficient, flexible, and available.
- The software vendor should be able to document the process by which a product was made user friendly, and such documentation should be understandable to the user.
- The user friendliness of software must be ultimately evaluated (whether implicitly or explicitly) in terms of the way people absorb and use knowledge (cognitive psychology).
- Formal models of the user, based on principles of cognitive psychology, are potentially useful for evaluating and developing software.
- A well worked-out metaphor or set of metaphors can be an effective means for allowing a novice to actively explore the capabilities of new software.
- To develop a computer-human interface (CHI) is to establish a means of communication with the user. Therefore, techniques of communication media, such as film, may be employed to enhance the communication process.
- The process of developing user-friendly software should follow three stages: early focus on the user, measurement of users' responses, and iterative design.
- A system should be structured so the novice can explore it without getting into serious trouble; it should also be terse enough for the expert.
- The form of instruction (whether it is a manual or a HELP menu on the screen) is less important than its clarity.
- There are trade-offs to be made between system security and user friendliness. With thought and planning, both can be accomplished.

The Quality of Working Life in the Electronic Office

CHAPTER 8

Coping with the modern electronic office may seem overwhelming, but upon reflection, it seems clear that we are in precisely the same situation as our forebears, who were coping with the problems of shifting textile production from the rural cottage to the urban factory. The observation that society is on the threshold of a new Industrial Revolution — a technological revolution — has been repeated so frequently that it now tends to be overlooked. Nevertheless, the term *pioneer* is completely appropriate for those who are at the technological forefront at this particular point in history. The office of 1920 was not that different from the office of 1960: a secretary 20 years of age in 1920 who dropped out of the workforce and returned in 1960 would not have had a great deal of trouble getting back to work. In the year 2000, the office of 1960 is likely to be unrecognizable. The changes in working conditions and work organization which have occurred thus far are only the tip of the iceberg compared to what is likely to occur in the relatively near future.

The driving force behind this technological revolution is, of course, the ever-increasing power, capacity, and speed of the computer, as well as its increasing affordability.

Although today's managers are, in some sense, standing in the same shoes as their forebears at the beginning of the Industrial Revolution, they are also heir to the decades of experience and changes in organizational philosophy that have led from the sweatshop to concern for the individual and for the quality of working life. Only the shortsighted will embrace the technology while ignoring the lessons of the past. A perceptive manager will immediately bring this historical perspective to bear on the introduction of any new technology.

What will be the effect of computer technology on the actual *conditions* of work — on the quality of working life? As Baetz has stated (1985), the structure of any office system — traditional or electronic — reflects underlying management philosophy. It is therefore reasonable to conclude that the introduction of computer-based office equipment will *accentuate* the existing office system structure and quality of working life. That is, if the situation is good already, automation can make it better; if it is bad, it may get worse.

This potential for extreme change places a special responsibility on managers and supervisors to insure that their underlying management principle remains that of *concern for people* — for the workers who will be benefiting or suffering from the new technology. In this chapter, we will be looking at the decreased job decision latitude, or control, and deskilling that can sometimes accompany the introduction of new technology into the office. Where bad chairs and poor air quality produce physical stress, these phenomena create stress in the *psychosocial environment*. How can psychosocial stress be managed? How can electronic systems of supervision be used appropriately? These are some of the special problems and opportunities encountered by supervisors and managers in the electronic office that will be investigated in this chapter.

Predicting the Effects of Change

The computer can be employed as an amazingly adaptive, almost awesomely powerful piece of equipment which continually challenges the user to explore the limits of their joint capabilities. But the same computer can be the taskmaster of an electronic sweatshop where oversimplified, highly repetitive, highly paced job demands closely resemble the worst industrial assembly lines. These assembly lines have been prime examples of work systems requiring behaviors which are primarily *childlike*, characterized by dependency, short time perspective, and abilities which are few and shallow. When childlike behaviors like these are required of fully functioning adults — either in the traditional assembly line or its more recent electronic manifestation — the result for the worker, according to organizational theorist Chris Argyris (1974), is conflict and frustration.

A degraded quality of working life is costly to both the individual and the organization — in two ways. It can result in psychosocial stress (as mentioned by Argyris, above) and/or physical stress (especially from inappropriate furniture, ambient environment, etc.). One result is employee health problems.

In the United States, for example, cardiovascular disease, which is widely held to be stress-related, accounted for $11 billion of lost output to industry during 1981. Workers compensation claims and disability retirements arising from job-related emotional distress are becoming more common. The cost of job dissatisfaction in terms of turnover and absenteeism has already been discussed (Chapter 6).

What changes in the workplace have led to this apparent increase in stress? Recent analyses point to the importance of the individual's reduced ability to *exert control* over the everyday details of his or her working life.

Job Decision Latitude and Job Demand

A useful and important analysis of the issue of control as applied to work has been provided by Karasek (1981). Using the results of survey research, Karasek carried out an extensive statistical analysis in which a large number of jobs — both white and blue collar — were classified according to two dimensions: job decision latitude and job demand. *Job decision latitude* was defined as "the working individual's potential control over his tasks and his conduct during the working day." Job decision latitude can be interpreted as *control*, not necessarily just concerning major decisions affecting the organization, but also over the moment-to-moment flow of daily life. It is the extent to which a person can decide what to do next on the job.

The range of job decision latitude can be illustrated by comparing a machine-paced assembly line worker with a freelance business writer racing against a deadline. Both have intense time pressures. However, for the assembly line worker, virtually every action is shaped by the need to keep up with the line. This is *low* job decision latitude. The writer, on the other hand, can allocate her resources as she wishes as long as the deadline is met. If, for example, her summary is not going well, she can switch to revising the introductory passages. She can even decide to take a nap now and work later into the night. This is an example of *high* job decision latitude.

Job demand, the other dimension of work, has three aspects: the pressures of meeting the demand of the workload itself, of dealing with unexpected tasks, and of coping with job-related interpersonal conflicts.

Karasek argues that previous researchers have focused on one or the other of these two dimensions, but have failed to realize that both must be considered *in combination*. Thus, four different categories of work must be considered: high demand–high control, high demand–low control, low demand–high control, and low demand–low control.

	High Demand	Low Demand
High Control	Manager: rush	Manager: slow
Low Control	Assembly line worker	Telephone clerk: slow

For example, during the holiday rush season, a retail store manager would have the pressures of high job demand, but would also have the freedom to allocate his time and effort (resources) in the way he or she saw fit. That same manager during the off season might exemplify low demand and high control. An example of low levels of both demand and control might be a telephone answering clerk in an office which is not busy. The clerk must stay beside the telephone in case a call comes through, but can spend the rest of the time reading a book or magazine. Finally, an example of a high demand–low control situation would be a person working on a high-speed assembly line, or doing data entry under time pressure and performance monitoring.

Karasek found that *the people most at risk for cardiovascular disease were in the high demand–low control situation*. The risk levels associated with people holding these jobs were, in fact, at least as great as the traditional risk factors for heart disease (smoking, age, obesity, etc.). Thus, the image of the high-powered executive being at risk for heart attacks is to some extent mistaken: the high-powered executive has a great deal of control, and while he or she may be at risk, the data entry person is at greater risk statistically.

Computer technology can either greatly *enhance* or greatly *diminish* the degree of control an individual has over his or her working conditions. Positive feelings of mastery and control result when an individual gains an understanding of how to use the computer system, and to get from it the things the organization needs. However, the consequences can be extremely negative when the computer system is used to exert control *over* people, rather than providing them with power that they can control.

Regaining Control

One solution to lack of control over work on the traditional assembly line was the *job enrichment* movement. Supporters of job enrichment proposed that work be redesigned so as to be more meaningful and challenging to the individual worker. In one of the most famous examples (the Volvo automobile plant in Sweden), the traditional assembly line was discarded. Small working groups took responsibility for integrated components of the final product (e.g., the electrical system or the interior), and individual group members were able to trade off different jobs.

The extent to which job enrichment has actually been effective is hotly debated. Its original assumptions have been challenged as oversimplified, and new, more complicated theoretical structures have emerged which attempt to explain when and if job enrichment will work. However, the concept of giving workers suitable control over and accountability for their own output is a valid one, and one which could be applied to situations where workers have tended to lose autonomy as a result of computerization.

Deskilling

Deskilling occurs when jobs which formerly required certain degrees of initiative and judgment are performed automatically. In its lowest form, deskilling is represented by the factory-like production center with rows of workers entering the same few characters into the same forms. These kinds of jobs are the electronic version of the paced assembly lines, and will likely present the same kinds of problems. Clerical deskilling has occurred when traditional secretaries with a wide variety of administrative duties and responsibilities have been required to learn a word-processing system — only to find that they have been downgraded to production typists.

However, deskilling can be found at a variety of job levels. Computerized problem-solving and decision-making routines have already been substituted for many professional, technical, and managerial functions, and rapid advances in the field of artificial intelligence make it likely that this process will continue. Management theorist Shoshanna Zuboff (1982) has described the way in which a collection agency structured its computer-mediated collection system so that major areas of discretionary authority which had formerly been the province of individual collection agents were eliminated by automated decision-making rules. Moreover, this phenomenon is not limited to the office, but may arise whenever electronic automation is employed. The collection agent who must now follow strict computer-based rules in servicing accounts shares the dissatisfaction of the highly paid commander of a commercial airliner, who complains that new automated controls make him feel like he's "only along for the ride."

The negative consequences to an individual of the loss of significant opportunities to exercise professional judgment and skill do not require a great deal of elaboration. They include, of course, a shift toward the low-control end of Karasek's classification. If job demand remains high, the individual may also move to a higher health risk category.

Zuboff points out negative consequences of deskilling for the organization as well. Risk-taking and creative alternatives to existing policies are less likely to emerge if all procedures are "frozen" in the computer. Interestingly, in the case of the collection agency, the system was implemented despite the perception of individual managers that the individual skill and judgment of collection agents was the prime factor in success in collecting from delinquent accounts! Thus, they computerized away what they considered to be their best asset.

Alternatives to Deskilling

The problems described above are not an inherent characteristic of the electronic automation of office procedures. They are a reflection of a particular management philosophy. In the case of the collection agency, it appears that the operational philosophy used to guide the development of the system program was not really intended by management. Implementation of this system was unfortunate for this company, since, as Zuboff points out, the company could just as easily have used the flexibility and power of their computer system to design a *supportive* information resource which "preserve(d) the entrepreneurial aspects of the collector's job while rationalizing its administration with on-line record keeping." Carrying this out, however, requires an understanding of the human cognitive and motivational factors discussed in the previous chapter. If, for example, the user-based program development approach suggested in Chapter 7 had been utilized by this company, involving input from the collection agents themselves at the outset, the outcome would probably have been a very different program: one that *supported* rather than replaced the individual skills of the agents.

Paul Fitts, one of the founding fathers of the human factors (ergonomics) profession in the United States, wrote a landmark report in 1951 about problems of automation of function for the U.S. Air Force. That report, which still has considerable relevance, laid out those job functions for which humans are likely to be better than machines, along with those functions for which machines are likely to be better than humans. Humans, Fitts wrote, surpass machines in their abilities to detect small quantities of light and sound, to recognize patterns of light and sound, to improvise, to store very large amounts of material for long periods of time, to recall relevant facts at the proper time, to reason inductively, and to exercise judgment. Machines, on the other hand, are better able to respond quickly to signals, to apply force smoothly, to perform repetitive, routine tasks, to store information briefly and then erase it, to reason quantitatively/deductively, and to do many different things at once.

In 1985, this list (with the possible exception of long-term memory capacity) could still serve as a set of guidelines to avoid the worst problems of deskilling and loss of discretionary judgmental abilities.

Supervision in the Electronic Office

Electronic Performance Monitoring

Machines in general, and computerized systems in particular, are especially good at keeping track of the time and frequencies of many different events, such as individual keystrokes. To the extent that a person interacts with a computer system, virtually every aspect of that interaction can be monitored. Thus, it is relatively easy, from a technical point of view, for a supervisor or manager to determine precisely at what time an operator sits down to work, how fast he or she is keying, what keystroke patterns are occurring, and when the operator stops for a break.

Moreover, as systems become more sophisticated, the increasing number of transactions of all kinds which take place under computer control will simply enhance the possibilities for such monitoring. It is now common practice in many places to monitor operators dealing with telephone inquiries (such as directory assistance), and in some cases operators are penalized for staying on the phone longer than some standard time. It is not far-fetched to imagine the same thing happening eventually to a stockbroker. As more and more office functions are automated, and as more and more functions such as data base manipulation, electronic mail, etc., work through a central computer, higher-level monitoring is possible.

The practice, and the possibility, of detailed, intensive monitoring has led to some very vehement reactions. A recent *Wall Street Journal* article was entitled "Productivity Spies: Computers Keep Eye on Workers and See If They Perform Well." It described typists whose detailed performance (keystrokes per minute, pages per day) was continuously monitored, and who became so angry that they sabotaged the system, creating false files and deleting other workers' files in order to inflate their own figures. Many of the workers who were subject to monitoring reported feeling that they were being spied upon and dehumanized. The comparisons with 1984 and Big Brother are obvious. Unions representing office workers have taken strong stands against electronic performance monitoring, and legislative proposals restricting such practices are beginning to emerge.

On the other side, management, somewhat defensively at times, talks of the need to save jobs by increasing productivity, and the advantage of having objective methods for determining and rewarding good performance.

A Different Approach to Electronic Performance Monitoring

Is it possible to reach any common ground in this controversy? Perhaps the following will serve at least as a clarification.

Consider the situation where a supervisor receives hourly keystroke rates from the computer system from each of the data entry clerks in her section, and her job is to admonish any clerk who is falling below some hourly standard, and to dock the pay of any who are consistently behind. From the perspective of Karasek's model, the individual workers under these conditions are under maximum strain conditions: continual high workload, and virtually no control. There is no choice but to keep working under the threat of being penalized.

There is nothing inherently noxious about one's performance being monitored, even by a computer. Many hundreds of thousands of people have eagerly placed hundreds of thousands of coins in performance-monitoring devices called videogames. Many athletes, both amateur and professional, are obsessed with their own performance statistics: runs batted in, shots on goal, attempted passes, etc. Olympians will work desperately to shave fractions of seconds off running, rowing, biking, or swimming times. Why should monitoring at work be any different?

The difference resides in their degree of control. In all of the examples taken from outside the office, the information provided by the monitoring system acts as *feedback*, a psychological concept which is known to act as a powerful motivator. The feedback provides the information which allows the individual to control his or her own behavior.

There is no reason to expect this to be any different in a work situation. The question is, can monitoring become feedback? Suppose that in a work situation, the hourly keystroke rates are given directly to the employee rather than the supervisor. All the supervisor sees is a cumulative monthly total. If the work standard is based on these monthly totals, the workload may be high, but the operator at least has some discretion — to speed up when feeling energetic, or slow down, or even to get up and walk around when feeling tired. If, in addition, specific target goals are set jointly by the operator and supervisor, and progress toward those goals is rewarded rather than slippage being penalized, the conditions have been established for what some experts believe will be a steady increase in performance.

In fact, in one specific labor-management dispute in which monitoring was an issue, the primary focus of concern was on the fairness of the monitoring *procedure*, and individual employees' lack of access to their own records. Labor and management have been able, in certain cases, to come to agreement on what constitutes fair monitoring practices.

Data entry work may be, as is commonly thought, at the bottom of the electronic office status heap. Nevertheless, if supervisors are supportive, if employees are treated as responsible, capable adults who will work toward goals when appropriate motivation is provided, if optimal physical conditions of work described earlier in this book are attended to, then there is no reason for even these unglamorous but essential jobs to be as bad as many report.

Electronic Supervision and Performance Appraisal

However, a broader perspective must be taken. As Baetz and Tapscott, Henderson, and Greenberg have pointed out in other volumes of this series, asking the machine for keystroke rates or time per operation may be asking the wrong question. Are those values really the best way of appraising performance? Keystrokes per minute or time per telephone call, being easy to monitor, are seized upon as the major measures of operator (and, by implication, system) effectiveness. Not only does this kind of measurement have the stress-generating potential already discussed, but it may also be giving misleading information as to the overall progress of the organization towards its goals.

For example, in a word-processing center, counting keystrokes per minute and pages per hour may seem to be reasonable measures of operator productivity. This, in turn, is seen as an essential component of overall office system productivity. However, these measures may not take into account the fact that the relative ease with which a *secretary* can make manuscript corrections will make it much more likely that the secretary's *boss* will make revisions. Where one or two drafts of a report were quite adequate in the past, there may now be seven or eight. The word-processing operation is more efficient; the system is not. Similarly, in a computerized telephone order entry system, the operators are held to a strict time limit per call. A loud buzzer goes off if they exceed their limits, and they are required to make up the excess on later calls. The average time to complete a call drops, but what increases is the number of customers who are given terse, abrupt, or even nasty responses to their inquiries, and who therefore decide to take their business elsewhere.

The overall result of these kinds of monitoring is a focus on *quantity* (easily measured) at the expense of *quality* (more difficult to measure) — to the ultimate detriment of individual *and* organization.

Using Supervision and Appraisal Effectively

Effective supervision and performance appraisal are, if anything, more complex and difficult in the electronic office. Traditional organizational patterns, job ladders, and chains of command are all in jeopardy. Traditional methods of work appraisal may not take into account the new demands on attention and learning required by automated systems, as well as the stress they induce. It has been argued that resistance, if not active hostility, can be expected from 20% of the workforce to any innovation, and this resistance must be dealt with in something more than a perfunctory fashion.

The very nature of the electronic medium makes work output somehow more abstract. The ease with which a day's work can disappear can induce some potent levels of anxiety and stress even in an experienced user. How much more support, then, is required by an unwilling novice who, already sure that this thing ultimately is going to cost him his job, fears that inadvertently hitting the wrong key combination will somehow destroy the machine.

However, if the challenges are enormous, the opportunities are equally enormous. Some management philosophies hold that the primary function of a supervisor is to support the people under him or her. Supervisors are to insure that workers have the proper resources — both physical, through good workstation design, and intellectual, through proper training — to perform their work as best they can. Supervisors are also to protect workers against undue outside pressures. If that philosophy is incorporated into a truly user-based system of program development, one outcome would likely be the kinds of operator programs which make use of, rather than override, basic human skills. A second outcome would be the kinds of supervisory support systems which can relegate routine paperwork to the computer, freeing up the supervisor's time to be spent more effectively by interacting with employees and planning/thinking about the real goals and objectives of the organization.

Finally, some researchers are beginning to question whether, in many situations, direct supervision (leadership) is really very effective. They discuss various mechanisms, called "substitutes for leadership" which have been observed to replace traditional forms of supervision. Specific examples of leadership substitutes include: a sense of professionalism among members of the work group, a high degree of knowledge and training among group members, and a clear expression of organizational objectives, goals, and policies (Kerr, 1976).

While these theorists have not necessarily written with the electronic office in mind, combining the substitute for leadership concept with the availability of current "intelligent" software would open up some potentially powerful management tools. Rather than thinking of the computer as supervisor, the computer would provide feedback, information, and training, as a sort of coach, to allow people to supervise themselves.

Management in the Electronic Office: A Perspective

A small bank had recently installed its first computer system and hired a programmer to service it. The senior administrative officer, a very thoughtful and dedicated employee, was concerned. He had worked at the bank for 20 years and, as a supervisor, prided himself on knowing every detail of every job. Now, however, he had to cope with an employee — the programmer — who did things which he simply couldn't comprehend, much less supervise. Moreover, the major operations of his bank were being taken over by a machine whose function he didn't understand, and didn't think he ever would.

A small college had also just received its first computer. Neither the vice-president in charge of the installation nor his young secretary had previous computer experience, and they began to learn the system together — although from different perspectives. However, the secretary spent more time on the system and learned more operational details. Both the secretary and the vice-president independently reported that the experience of mastering the system together changed their relationship with each other so that they felt much more like colleagues than boss-and-secretary.

These examples illustrate some of the broader problems — and opportunities — encountered in an office where work is accomplished by means of computer-based systems. Of course, similar situations could always be found before the electronic office came into being, but in the current era of transition, there will be many managers who will not understand what some employees and their equipment are doing, and many other managers who will be mastering systems together with their assistants.

The thoughtful manager is faced with the dual challenge of implementing the technology as effectively as possible while at the same time harnessing the inherent enthusiasm and creativity which, if first allowed and then encouraged, most individuals will naturally bring to their work. The premise of this book and of the others in the Converging Technology Series (Baetz; Tapscott, Henderson, and Greenberg) is that these dual goals can be *complementary* and *mutually reinforcing*. The task, for management, is to take seriously the question raised by Paul Fitts so many years ago as to what people do best and what machines do best.

Systems should be designed which give people a greater sense of control over their work, and which free them from the sense of being controlled by it. The natural trend should be towards work requiring increased rather than decreased levels of human skill. Even for jobs such as data entry which are inevitably routine and repetitious for the employees who hold them, there are still many areas in which enlightened management can improve the quality of working life.

New Directions for the Electronic Office

CHAPTER

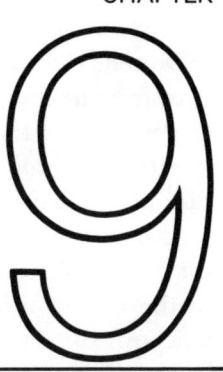

It is now several years in the future. The Leming Corporation has been taken over by a progressive management group which instituted major environmental and structural changes. Elizabeth, who had been just barely hanging on until she could retire, blossomed under the new enlightened management, and has recently been promoted to the management-level position of section administrative officer.

Elizabeth arrives at her office, sits down, and adjusts her ergonomic chair and desk. She turns on her computer system, which is now little more than a lightweight keyboard, and arranges the four flat panel display units on her desk so that they can be read easily. Each screen is capable of displaying high-resolution graphics, as well as print-like text, and can be assigned, through her keyboard, to one of many systems available to her. The screens are also lightweight; each has its own height-adjustable stand. What she has, in effect, is an "intelligent workstation."

Elizabeth first calls up her personal calendar display by speaking the word CALENDAR. A voice recognition program, tailored for the unique sounds of her voice, activates, loads, and displays the program. The display itself actually looks like a calendar page, with solid borders, different styles and sizes of typefaces, and differently colored entries. This program, which is continually updated by her secretary, indicates that the annual report, which her section has the responsibility for preparing, needs to go to the president for final approval the day after tomorrow at the corporate management retreat. She also sees that the financial summary statement is still listed on her schedule as needing her preliminary signoff.

Elizabeth then calls MAIL and a list of the items being held in her electronic mail file is displayed. She notes, with irritation, that the financial statement is not present. Since the mail display is up anyway, she quickly scans the title, originator, and priorities of items currently in her file. One file needs immediate attention, since it is from the president's personal assistant. She checks the file, notes that it is, as she expected, the cover letter from the president for the annual report, and transfers the letter to her personal text editor file. However, she still has to get Fred to take care of the financial statement.

Elizabeth says VOICE and her store-and-forward message system display appears. She gets into the SEND mode and indicates that a priority interrupt message should be sent to Fred, who is responsible for the financial statement. Although Fred reports to Elizabeth, his office, in the financial services compound, is in another city 500 miles away. The priority interrupt message, which is limited to managers at her level, will interrupt any ongoing activity at Fred's workstation and, in effect, act as an intercom. She then asks Fred for the status of the report which was due yesterday. There is no immediate response, which means that Fred is either out of the office or not answering.

Heaving a sigh, she realizes that this will have to be done the hard way. Calling in her secretary, she instructs her to use the management search procedure and examine the contents of Fred's working file directory. This will take a little time, so she returns to her mail file. She proceeds through three general memoranda from headquarters, scans each quickly, and then consigns them to her electronic trash buffer. The fourth memo, which requires action, refers back to the third. Using her keypad, she retrieves the third memo from the trash buffer and displays both documents side by side on two separate screens. Putting her own text editor on a third screen, she composes a brief report, calls up her personal file storage menu, and stores her memo along with the two relevant supporting documents. She then returns to her electronic mail menu and sends the report to its destination, with copies to two interested parties.

The secretary indicates that she has gained access to Fred's directory, so Elizabeth clears her own screens, and is now able to examine all of his current working files. She quickly finds the one marked "Annual Report" and examines it. She notes, with dismay, that it still needs two or three hours more work. She checks the log and notes that he has not even called up the file for two days. She makes a mental note that this is probably the time to re-assess Fred's work.

Meanwhile, one of her screens is flashing, indicating a priority voice message for her. Checking her screen, she sees that several voice messages are in storage, ready for her to listen to them. However, the priority message is from the president himself. She gives the SPEAK command.

"Elizabeth, we'd like you to join us at the corporate retreat. Come down this evening, if you can get a plane, and stay the week. We've got a room reserved."

Elizabeth is startled and pleased. She did not think that managers at her level were invited to the annual retreat, which is being held at a fancy resort hotel in the Bahamas. She calls in her secretary and asks her to make the arrangements. Elizabeth then walks down the hall to the teleconference area for a half-hour conference with other administrative managers dealing with progress on the new voice recognition data entry system to be used in the warehouse.

In the teleconference area are several small television studios. The studio scheduled for this conference has a technician in the control room, a workstation and chair, and various cameras and television screens. On the desk is an intelligent workstation which can be linked to her own computer system back in her office.

Elizabeth sits behind the desk, alone, and, after a few moments of signal checking by the technician, sees, on a large screen on the opposite wall, the separate images of six of her colleagues at different locations around the world. The displays are side-by-side and blended so as to approximate the appearance of one side of a conference table. A much smaller display of herself is off to one side, so that she can see the image of herself that the others see. She checks her appearance briefly, as in a mirror.

Elizabeth and her fellow managers greet each other casually. A carefully constructed stereo sound system causes each person's voice to seem to emanate from his or her visual image. It is not exactly like a face-to-face meeting, but Elizabeth is getting used to the system, and there are moments in a heated discussion when she forgets that she is only talking to a television set.

Carlos, the senior manager who is in charge of the meeting, allows a few moments of informal chat, and then starts the meeting by displaying, on everyone's desk terminal, a copy of the agenda. He then launches into a summary report of progress on the warehouse system. Graphs and charts appear on the desktop screen. Elizabeth gives these only a cursory glance, since she knows all of this material will automatically become part of her own meeting file.

The flow of the meeting is interrupted by Andrew, who objects to the interpretation of one of the graphs. He is able to load into the system one of his own graphs — which thereby automatically becomes a part of the file. Others comment, and some also add bits and pieces of their own data. Finally, Carlos is able to get some resolution on the question. He types a short note on his screen summarizing the position. The note also appears on everyone else's screen. After a brief flurry of group editing, they arrive at a consensus. However, the time scheduled for the meeting is almost over, and it is necessary to reschedule a follow-up meeting.

Following a request from Carlos, Elizabeth uses the terminal to make contact with her personal files in her office, and loads in her updated calendar. Each of her colleagues does the same. Each calendar is automatically stored in a master teleconference schedule program which also has updated information as to availability of conference rooms at each location. The program's task is to search for the next free half hour for both people and rooms, and automatically enter it in everyone's calendar. This would normally be very difficult. However, each manager has a priority value from 1 to 5 which he or she assigns to each appointment. Since the next meeting has a priority 2 automatically assigned by top management, all appointments with priorities of less than 2 are automatically reassigned on everyone's calendar. Each person has a chance to object to the reassignment, but careful original assignment of priorities means that this rarely occurs.

Meanwhile, Elizabeth's secretary returns to her own desk and calls up her "Travel Advisor" program, a new *expert system* just delivered from the artificial intelligence group. The program, which is tied in to the airlines' main computer, leads her through a series of steps, asking her for pertinent information regarding the planned itinerary. The program displays five alternative flights, indicating all connections, times, and costs. Once a decision is made, the program orders and confirms the flight. A further series of questions, based in part on stored information regarding Elizabeth's travel patterns in the past, leads to arrangements for a rental car in the Bahamas and a taxi from her home to the airport, allowing her to drive home and pack. Meanwhile, the funds for all of the above have been transferred from the section travel budget, and an additional amount has been transferred from Elizabeth's personal bank account to her housekeeper's account, since she won't be home to pay her as usual.

The secretary gives Elizabeth a printout of the above information. It is the first piece of paper either has used all day. Elizabeth will use the confirmation number at the curbside computer terminal at the airport to get an automatically printed paper copy of her ticket. Her "smart" bank card will be inserted in the terminal for identification purposes. Only the cab driver's tip will have to be paid in cash.

It is 9 o'clock the next morning somewhere in the Bahamas. Elizabeth has returned to her hotel room from the beach, where she has enjoyed an early morning swim. The first meeting with the president will not start until 10. Now there is time for work. Elizabeth unpacks her portable personal computer and plugs the modem connection into the phone jack. In a moment, she is effectively back in her office. She again checks her files and notes that Fred's report has still not arrived. She then sends a voice message to Debbie, a senior analyst in Fred's office, asking her to finish up the work on an emergency basis.

By 2 o'clock, Elizabeth has been to her meetings, has had some more beach time, and is back at her computer. Debbie has managed to complete a draft of the missing section, and they each put their screens in dual edit mode and together go over the material, speaking to each other through the voice channel, and alternately making corrections on the screen. The document is finished, the annual report is ready for final processing, and Debbie is, in Elizabeth's mind, headed for a promotion. Matching action to thought, she sends a voice message to Chan, the personnel officer, on the confidential circuit, in which she suggests the promotion while at the same time inquiring about Fred's status. (The confidential circuit has an electronic "scrambler" on either end which operates when both Elizabeth and Chan have inserted their "smart" company identification cards in their respective terminals.)

Chan must now make a decision as to whether he should, within the guidelines of company policy, promote Debbie. He also must decide what to do about Fred. He locates both personnel files from master storage, and loads both into his decision support program. Examining Fred's file, he sees a notation indicating that the electronic version of the file is incomplete. Fred has been with the company so long that portions of his file have never been entered into the computer system. Chan goes to a small metal cabinet, checks a cross-reference number, and takes out a piece of stiff cardboard in which several tiny pieces of film are embedded. These are micrographic copies of the original paper files which are now stored miles away in a warehouse. Chan places the film into a reader, punches in the cross-reference coordinates, and the images of Fred's record come up on the screen.

After a few minutes of checking the micrographic record against the computer screen, Chan determines that 10 pages of the original file are missing from the computer file. He identifies the page location, enters a "copy" command, and a full-size photocopy of each page is produced. He reads over the paper copy, and notes that it includes medical and psychological data indicating that Fred does not function well under pressure. Chan ponders this while automatically activating the optical character reader (OCR). He feeds each of the 10 pages into the OCR, and the material is automatically converted to electronic images.

Chan is now ready to prepare a decision analysis. He starts with Debbie's information. Her current salary, seniority, qualification summary, performance summary, test scores, and other pertinent information are compared against others in the division, and company wide. Next, the implications, both financial and in terms of company personnel targets, of her promotion, are explored. Since this work is a major part of Chan's job, the decision support program is set up precisely to give this kind of information. The computer analysis is done with a few keystrokes. Elizabeth's recommendation, coupled with other favorable comments in Debbie's file, make the promotion a logical step.

Fred's case is a little more difficult. Chan decides that Fred shouldn't have been assigned to the job he has now, but would probably do well in a less-pressured assignment. He activates a company-wide search for personnel openings which match Fred's qualifications. Several openings appear on his screen, and he notes that two are in the same city where Fred is now living. He now sets up a second analysis which projects the implications of Fred's departure from the division. At this point, he is convinced that the transfer can be made. He now calls up a standardized recommendation and analysis form, and with a few keystrokes, summarizes the results of his work. He has carried out a difficult analysis within 30 minutes, and with a minimum of keystrokes. Now he will speak with Fred and make a judgment as to whether this move is the best thing to do. He is concerned because Fred's performance has deteriorated in recent months and so he sends a message to Fred's mail file requesting a personal meeting so they can discuss the situation privately. . . .

These are among the new directions in which the electronic office may move, from the perspective of 1986. This is not just a flight of fancy: virtually all the systems described above could be put together today. Computer networking and teleconferencing are already common. Interacting with voice-responding computers has advanced to the state where a person can pay the mortgage and other bills from home over the phone, and touch control monitors are installed in hotel lobbies to provide tourist information.

All of these electronic marvels and, no doubt, many more, will be marketed, and will go through cycles of being remodeled, streamlined, and miniaturized, most of them by more than one manufacturer; thus, they will take myriad forms. Each will pose a special ergonomic challenge for those who design or use it.

The future of the office is being radically changed through this technology. Terminals are getting smaller, lighter, and cheaper. Flat panel screens with less glare and better resolution will surely become commonplace; their compact size will free up more accessible work space — probably for additional flat panel screens!

Among the hot issues will probably be how to use voice recognition effectively. Some unthinking people may want to have the last data entry jobs done by people talking for days on end into microphones. If this happens, throat-soothing medications will replace eye drops and aspirin as the stop-gap solutions to the day's ergonomic problems. Eventually, voice recognition will probably be used in some combination with keyboard entry or optical character recognition (a process through which printed characters can be read into the computer directly). Voice recognition will have other special applications, particularly in circumstances where people literally have their hands full.

The nature of jobs may change as well. Data entry may no longer occupy so many work hours, as society becomes relatively paper-free. The smart bank card will allow direct approval and transfer of funds without the intermediate paper transactions. Portable computers and telephone links will allow customer order entries to be entered directly into the vendor's computer system, and confirmed via the customer's own electronic mail. There will be more and more sophisticated expert programs, and a major problem will be the allocation of decision making, either to humans or to intelligent programs.

To the extent that transactions of any sort are transmitted via electronic means and everyone's workstations can be interconnected by modem, people's physical locations become increasingly irrelevant. (In the scenario above, Elizabeth was able to run her organization almost as effectively from her hotel room in the Bahamas as she could from her desk.) People have already begun working at home — in "the electronic cottage" (which, itself, can either be a sweatshop or a haven) — rather than travelling to an office.

One of the things that can happen as electronic links proliferate and as remote branch offices are directly tied in to the home office, is that many of the messages across these links will be devoted to socializing or personal conversations.

Management response to this occurrence may well be to set up and stringently enforce policies that would restrict communication channels to business use only. If so, shutting down these channels will almost certainly act to the detriment of the banning organization. The reason is that, as more and more interaction goes on by computer, a major emergent problem is likely to be *social isolation*. Very little interpersonal contact was described in the scenario above; virtually all of the business was conducted via the terminal system, and even the contact with the secretary could have been computer-mediated. This does not, of course, have to be: electronic devices could be used to free up time which could then be spent in face-to-face discussion, supervision, and good old-fashioned fun. However, the potential for social isolation is clearly present. Conversely, the monitoring and lack of privacy issues discussed in Chapter 8 take on a new dimension. In a totally electronic work environment, virtually everyone's activity is theoretically open to scrutiny.

What are the human implications of all this?

One thing that will not change appreciably is the human body — the same one people have inhabited for centuries. It may get a little taller or thinner, but most of the constants will remain. People will still have backs that hurt if they bend over too much. They will still have eyes that hurt from too much use under poor visual conditions. There will still be a carpal tunnel that needs to be protected, and legs that go to sleep if the circulation is not sufficient.

But the human being is more than just a biological chip tossed in among the microchips. Humans will still need both privacy and socialization. They will still need a sense of accomplishment, of mastery. They will still get tired, be subject to stress, and find that there is only so much attention one human being can allocate to a task. Each human being will still be unique.

So the ergonomist of the future will have much to deal with, as he or she tries to see that new technology meshes with human needs and human capabilities. In the best of all possible worlds, ergonomic research will have gone forward, knowledge about human capabilities will increase and be more systematized, better furniture and other support systems will be known and will be widely available. User friendliness will be the norm.

The managers of the future will have to cope with the changes as well as the constants. The successful ones will understand and use effectively all those tools which enhance both productivity and the quality of working life.

APPENDIX I

Assessing Research Results

(NOTE: The following is not a comprehensive treatment of general scientific methodology, but a guide to some specific aspects of ergonomic research assessment which might be useful for managers.)

As mentioned in Chapter 2, scientific research may make use of either of two different research *methods* — observational and experimental — and two different research *settings* — field and laboratory.

Observational research is done when the researcher takes measurements or makes observations without intervening or changing the conditions under investigation. Astronomers are all observational researchers. In ergonomics, this type of research might involve looking at absenteeism rates at two different office sites, each with different kinds of terminals and furniture. Observational research is typically done in field settings. Health questionnaires are an example of such research (although it can be argued that simply giving out the questionnaires changes the situation, since it both expresses interest, and makes the workers more conscious of the situation).

Experimental research, on the other hand, implies the capability to intervene directly in, that is, to control, the conditions of measurement. If it were possible to assign well-designed ergonomic furniture randomly to one group of workers, and poorly designed furniture randomly to a second group, and measure the outcome in both groups, this would constitute an experiment. Experiments can be carried out either in the laboratory or in the field, although the latter tends to be more difficult.

Assessing validity. Suppose that the findings of a research experiment show that a measured change in A was associated with a measured change in B. Two basic types of issues must be examined in assessing such results (Cook and Campbell, 1979).

The first issue is this: Could something else have accounted for these results? That is, are the changes in A really associated with changes in B? Was the experiment adequately controlled? (These questions are about the *internal validity* of the experiment.)

The second issue is the following: Can these results be generalized? Do the results obtained under the particular conditions of this study apply to other situations, or is the experiment so narrow that it is inapplicable to the real world? Do the results fit into — or do they negate — any overall theory or conceptual framework? (These questions have to do with *external validity*.)

Many aspects of these two issues are highly technical; however, the manager will find these three questions useful in assessing research in ergonomics:

1. Was the experiment adequately controlled?
2. Is there anything else which could account for the results?
3. Do the results fit into the current conceptual framework? If so, what else might be logically expected, and if not, how do they change the theoretical framework?

These questions are the backbone of the assessment process.

Let's take as an example the statement that VDT workers have an inordinate amount of stress and many physical ailments. The important question is "Compared to whom?"

The answer to that question, "Compared to whom?" or "Compared to what?", is the definition of the controlled experiment, one of the most basic concepts in science. The *experimental group, sample, or condition* must be compared to another *control group, control sample, or control condition*, which is the same as the experimental *in every possible respect* except for the variable you are trying to test. In this way, scientists can essentially *subtract out* everything except the particular thing they are examining.

Schematically, a well-controlled experiment might look like this:

Experimental	**−**	**Control**	**=**	**Difference**
Environment		same		nil
Lighting		same		nil
Copyholder		same		nil
Wrist rest		same		nil
Adjusted workstation		same		nil
Adjusted chair		same		nil
Monitor		same		nil
Task		same		(measure performance)
Grandjean keyboard		QWERTY keyboard		?

Here, if one subtracts the control values from the experimental values, one finds that any measured difference in task performance is caused by the difference between the standard QWERTY keyboard and the keyboard modification by Grandjean. (Both keyboards are described in Chapter 4.) That which is varied by the researcher, in this case the keyboard, is sometimes called the independent variable. The measured difference — in this case, task performance — is the dependent variable.

However, it is common to read or to be told that, for example, at a certain company, a field survey was done which showed that 70% of all people working at VDTs have eye strain, back, and shoulder problems. Here again, the manager has to ask: "Compared to whom?" And in fact, when the number of such complaints of *non-VDT office workers* are subtracted from those of VDT workers, the percentage of complaints attributable to VDTs decreases. Here, non-VDT office workers were used as the "control" group. What we have shown is that other office workers have health problems, too, but they are fewer than those of VDT workers. (In this Appendix, we will not focus on the number of complaints of office workers or VDT workers: our purpose in these examples is strictly to show how experimental assessment applies to ergonomic research with VDTs.)

The next logical question is this: Are non-VDT office workers an *adequate* control for VDT office workers? The criterion for an adequate control is that it be *in every possible respect* the same as the experimental, except for the variable you are trying to test.

Even when you try to ensure that the tasks to be carried out are similar (such as having participants read/edit/enter copy), there are significant ergonomic differences between typing and working at a VDT. General office workers usually have greater variety in their jobs, and are able to move about physically more than their VDT counterparts. As we mentioned before, the typist's workstation, with its lower typing surface, is usually more adequate. The VDT worker is also viewing finished copy from a light-emitting, highly reflective glass surface, in a vertical plane, rather than reflected light from a matte-finished paper coming out of a typewriter. The VDT copy being read is usually composed of light characters on a dark background, rather than the reverse. Other differences include the feel of the keyboards, the readability of the type, the type of feedback to the worker from the machine, the ease of correction, and the knowledge base (and therefore the mental concentration) required to operate the machine.

This analysis leads to the conclusion that the components of the tasks are different at a typewriter and at a VDT; the nature of the work, as well as its component parts, is different. Thus, it is not meaningful to use a typewriter as a control for a VDT in an experiment, and it is apparent that the VDT terminal changes the nature of the physical environment and the task environment.

The nature of problems related to VDT use can be determined only through a series of careful research investigations which assess the effects of each task component both individually and in combination. Moreover, given the sheer number of differences between VDT work and non-VDT work, it is logical to conclude that the only adequate control for a VDT worker is another VDT worker! In order to isolate any one factor, such as glare on the monitor, to see whether or not it affects VDT workers in terms of eye strain or performance, the control must be other VDT workers doing the same task under identical conditions, but without glare.

The problem with this approach is that there are so many possibilities that a comprehensive research program would take many years to plan and execute. For this reason, an important first step is the controlled experiment involving a *global comparison*. This kind of experiment is designed to answer the question, "Do *any* of a certain group of ergonomic changes cause fewer health complaints or better performance?" The experimental design looks like this:

Experimental Group	**Control Group**
Data entry task	Same
Ergonomic factors:	
Adjusted ergonomic chair	Ordinary chair
Adjusted ergonomic table	Computer on desk
Wrist rest	No wrist rest
Well-placed copyholder	No copyholder
No glare on monitor	Glare
Contrast-enhancing filter on monitor	No filter

If the experimental results showed no difference, we could assume that *none* of these ergonomic "improvements" had made any difference, or, by some strange circumstance, they had precisely canceled each other out. If, on the other hand, there were a difference (and, in fact, there is), it would indicate that something among the group of ergonomic changes, or perhaps more than one thing, accounted for the difference in performance. Subsequent experiments could then be done to determine which factors caused the difference in performance. In each experiment, fewer factors would be varied. In this sequence, the laboratory studies become increasingly specific.

It is possible to describe a continuum of scientific observation and experimentation, going from the general to the particular. Field surveys identify "hot spots" within the general population or a population of similar workers. Global experiments explore causes, and specific experiments zero in on them.

In assessing any scientific claim, the manager needs to know where along this continuum the observation or experiment occurred. A statement such as "VDT workers have lots of health complaints" is cause for concern, but it gives no information about how unusual the phenomenon is, or what to do about it. A further refinement, "More VDT workers than other office workers have health complaints, and office workers in general have more health complaints than bricklayers," is much more illuminating, and tells us that maybe we'd better worry about all our office workers, especially those at VDTs. But if an adequately controlled scientific experiment tells us that reducing the level of glare on the monitor results in appreciably less eye strain in people working at VDTs when compared to a comparable group of VDT workers who experience higher levels of glare, that is something we can understand, and something for which we can seek a solution.

Although any adequate control group will increase the accuracy of a conclusion, scientists use different kinds of controls in different situations. Each has its strengths and weaknesses.

One powerful control consists of using populations that are matched for occupation, family size, age, and other variables. Elizabeth and Susan, the two office workers mentioned in this book, were matched in this way. Only their working conditions and, specifically, the design of their workstations differed. It should be noted, however, that one pair of workers does not constitute a statistical sample. In evaluating evidence, statisticians can calculate the likelihood that a certain quantitative value (such as the difference in work performance between two differently designed workstations) reflects a real difference, rather than chance fluctuations in performance. This calculation is called the *statistical significance*. One often hears that a certain difference between two conditions was "significant at the 5% level." This statement means that, all other things being equal, a difference as large as the one which was obtained could be expected to arise purely by chance only 5 times out of 100.

In general, the larger the number of observations (sample size), the more likely it is that, if a real difference is present, it will be detected. For example, suppose that Elizabeth's and Susan's work performance are being compared on a day during which Susan is suffering from a bad cold. Although Susan's workstation is better designed, she is so ill that her work performance is actually 10% lower than Elizabeth's. If this were the only measurement used, we would draw the mistaken conclusion that well-designed workstations cause poor performance! (In this case, Susan's lower performance would be considered an example of a chance fluctuation.)

However, if we take ten of Susan's co-workers, and measure their *average* performance over several days, it is highly unlikely that all of these people will be suffering from colds on all of these days. Thus, if the difference in ergonomic design of workstations really influences work performance, comparing this *group* of workers with a group of ten of Elizabeth's co-workers will be more likely to show improved performance levels from those with the better workstations. The reason, of course, is that with a larger number of observations, extraneous factors affecting performance, like having a cold, are as likely to occur among Elizabeth's co-workers as among Susan's.

Another way of canceling out the differences between people is to *use people as their own controls*. For example, Elizabeth's work output could be measured first in her regular workstation and then in an ergonomically improved workstation. The measurements would have to be taken as close in time as possible, and perhaps repeated, to minimize the effect of Elizabeth's own variability.

To cancel out the effect of such factors as learning and fatigue, which vary with time, scientists will often undertake a *counterbalanced experiment*, measuring a worker's performance first in the old, regular (R) workstation for a day, then in the new, good (G) one for two days, then back in the regular one, the sequence being RGGR. The effect of learning or improving skills on the fourth day is high, and balances the low figure on the first day. Similarly, the changes from day 2 to day 3 can be averaged. Thus, any difference between the average of the two R's and the average of the two G's would presumably be due only to those factors differentiating R from G. This kind of data is particularly illuminating when compared to that of workers being observed in the sequence GRRG.

A second type of experiment in which people serve as their own controls is the workplace intervention. The control, or baseline performance, is measured over a period of time in the setting to which the workers are accustomed. Then some type of change, or intervention, is made, and the performance of the same workers is again measured using the new situation.

The use of a workplace situation provides fertile ground for answers to the second key assessment question, "Is there anything else which can account for the results?" Many people cite the Hawthorne effect as a basis for questioning intervention experiments. This effect takes its name from an important long-term study done at the Hawthorne plant of Western Electric in the 1920s and 1930s. Part of the study included observation of a small group of women who were assembling telephone relays; they worked under closely monitored conditions of heat, humidity, lighting, and other variables, and they were closely observed. It was found that, over the course of the experiment, *any* change, positive or negative, in physical circumstances (such as increasing or decreasing light levels), incentive pay, rest breaks, working hours, and even reversion to former conditions, caused an increase in productivity — except one, when the lighting was reduced to semi-darkness.

Some people have interpreted these increases in productivity as evidence that any interest that management takes in the employees will cause an increase in productivity, and that within certain broad limits (such as having too little light), the physical conditions of the workplace are irrelevant. If this were, in fact, the case, how could the effects of any ergonomic intervention be distinguished from the Hawthorne effect? The only way to insure that such a distinction could be made would be to intervene in similar, but not identical, ways in the workplace of a control group and an experimental group. For example, new furniture might be bought for all employees, but half would get ergonomic furniture and the other half attractive but non-adjustable furniture.

In practice, few companies will decide to invest in a lot of new furniture, half of which might turn out to be enormously inferior, and the other half of which might be enormously expensive, in order to prove the point. However, there have been instances where ergonomic furniture has been introduced without the workers being properly instructed as to its use (see Chapter 4). Their subsequent dissatisfaction and continuing health complaints would lead one to believe that the Hawthorne effect, at least in this situation, did not occur. Likewise, in the Springer experiment described in Chapter 2, new, non-ergonomic furniture was introduced into the workplace and no difference in performance was observed.

In fact, the interpretation of the Hawthorne effect summarized above has been the subject of much criticism. A different interpretation is that the women singled out for the study were removed from routine assembly line jobs and given a new, participative, consultative role with regard to their work and their relationships with management and the experimentors. In essence, their new working conditions were not unlike those of members of a modern quality circle. This dramatic psychosocial change, and the group dynamics that resulted, were so powerful that productivity increased in all circumstances except where physical hardship was imposed. This interpretation brings us back to the concept of eustress. (There are, in fact, many more interpretations and reinterpretations of the Hawthorne studies, which cannot be covered here.)

An ergonomist looking just for the pure physical effect of the furniture in a field intervention study would thus have to minimize opportunities for group interaction while the furniture was being introduced, and/or look for confirmation of the strictly ergonomic factors in other experimental circumstances. In a controlled *laboratory* experiment, where the experimental subjects do not interact with one another and no group dynamic therefore exists, the interpretation of the Hawthorne effect described above would not be relevant.

In the practical context of the workplace, one would not want to eliminate interpersonal or group dynamics, which have an intrinsic value. However, the point remains that in experimental methodology, it is difficult to isolate this kind of *psychological* effect from the beneficial *physical* effects of ergonomic changes alone.

In theory, then, there are clear differences between the different types of data and experiments that can be applied to office ergonomics. In practice, however, trade-offs occur in some of these methods.

General field surveys may be broad-brush and descriptive. To assess their conclusions, one must always be aware of baseline levels and the presence or absence of control groups. In this, as in other methods, the larger the number of people observed, the more likely it will be that individual differences between people will cancel out.

In workplace interventions, there is always the possibility of the Hawthorne effect, but other difficulties also present themselves. In general, one cannot forget the goals of the company or organization at whose place of business the intervention is being carried out: few businesses want their workflow interrupted in the interest of pure science. On the other hand, the workplace intervention has the advantage of an excellent, long-term baseline and the possibility of long-term follow-up. It also offers "real life" tasks, worker experience, and realistic workdays, among other things, which would be difficult to match in controlled laboratory experiments.

The laboratory experiment has many advantages, the foremost being that conditions can be tightly controlled. On the other hand, time and money, in terms of grants for experimental work, are limiting factors; thus, the size of samples is usually smaller. Individual subjects who are hired or recruited for an experiment may vary greatly in the skills (such as typing skills) that they bring to the task, and the possibility that they may have to learn the task (rather than its being a familiar one) must be considered. The brevity of the experiment itself may prevent the observation of certain health complaints, which under normal working conditions manifest themselves only over a long period of time. (Typical ergonomic experiments should not involve health hazards which are any worse than those in an ordinary non-ergonomic office. Nevertheless, for ethical reasons, a formal experiment requires informed consent from participating subjects.)

Given all of the above, it is clear that there are many different paths of scientific investigation, that constructing a research study is as much an art as a science, and that assessing validity — both internal and external — is rarely a clear-cut process, but is typically based on questions of degree. The person who is not sufficiently critical and who fails to ask pointed questions about research methodology risks falling into the trap of accepting an incorrect finding. On the other hand, the person who is too critical risks rejecting explanations which may, in fact, be correct.

The latter has presented a particular problem in VDT research. As discussed in Chapter 5, for example, it has been very difficult to find clear-cut evidence of visual fatigue associated with conditions of VDT use. One could argue, therefore, that there are no visual problems related to VDTs. However, a more reasonable alternative explanation is that the concept of visual fatigue itself has been, historically, very difficult to quantify. But this does not mean that visual fatigue does not exist as a practical problem.

In research design and research assessment, a fine balance must be struck between being too critical and not critical enough. In this book, many research investigations using different methodologies and samples are discussed. Although each may have its own flaws, conclusions from a number of different studies that point in the same direction would suggest a reasonably sure general conclusion.

Some of the complexities in striking this balance are illustrated in assessing the work of Brill and the BOSTI group. These studies, discussed in Chapters 2 and 6, represent an enormous effort at providing a solid research-based link between *ergonomics* and *economics*. However, some cautions must be raised.

There is a particular problem associated with scientific research which has direct and immediate application to the real world. This problem is communication — in particular, the dual communication responsibility of the applied scientist. On the one hand, research results must be communicated to potential *users* (designers, programmers, managers) in a format which is rapidly and easily accessible. Accordingly, for any applied research, there is always a mass of supporting technical details regarding procedures and analyses which the typical user of the study does not want or need to see.

On the other hand, the very nature of scientific research dictates that such technical details be made available to scientific colleagues. In fact, the general rule is that a scientific study must be described in sufficient detail that it could be repeated by someone else and that the data presented could be reanalyzed by someone else. It is this characteristic of complete openness and exposure of every detail of scientific research to critique and review that gives the scientific method its enormous power.

For most applied research, this problem is solved by the researcher's preparing two different reports for two different audiences: a user-oriented summary and a detailed technical report. The Notes and Bibliography of this book, for example, provide sources for those interested in pursuing the scientific bases of the statements contained here.

In the case of the BOSTI study, however, the description of procedure and analysis is insufficient to allow a complete critical review by scientific criteria. Although the only published report at this date contains 400 pages, including many tables and charts, it can be classified only as a user-oriented summary. (The enormous size of the data base probably led to the exclusion of certain details to limit the length of the report.) However, certain discrepancies in reported sample sizes and composition of control groups have been reported which require such detail in order to be fully resolved.

Does this mean that the results of the BOSTI study are invalid? Probably not. There is no question that detailed scientific analyses and reviews of the study's procedures must still be done. Nevertheless, at least on a tentative basis, the BOSTI data can provide useful information, for the following reasons:

- The direction and substantive content of many of the major findings are in agreement with other findings in the literature. For example, a review by Becker (1981) documents several studies that agree with the BOSTI findings regarding general dissatisfaction with open offices. (If studies had been in direct contradiction, the concerns about validity would have been greater.)
- The general procedures and rationale for the linkage between "bottom line measures" (performance, job satisfaction) and specific costs are, in fact, accepted methodologies and have appeared in several texts.
- There is an accumulating body of evidence suggesting that positive financial benefits can be achieved through proper ergonomic design.

Some of these were discussed in Chapter 2. In addition, a recent article by Schneider (1985) lists a number of case studies showing significant productivity gains through application of ergonomic design principles.

There are a number of areas of uncertainty in the chain of financial and behavioral reasoning that went into the BOSTI study. However, for a variety of reasons, their analyses may as likely be an underestimate as an overestimate of the potential benefits. For instance, BOSTI deliberately underestimated the value of work performance for highly paid professionals and deliberately chose a highly expensive building site, and state-of-the-art ergonomic furniture was unavailable during the period of the study. In any case, these *ergonomic* cost/benefit estimates are perhaps on a par with the cost/benefit analyses that might be used to justify the much larger expenses associated with, for example, a new computer system. Thus, the bottom line of the BOSTI study is that the approach is valid and the findings seem reasonable but subject to verification.

As stated previously, the manager as a consumer of scientific research is in very much the same position as the manager as a consumer of legal advice. The three basic questions outlined at the beginning of this appendix (regarding adequate controls, consideration of alternate explanations for the results, and consistency with a theoretical framework) are questions the thoughtful manager can ask. However, assessment is not always easy or straightforward. If questions or doubts persist, these might best be explored with a consultant.

APPENDIX II

Anthropometric Data:
U.S. Civilian Body Dimensions: Female/Male in Centimeters or Kilograms, for Ages 20 to 60

	Percentiles	
	5th	**50th**
Stature (height)	149.5/161.8	160.5 /173.6
Eye height	138.3/151.1	148.9 /162.4
Shoulder (acromion) height	121.1/132.3	131.1 /142.8
Elbow height	93.6/100.0	101.2 /109.9
Knuckle height	64.3/ 69.8	70.2 / 75.4
Height, sitting	78.6/ 84.2	85.0 / 90.6
Eye height, sitting	67.5/ 72.6	73.3 / 78.6
Shoulder height, sitting	49.2/ 52.7	55.7 / 59.4
Elbow rest height, sitting	18.1/ 19.0	23.3 / 24.3
Knee height, sitting	45.2/ 49.3	49.8 / 54.3
Popliteal height, sitting	35.5/ 39.2	39.8 / 44.2
Thigh clearance height, sitting	10.6/ 11.4	13.7 / 14.4
Head breadth	13.6/ 14.4	14.5 / 15.4
Head circumference	52.2/ 53.8	54.9 / 56.8
Interpupillary distance	5.1/ 5.5	5.83/ 6.20
Forward reach, functional	64.0/ 76.3	71.0 / 82.5
Elbow-fingertip length	38.5/ 44.1	42.1 / 47.9
Hand length	16.4/ 17.6	17.95/ 19.05
Hand breadth, metacarpal	7.0/ 8.2	7.66/ 8.88
Hand circumference, metacarpal	16.9/ 19.9	18.36/ 21.55
Chest depth	21.4/ 21.4	24.2 / 24.2
Elbow-to-elbow breadth	31.5/ 35.0	38.4 / 41.7
Hip breadth, sitting	31.2/ 30.8	36.4 / 35.4
Buttock-knee length, sitting	51.8/ 54.0	56.9 / 59.4
Foot length	22.3/ 24.8	24.1 / 26.9
Foot breadth	8.1/ 9.0	8.84/ 9.79
Weight (in kg)	46.2/ 56.2	61.1 / 74.0

SOURCE: Kroemer, K.H.E., & Price, D.L. (1982, July). Ergonomics in the office: Comfortable work stations allowed maximum productivity. *Industrial Engineering.* By permission. Courtesy of J.T. McConville, Anthropology Research Project, Yellow Springs, OH 45387, and K.W. Kennedy, USAF-AMRL-HEG, WPAFB, OH 45433.

*Estimated by Kroemer.

ANTHROPOMETRIC DATA   181

	95th	Standard Deviation
	171.3/184.4	6.6 / 6.9
	159.3/172.7	6.4 / 6.6*
	141.9/152.4	6.3 / 6.1*
	108.8/119.0	4.6 / 5.8*
	75.9/ 80.4	3.5 / 3.2*
	90.7/ 96.7	3.5 / 3.7
	78.5/ 84.4	3.3 / 3.6*
	61.7/ 65.8	3.8 / 4.0*
	28.1/ 29.4	2.9 / 3.0
	54.4/ 59.3	2.7 / 2.9
	44.3/ 48.8	2.6 / 2.8
	17.5/ 17.7	1.8 / 1.7
	15.5/ 16.4	.57/ .59
	57.7/ 59.3	1.63/ 1.68
	6.5/ 6.8	.44/ .39
	79.0/ 88.3	4.5 / 3.6*
	46.0/ 51.4	2.2 / 2.2*
	19.8/ 20.6	1.04/ .93
	8.4/ 9.8	.41/ .47
	19.9/ 23.5	.80/1.09
	29.7/ 27.6	2.5 / 1.9*
	49.1/ 50.6	5.4 / 4.6
	43.7/ 40.6	3.7 / 2.8
	62.5/ 64.2	3.1 / 3.0
	26.2/ 29.0	1.19/ 1.28
	9.7/ 10.7	.50/ .53
	89.9/ 97.1	13.8 /12.6

In a given office, adjustments may need to be made if the dimensions of a group of workers vary greatly from those shown here.

Conversion Table
1 inch = 2.54 cm
1 lb. = 0.4536 kg
1 cm = 0.3937 inches
1 kg = 2.2046 lb.

| | Standard |
95th	Deviation
171.3/184.4	6.6 / 6.9
159.3/172.7	6.4 / 6.6*
141.9/152.4	6.3 / 6.1*
108.8/119.0	4.6 / 5.8*
75.9/ 80.4	3.5 / 3.2*
90.7/ 96.7	3.5 / 3.7
78.5/ 84.4	3.3 / 3.6*
61.7/ 65.8	3.8 / 4.0*
28.1/ 29.4	2.9 / 3.0
54.4/ 59.3	2.7 / 2.9
44.3/ 48.8	2.6 / 2.8
17.5/ 17.7	1.8 / 1.7
15.5/ 16.4	.57/ .59
57.7/ 59.3	1.63/ 1.68
6.5/ 6.8	.44/ .39
79.0/ 88.3	4.5 / 3.6*
46.0/ 51.4	2.2 / 2.2*
19.8/ 20.6	1.04/ .93
8.4/ 9.8	.41/ .47
19.9/ 23.5	.80/1.09
29.7/ 27.6	2.5 / 1.9*
49.1/ 50.6	5.4 / 4.6
43.7/ 40.6	3.7 / 2.8
62.5/ 64.2	3.1 / 3.0
26.2/ 29.0	1.19/ 1.28
9.7/ 10.7	.50/ .53
89.9/ 97.1	13.8 /12.6

In a given office, adjustments may need to be made if the dimensions of a group of workers vary greatly from those shown here.

Conversion Table

1 inch = 2.54 cm
1 lb. = 0.4536 kg
1 cm = 0.3937 inches
1 kg = 2.2046 lb.

APPENDIX III
Case Study: Putting Together a VDT Workstation

The task of assembling many components and putting them together into the integrated whole called the ergonomic workstation is very much like solving a jigsaw puzzle — all the pieces must fit with each other. One does not solve a jigsaw puzzle by reading about it; the pieces have to be picked up and moved about. The same principle holds for solving the workstation design puzzle: to gain a reasonable understanding of the problems involved in trying to comply simultaneously with many different ergonomic criteria, it is necessary to move things around actively.

The step-by-step assembly of a VDT workstation described in this appendix provides such an opportunity. The reader is asked to follow along with pencil and graph paper, thereby participating with us in the design process, and, very possibly, coming up with even better solutions. We do not pretend to have presented the perfect solution to workstation integration in this appendix. Instead, we have provided an example of a possible solution — one which rests heavily on specific assumptions and boundary conditions which may be different in other situations.

Selection of Components

As a general rule, maximum flexibility of all workstation components would make the workstation more adaptable for more people. Greater flexibility is also a good hedge in areas of controversy or where personal tastes are likely to vary. Unfortunately, it also usually costs more. This means that trade-offs need to be made between ranges of adjustment and costs.

These are the VDT workstation hardware components about which decisions must be made.

1. *The computer terminal.* Which one should be selected and which parts of it must be accommodated on the worksurface (keyboard, monitor, and perhaps computer-disk drive)? *It is absolutely crucial that the keyboard and monitor not be one integrated unit,* as

Elizabeth's was, because this imposes ergonomic restrictions which cannot be circumvented, and which make the unit unsatisfactory for continuous use. The print generated should be readable at convenient distances. The keyboard should be well designed: computer functions and special computer keys should be separated from the traditional typewriter keys.

2. *The worksurface*. It should have two adjusting levels — one for the keyboard and the other for the monitor — or one adjustable level for one component plus a supplementary adjustable level for the other, if needed.
3. *A chair* (see Chapter 3).
4. *A footrest*. This should be provided, if required, for short workers. Some footrests are built into the chair or workstation. If the worker is required to operate a foot pedal with the feet, as in the case of some dictating machines or electric copyholders, then the footrest must be able to accommodate the foot pedal.
5. *A wrist/palm rest* should be included (unless the keyboard is thin enough for the table surface to provide support).
6. *A copyholder*.
7. *A task light*, if required.

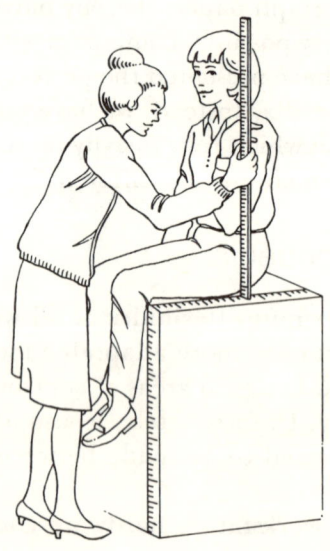

Figure III-1.
Taking measurements relevant for workstation design. With this simple set-up, it is possible to measure augmented popliteal height, seated elbow height, seated eye height, thigh clearance, and buttock-popliteal length very quickly. The subject must sit as far back on the table as possible, so that the edge of the table is at the crease behind the knee.

Anthropometry

In order to custom design your company's workstations to fit your employees' needs, you will also have to acquire basic anthropometric data from an appropriate source. The usual procedure is to accommodate a certain percentage of the population by selecting the relevant measurements from anthropometric tables. This must be done with the realization that if, for example, you have a large number of short people in your population, you should favor, or perhaps extend, the lower end of the range. Appendix II contains a convenient table of anthropometric measurements for North American civilians compiled by Kroemer. These are the measurements that we have used in the current example.

Alternatively, you could compile the measurements yourself. If the workforce is large enough and/or different enough from the existing measured populations, it may be appropriate to have this done by specialists. On the other hand, if you suspect that there are some employees who are above or below the range of existing anthropometric tables, it may be helpful to use the procedures listed below to estimate their dimensions. These measurements will be less accurate than those done by professionals, but should certainly be accurate enough, if done carefully, to make practical decisions. With the simple set-up seen in Figure III-1, each worker could be measured in less than two minutes. These are the measurements to be taken:

1. *Popliteal height with shoes (augmented popliteal height).* Just ask each worker to sit on a table with the crease behind the knee at the table edge, and the leg dangling straight down, and measure from the table top to the bottom of the heel of the shoe. The worker's *typical* work shoe should be worn. (An alternative is to measure without shoes and then apply a standard correction. This will be done in the case described later.)
2. *Seated elbow height.* Have the worker sit up in a straight but lordotic position on the table, but in a relaxed enough posture to key in for an extended period of time. Then measure from the table top to the elbow (this is easier to measure if the worker puts the hand up to the collar bone, and lets the upper arm drop vertically).
3. *Seated eye height.* With the worker seated as in (2), measure from the table top to the outer corner of the eye.
4. *Thigh thickness* can be determined quickly with the worker seated as above. Measure from the top of the table upon which the worker is sitting to the thickest (tallest) part of the thigh. A thin board placed across the thighs may be helpful in taking this measurement. Thigh

thickness is measured to make sure that the thighs are not compressed by the underside of the keyboard support surface.
5. If the table surface upon which the worker is seated is ruled (see Figure III-1), the distance from the popliteal area (behind the knee) to the rear of the buttocks can be determined at a glance. This measurement is used to make sure that seatpan depth is not too great.

Putting the Pieces Together

At this point, the actual integration of workstation components begins. To gain the most benefit from this exercise, the reader should obtain the following materials:

1. Several sheets of graph paper. A "fine" ruling (e.g., 10 squares to the centimeter) should be selected.
2. Pencils and erasers.
3. Protractor and ruler.

In all cases, a *side view* of the workstation will be assumed. Your sketches should look something like Figure 4-1. All your intermediate calculations should be done in the metric system (1 inch = 2.54 cm). (For ease of comprehension, both metric and inch-pound measurements appear here. However, the inch-pound measurements should not be used in your calculations, as they are slightly inaccurate due to rounding.)

To make this exercise more "user friendly", we have provided specific sketching instructions, which appear periodically throughout the rest of this appendix. (The instructions are in italics and are identified with a double asterisk (**).) Read through the material until you encounter an instruction, then carry out the instruction before reading the section that follows it.

** *On the graph paper, use a scale of one square per cm, and label each 10 squares up the left margin as 10 cm increments from 0 to 140 cm. The long dimension of the graph paper should be vertical.*

Selection of Chairs

As was discussed in Chapter 3, desirable support characteristics of chairs include adjustable backrest height and tilt with lumbar support, adjustable seatpan tilt (forward and back), and tapered (waterfall) front. It should also be possible for the worker to make all adjustments while seated and the adjustment controls should be non-strength dependent. (For a more comprehensive list, see the end of Chapter 3.)

As discussed earlier, seatpan height is determined by popliteal height. If a person sits in an upright posture and the chair is at his or her popliteal height, the feet/shoes should be resting flat on the floor with hip and knee angles at 90 degrees. We will start by assuming that our population of employees falls within the range of 5th percentile female to 95th percentile male. Civilian anthropometric data for the U.S. (see "Popliteal height, sitting" in Appendix II), indicates that the 95th percentile male popliteal height is 48.8 cm (19 inches), while the 5th percentile female popliteal height is 35.5 cm (14 inches). These values are measured without shoes, so Kroemer adds a 2 cm (0.75 inches) increment for shoe height to each. Thus, a starting place for chair selection on the basis of seatpan height is a chair with a lower limit of 37.5 cm (15 inches) and an upper limit of 50.8 cm (20 inches). (If you have done your own measurements, these latter figures correspond to the minimum and maximum measurements of popliteal heights with shoes.)

Unfortunately, in the real world, it is rarely possible to adjust chairs within such a wide range. Adjustability of chairs is accomplished through pneumatic gas cylinders — the same devices which are used to open the hatch part of hatchback automobiles. The current state of the art in cylinders used for standard office chairs (as opposed to drafting stools) permits a range of adjustment of only 11.43 cm (4.5 inches), whereas the range of adjustment called for between the high of 50.8 cm (20 inches) and the low of 37.5 cm (15 inches) in the preceding calculation is 13.3 cm (about 5 inches).

Several compromise solutions are possible. For example, a chair might be selected which adjusts through the range 40.6 cm to 52.1 cm (16 to 20.5 inches). If a fifth percentile woman is seated in this chair at its lowest setting, with 2 cm (0.75 inch) heels, her feet will be 3.14 cm (about 1.25 inches) off the floor. Thus, for the shortest woman, a footrest will be required. And, as will be seen, this footrest will need to be height adjustable. Similar calculations show that this chair is adequate for the 95th percentile man.

**At the left side of the graph paper, indicate the range of adjustability of the chair.*

Another solution is to buy two types of chairs, one which adjusts in the upper range and the other in the lower range. This may lead to administrative problems in workstation assignment if workstations are shared (multi-user), but it increases the total range of adjustability of seatpan height.

Measuring the seatpan height of a contoured, padded seat is much more complicated than it seems. The measure obtained will vary, depending on the angle of the seatpan, where on the seatpan the measure is taken, and how much weight is on the seat. The furniture industry, fortunately, is in the process of developing a standardized measurement procedure, but, until then, there will be an inherent degree of uncertainty in the comparison of seatpan heights of different chair models.

Selection of Worksurfaces

The next stage is to select worksurfaces. Here, also, several options are available. These range from fixed-height platforms to desks with adjustable keyboard shelves, to dual-level, fully adjustable worksurfaces which allow for independent height and tilt adjustability for both keyboard and screen.

The Dutch ergonomist Vellinga (1984) proposed a workstation design using a table which has only one surface, adjustable through a range of 62.5 to 82.5 cm (24.6 to 32.5 inches). The central portion, on which the monitor and keyboard rest, is rectangular, measuring 45 cm (about 18 inches) wide by 90 cm (35 inches) deep. Two side panels, 75 cm (29.5 inches) in depth and variable in width, angle off at 135 degrees, forming a truncated "V". Vellinga's rationale for a single surface is based on a field study in which it was observed that VDT operators provided with dual-level adjustability tended to adjust both the keyboard holder and the monitor holder in the same direction, and by the same amount. Accordingly, Vellinga assumed that it would be more effective (and less expensive) to have only one surface which was continually adjustable, but to provide a supplementary support stand to be placed on the table to raise the monitor. The single-level table is a very effective worksurface, because the working level is not split up. Thus, if non-VDT tasks are being done, the table can be adjusted to a different height if that is appropriate. If VDT work is a secondary part of the task, the terminal can be put on the side, and unbroken space is then available for papers and reference materials either to the left or the right (depending on whether the worker is left- or right-handed).

***At the left side of the graph paper, indicate the 62.5 to 82.5 cm (24.6 to 32.5 inches) range of adjustability of the Vellinga table.*

Integration of Components

The **chair and worksurface** can now be put together. The goal, given the importance of proper orientation of the hand and elbow, is to put the surface of the table at the level of the elbow. In this way, either the relatively flat keyboard or a thicker keyboard with greater angle could, with a wrist/palm rest, provide sufficient support. In addition, if the chair has armrests, they should be very short, so as not to bump against the table.

The key anthropometric dimension to be considered here is seated elbow rest height (see "Elbow rest height, sitting" in Appendix II). This is the distance from the surface of the seatpan to the tip of the elbow while the subject is seated in a standard upright posture. Ninety-fifth and fifth percentile values for this dimension are, respectively, 29.4 cm (11.5 inches) and 18.1 cm (7 inches). However, a Finnish field study (Launis, 1984) showed that, for people who are actually working in an upright posture, measured elbow rest heights were an average of 3.9 cm (1.5 inches), less than those measures in more rigid standard anthropometric posture. Therefore, the seated elbow heights listed above should be corrected for this factor. The resulting values are, respectively, 25.5 cm (10 inches) and 14.2 cm (5.5 inches).

The small (5th percentile) woman should now be visualized sitting in a chair which has been pulled up to the table. With the chair at its minimum height of 40.6 cm (16 inches), we add the 14.2 cm (5.5 inches) increment for elbow height. The resulting value, 54.8 (21.5 inches) puts the elbow 7.7 cm (3 inches) below the lowest adjustment of the table (62.5 cm, or 24.6 inches). This problem can be solved with an 11 cm (4 inches) high footrest. This allows us to raise the chair about 8 cm, to a seatpan height of 48 cm (about 3 inches, to 19 inches), placing the elbow height at 62.2 cm (24 inches), which is close to the lower limit of the table. In this way, we can meet simultaneously the criteria of hand and arm support, and trunk and back support.

**At this point, you should sketch the appropriate seatpan/popliteal heights, footrest, elbow rest and table heights for the 5th percentile woman. For simplicity, draw the elbow joint directly above the rear of the buttocks.*

It is important to check whether or not this arrangement allows sufficient thigh clearance. Thigh thickness measured above the seatpan for a 5th percentile woman is 10.6 cm (about 4 inches). See "Thigh clearance height, sitting," in Appendix II. If this is added to the seatpan height, the result is 58.6 cm (23 inches) from the floor to the top of the thigh. The lowest position of the table is 62.5 cm (24.6 inches) and it is 2 cm (0.75 inches) thick. This puts the underside of the table at 60.5 cm (23.8 inches) above the floor. Thus, the distance between thigh height

(58.6 cm, or 23 inches), and the undersurface of the table (60.5 cm, or 23.8 inches) is 1.9 cm (0.8 inches), and thigh compression is avoided. (Thigh compression is usually avoided if the worksurface is thin and if there are no drawers above the thighs.)

The same calculation should now be done for the large (95th percentile) man, as follows.

**Sketch this on a separate sheet of graph paper, as above.*

His popliteal height with shoes is 50.8 cm (20 inches), and the chair can be set to this seatpan height. If the corrected seated elbow height (25.5 cm, or 10 inches) is added to the seatpan height, his elbow is located at 76.3 cm (30 inches), which is 6.2 cm (2.4 inches) below the maximum height of the table. However, this presents no problem — the table can be adjusted to 76 cm (29.9 inches). The resulting thigh clearance (17.7 cm, or 6.9 inches) is quite adequate.

The next step is to fit the **VDT and copyholder** into this scheme. This requires the determination of another anthropometric dimension called the *seated eye height* (see "Eye height, sitting" in Appendix II). This measure locates the position of the eye above the seatpan while the worker is sitting in the standard upright posture. Kroemer suggests reducing this by 2 cm (0.75 inches) for normal (more relaxed) sitting. Therefore, the resulting corrected values for the 95th and 5th percentile males are 82.4 cm (32.4 inches) and 65.5 cm (25.8 inches). Added to the appropriate seatpan heights (48 cm, or 19 inches, for the 5th percentile female and 50.8 cm, or 20 inches, for the 95th percentile male), this puts the eyes at 133.2 and 113.5 cm (52.4 and 44.6 inches) above the floor, respectively.

**Locate the seated eye height for both individuals by drawing a vertical line from the seatpan which connects the rear of the buttocks with the elbow joint, and by marking the appropriate eye height on this line above the seatpan. This point is called the Eye Height Reference Point. The actual position of the eyes is closer to the terminal than this point. This location can be determined by drawing a line perpendicular to the Eye Height Reference Point in the direction of the terminal. The eyes should be approximately 12 cm (4.7 inches) and 16 cm (6.3 inches) along this perpendicular line for 5th and 95th percentile persons, respectively. (The anthropometric basis for this correction is an approximation based on 80% of the measured distance from the eye to the back of the head, found in the NASA tables (Webb Associates, 1978).)*

The **monitor and keyboard** must now be located with respect to the worker. We have chosen a terminal with a keyboard 3 cm (1.1 inches) high and 10 cm (4 inches) deep, although a thicker one could have been used, as will be seen. The monitor is 40 cm (15.75 inches) high by 28 cm (11 inches) deep. The display screen area is between 15 cm (5.9 inches) up from the base and 5 cm (about 2 inches) down from the top. Again, the monitor and keyboard must be separate units for any adjustment to be possible.

The operator should be sitting in standard position with the forearm parallel to the floor and at a 90 degree angle with respect to the upper arm. The viewing angle to the center of the screen should be 20 degrees below the horizontal. The monitor and keyboard must be positioned in such a way as to satisfy each of these criteria. The solution for the 95th percentile male will be described first.

The anthropometric table in Appendix II lists a value of 51.4 cm (20.2 inches) for "Elbow-fingertip length" of the 95th percentile man. This dimension can be used to position the keyboard. The rear edge of the keyboard can, in turn, define the front edge of the monitor. For purposes of this problem, locating the rear edge of the keyboard at 8 cm (about 3 inches) beyond the ends of the fingertips, or 59.4 cm (23 inches) beyond the elbow, seems reasonable.

**For the next step, it would be easiest to take an extra piece of graph paper and cut out the overlay of the monitor measuring 40 cm × 28 cm (15.7 inches × 11 inches). Indicate the location of the display screen on the overlay.

The line of sight can be indicated by using the protractor to draw a line from the eye 20 degrees below the horizontal. Now locate the rear edge of the keyboard, as indicated above, a distance of 59.4 cm (23 inches) from the elbow along the desk. Place the monitor overlay right behind the keyboard. It should be apparent that the monitor is too low. However, if a supplemental monitor stand is used to tilt the monitor 15 degrees upward and to add an extra 8 cm (3 inches) to the monitor height, so that the top and bottom of the screen are equidistant from the eye (minimizing character distortion), we find that the 20 degree line intersects the center of the screen at an approximate viewing distance of about 55 cm (21.6 inches). To draw this in, first add the 8 cm (3 inches) of height to the monitor stand; then, using the rear edge of the monitor, draw a line 15 degrees upward.

At this distance, the characters on the screen must be at least 2.55 mm (0.10 inches) high, in order to occupy a visual angle of 16 minutes of arc. (See Chapter 4.) The monitor we have chosen generates characters that are larger than this.

A crucial item to check at this point (as our lunchtime friend at the beginning of Chapter 4 knew) is whether the monitor (or more precisely, in this instance, the supplementary monitor support), keyboard, and wrist rest will fit on the Vellinga table we have chosen! With 5 cm (about 2 inches) of table to support the wrist in front of the thin keyboard (or a 5 cm deep wrist rest for a thicker keyboard), with a keyboard 10 cm (3.9 inches) deep and a monitor support 30 cm (11.8 inches) deep and large enough to accommodate the 28 cm (11 inch) deep monitor, we find this 90 cm (35.4 inch) table deep enough to support this set-up. If we needed more flexibility in terms of viewing distance, we might find a clamp-on floating monitor support, which works like a clamp-on light and holds the monitor above desk level.

Ordinarily, the copystand would be placed somewhere near the monitor, and within the tolerance zone for depth of focus. (This is the 10 cm (3.9 inch) tolerance zone in front of and behind the monitor.) However, if the task is the one discussed in Chapter 4 (entering data from a phone book), the placement of the copyholder holding the book will give rise to some problems. Because the print is so small (1.15 mm, or 0.05 inches), the copy will need to be only 24.9 cm (9.76 inches) away to maintain a 16 minute visual angle. Thus, there is a considerable discrepancy between the viewing distances required for copy and screen.

There are some creative solutions to this dilemma. If the task is primarily one of data entry, the copy, not the screen, should be in the primary viewing position. A "floating" copystand could be located directly above and in front of the keyboard at the appropriate distance, and the monitor shifted to one side and moved closer. If reading phone-book-sized text will be a frequent part of the operator's task, automatic copyholders are available which include magnifying line guides which can be moved under foot-pedal control.

In the case of the small woman (5th percentile) her elbow-fingertip distance is 38.5 cm (about 15 inches). Adding 8 cm (about 3 inches) places the edge of the keyboard at 46.5 cm (about 18 inches). Referring again to "Eye height, sitting" in Appendix II, the woman's eyes should be at a height of 113.5 cm (44.6 inches) above the floor and they should be 12 cm (4.7 inches) forward.

*Draw the same type of sketch for the 5th percentile woman as for the 95th percentile man. If you again place the monitor behind the keyboard and draw a 20 degree line of sight, you will discover that the monitor must now be raised 6.5 cm (2.6 inches) and angled 17 degrees upwards.

The resulting viewing distance is 45 cm (17.7 inches). This operator will probably continue to have problems reading the telephone book, which requires a viewing distance of 24.9 cm (9.80 inches). However, given a 10 cm (3.9 inch) tolerance zone, the discrepancy is not as great as in the case of the 95th percentile male.

In each of the cases above, the chair is upright. What would happen, however, if a 15 degree backward tilt were added? In the case of the 95th percentile man, the viewing distance would be increased by 11 cm (4.3 inches), resulting in a viewing distance of 66 cm (25.9 inches). This increased viewing distance would lead to problems in seeing the text, if not the screen. On the other hand, using a 5 degree forward tilt results in a 48 cm (18.9 inch) viewing distance, bringing him 7 cm (2.75 inches) closer to both screen and copy.

Not all visual tasks are as demanding as reading from a phone book. Suppose that the paper copy is a typed manuscript with a minimum character size of 0.2 cm (0.08 inch). The appropriate viewing distance, for a 16-min visual angle, would be 43 cm (16.9 inches). Thus, in the upright posture, the operator could locate the copyholder at this position and be very close to the 10 cm (3.9 inch) tolerance zone for focusing on the screen. Leaning forward slightly would put him within the zone. If the chair were tilted forward 5 degrees, he would, of course, be clearly within the zone. However, in the backward tilt position, the viewing distance of the screen is 66 cm (25.9 inches) and the edge of the tolerance zone is 56 cm (22 inches). Since the copy needs to be located 43 cm (about 17 inches) from the eye, it will be 13 cm (about 5 inches) closer to the user's eye than the edge of the tolerance zone.

**Redraw the line between the rear of the buttocks and the Eye Reference Point for the 95th percentile man. This line should be vertical. Now, measure an angle of 15 degrees backwards from the buttock point, and draw a line of equal length. The top of this line locates the new Eye Reference Point, and, as before, the new eye position will be located at a point 16 cm (6.3 inches) in the direction of the screen on a line drawn horizontally from the Eye Reference Point. Repeat the procedure for a 5 degree forward tilt. Locate the 10 cm (3.9 inch) tolerance zone in front of the screen center and the various viewing distances.*

In the case of the 5th percentile woman, the viewing distance at 15 degrees backward tilt amounts to 57 cm (22.4 inches), an increase of 12 cm (4.7 inches) from the upright posture. For the 5 degree forward tilt, the new viewing distance should be 40 cm (15.7 inches), a 5 cm (about a 2 inch) decrease. The manuscript copy, at a required viewing distance of 43 cm (16.9 inches) would be well within the tolerance zone for upright and forward tilt, but would be 5 cm (2 inches) distant for the backward tilt.

***Sketch the above procedure for the 5th percentile woman. Recall that the eye location correction value is 12 cm (4.7 inches) from the Eye Reference Point.*

Thus, if the chair is in the backward tilt position, the operator may either have to move the monitor and copy closer or lean forward, away from the back support. This will present a greater problem for larger workers.

At this point, with the chair we have selected, the Vellinga table, the adjustable monitor stand, and an adjustable footrest, we can be reasonably certain that we can meet many of the ergonomic criteria for the people who fall between the 5th percentile female and the 95th percentile male. The greatest potential problems would arise in the area of matching the copy and screen viewing distances. Here, the nature of the visual task, as well as the operator's visual abilities and optical status, become important concerns. (See Chapter 5.)

The need for an adjustable footrest provides an interesting example of the interaction between components which must be considered in a complete problem solution. In order for the small woman's elbows to be level with the minimum height of the table, a rather high (11 cm, or 4.3 inch) footrest was required. It would be convenient (and much less expensive) if this footrest were fixed in height, and used by the smaller people, but not by the larger people. Given the ranges of adjustability of the table and chairs, it might appear, at first glance, that this approach is reasonable. However, an extrapolation from Appendix II indicated that this is not the case. For example, the augmented popliteal height (popliteal height with shoes) for a 10th percentile male is 42.61 cm. Thus, he would be able to sit comfortably in the selected chair without using a footrest. However, since his corrected elbow rest height is 16.55 cm, the resulting elbow location, 59.16 cm, is below the minimum level of adjustability for the desk. (These values were mathematically derived from the table, using the 50th percentile measurement ± 1.3 standard deviations. Note that the measurements are for the 10th percentile.) However, if the 11 cm (4.3 inch) footrest were used, the combined popliteal height plus footrest height (53.61 cm, or 21.1 inches) would be higher than the upper range of adjustability of the chair.

It appears that these problems would occur, at least for males between the 10th and the 20th percentiles, and for females between the 40th and 50th percentiles. Thus, either an adjustable footrest is required, or, alternatively, a series (how many is not clear) of fixed footrests of varying heights.

Finally, it must be emphasized that all of the above calculations help us come to *theoretical* conclusions. The results we obtained should work, but *unless they are actually tried out in a real-life situation, we cannot know this definitely*.

Given all the details which must be brought together, and which affect each other, it is quite easy to overlook something in working through a case study like this one. Because workstations are a long-term investment, trials using sample equipment at the worksite are an absolute necessity. Even if all the chosen workstation components fit together well in theory, there is the possibility that overhead lighting fixtures might render the monitor position unsatisfactory, that the type of hard copy used in the particular office cannot be accommodated on the worksurfaces, or that some other detail interferes in some way. That is why it is essential that worksite trials using the actual task be carried out. As discussed in Chapter 3, these trials should include a cross-section of employees performing actual tasks for at least a week each.

Glossary

The words in this glossary will be defined informally, and only in terms of their use in this book, rather than having general, all-inclusive definitions. Words which are used only once, and are defined on that page, are not included here; they may be found in the index. Some words are defined here only because they may need to be differentiated from other commonly used words. (For instance, "computer" is defined in order that it may be differentiated from "computer terminal").

Accommodation. Muscular contraction which changes the shape of the lens of the eye in order to focus. Weakness of accommodation leads to farsightedness.

Adaptation. Adjustment of the retina of the eye to high or low light conditions.

Ambient. The surrounding (environment), including air, temperature, and noise — as opposed to the proximate, or immediate, environment.

Anthropometry. Measurement of the physical dimensions of human beings which are relevant for designing things people use and wear.

Applied research. Research which applies the techniques and results of basic science to practical problems.

Arc. *See* degree(s) of arc.

Artificial intelligence (AI). Computer programs with the capability of performing human-like cognitive functions (such as playing chess). The delineation between *AI, intelligent programs,* and *expert systems* is indistinct.

Augmented popliteal height. The distance from the floor to the crease behind the knee when a person wearing shoes is sitting with the knee bent at a right angle and the feet (shoes) firmly on the floor.

Biomechanics. The interpretation of how mechanical forces (such as gravity) act on a living organism, based on a view of the organism as a system of weights, levers, etc.

Bullpen. An open office plan, with little or no enclosure for individual workspaces.

Candella per square meter. A measure of luminance. Abbreviated cd/m^2.

Carpal tunnel. A structure in the wrist carrying nerves, tendons, and blood vessels that supply the fingers. The carpal tunnel is very sensitive to trauma, including prolonged bending of the wrist.

Cathode ray tube (CRT). A device in which an electron gun emits electrons, which in turn excite a phosphor, producing a display on the screen. The gun must be several centimeters/inches from the screen; this accounts for the depth of the CRT. Television sets and most current VDT monitors are applications of CRTs.

Character. A letter, number, or symbol. *See* typeface *or* font.

Cognition. The process of gaining information or knowledge. (*Adjective*: cognitive.)

Cognitive psychology. The study of the ways in which people pick up information in the outside world, store it, integrate it into existing memory structures, use it for decision making, and act on decisions.

Computer. An electronic information processing device. A computer may also include a keyboard and a monitor, a central processing unit, and other components. It is not to be confused with a *terminal*, which consists only of keyboard and monitor and cannot function without being linked to a central computer.

Computer-human interface (CHI). The components of software systems through which the human interacts directly with the computer. Some people use a broader definition, which includes physical aspects of the terminal, workstation, and chair, as well as the task.

Computer terminal. Consists of a keyboard, monitor, and associated devices that are hooked up to a central computer.

Conceptual framework. A reference base from which to view ergonomics (or some other subject), which integrates the available information, makes it understandable, suggests avenues for further research, and forms the basis for future hypotheses. Also called a *theoretical framework* or a *set of working hypotheses*.

Contrast. The difference between the amount of light received from an object and that received from its background.

Control. To verify by comparison with another group or condition. *See* controlled experiment.

Controlled experiment. An experiment in which the variable being investigated is compared under two or more conditions, with all the other variables being held constant. In an ideal controlled experiment, everything in one group (the experimental group) is identical to everything in the other (control) group, except that one variable which is expected (hypothesized) to make a difference; that difference is then measured. (See Appendix I for further discussion.)

Convergence. Occurs when the eyeballs point at the object being viewed. Convergence is most evident when you try to look at a finger close to your nose, but also occurs when you look at something farther away.

Copy. Documents, usually on paper, as opposed to text on a screen. *Paper copy* and *hard copy* are synonyms.

Cornea. The front surface of the eye; a part of the eye's optical system which does not change focus.

Counterbalanced experiment. An experiment in which two conditions (for example, A and B) are alternated, usually in the patterns ABBA or BAAB, on successive days (or other time periods), using the same subject(s) in both conditions. The difference between the two conditions can be obtained by subtracting the average of the two A days from the average of the two B days. In this way, each subject serves as his or her own control, and time-dependent effects (such as learning and fatigue) are theoretically canceled out.

CRT. Cathode ray tube.

Cursor. The blinking line, dot, or square present in most programs, which tells the operator where the action is: where newly keyed in material will be inserted, where material will be deleted, etc. The cursor can be moved by the operator.

dB and dB(A). *See* decibel.

Data base. Usually, an organized body of information, stored so that it can be retrieved (accessed) in a variety of ways. *Example*: A list of customers might be retrieved alphabetically, by size of purchase, or by zip code.

Decibel. A unit of sound, abbreviated **dB**. An A-weighted decibel (abbreviated **dB(A)**) is weighted according to human sensitivities to various sound frequencies.

Degree(s) of arc. One degree is 1/360 of the circumference of a circle. There are 60 minutes per degree of arc. Used to measure the size of characters in text. (*See also* visual angle.) The number of minutes of arc equals 3450 multiplied by the character height (or width) divided by viewing distance.

Depth of field. The tolerance zone of distance forward and beyond the object being focused upon, within which the image is clear (not blurred).

Depth of focus. Similar to depth of field, but refers to the image on the retina.

Descender. That part of a printed or written character which falls below the baseline on which non-descending characters rest. (For example, the bottom parts of *y*, *g*, and *p* are descenders.)

Design solution. The end result of planning/designing — ideally, the result of an interactive process involving dialogue among informed user, manager, and designer.

Disc. The flexible, fluid-filled membranes between the vertebrae, which cushion the spinal column.

Disk. A plastic device which looks something like a phonograph record, used for storing data or documents for a computer. Also called a *floppy disk*.

Display screen. The piece of equipment which looks like a television screen, and upon which the images which are keyed in on the keyboard are projected. Also known generally as the monitor or CRT (cathode ray tube).

Dot matrix. A system of dots generated by a printer, a VDT, or a CRT, which are used to form letters of print.

Down. A computer or computer system is "down" when it is inoperative as a result of software or electrical problems. Sometimes called a "crash."

Dynamic motion (of a chair). When the chair's movement follows the movements of the user without the user's making adjustments.

Dynamic work. Muscle work accompanied by increase in heart rate and breathing rate, resulting in increased blood flow. *Examples*: Running and walking.

Electromyography. Studying the activity of muscles by means of the electrical impulses that travel through them and initiate muscle contraction.

Electron gun. An electronic device which shoots the charged particles that create a display on a CRT screen.

Electronic. An electrical device which also uses vacuum tubes,

transistors, or photoelectric cells.

Enclosure. The degree to which a person's workspace is separated by walls or dividers from the workspaces of others.

Ergonomics. The fit between the human being and those inanimate things, especially machines, with which he or she interacts. (See Chapter 1.)

Eustress. Stress (i.e., anything requiring adaptive change in an individual) of a pleasant nature, such as getting married, being promoted.

Expert system. A computer program which makes decisions based on logic programmed into it plus information supplied by the user. *See* artificial intelligence.

External validity (of an experiment). The extent to which the results of an experiment can be generalized, and the extent to which they fit into a theory or conceptual framework.

Femur. The thigh bone.

Field. On-site (as opposed to *in the laboratory*).

Font. A style of type produced either on a typewriter, on a computer printer, or in typesetting. *Also called* a typeface.

Flat panel display. A monitor which does not use a CRT, and can therefore be flat. It is similar to the display on a digital watch, although different principles are involved. Currently, this type of display is more expensive than CRT-based displays, but the cost is decreasing.

Footcandle (fc). A measure of illuminance (in the inch-pound (English) system); one footcandle is approximately 10.8 lux (in the metric system).

Footlambert (fL). A measure of luminance (light coming from a surface) in the inch-pound (English) system. One footlambert is approximately 3.4 candellas per square meter (in the metric system).

Format. The arrangement of written material on a screen or on paper. May be used as a verb.

Glare. Unwanted light that interferes with vision or causes discomfort.

Global comparison. An overall comparison. An investigation of several variables at once, such as an experiment designed to find out whether adjustable chairs and workstations, wrist rests, and non-glare filters, taken together, cause a difference in task performance.

Hard copy. Information or data written on paper (also known as *paper copy*), as opposed to copy on a VDT screen.

Hertz (Hz). A measure of rate of repetition, or frequency, such as sound waves, radio waves, or raster scan (refresh rate) on a CRT. Measured in cycles per sec.

Home row. The vertical center row of the VDT or typewriter keyboard (the ASDF row of a QWERTY keyboard).

Human engineering. Ergonomics, or human factors.

Human factors. Often used as a synonym for *ergonomics*.

Hypothesis. A prediction that if one thing is true, then another is true. Hypotheses are not accepted as fact without experimental proof.

Hz. Hertz.

Illuminance. A measure of the light falling on a surface (measured in footcandles or lux).

Intelligent programs. Software programs capable of making decisions. The borderline between *intelligent programs, expert systems,* and *artificial intelligence* is indistinct.

Internal validity (of an experiment). The extent to which an experiment was adequately controlled. *See also* hypothesis.

Intervention, workplace. Making a change in the workplace. It can be, but is not necessarily, part of a research study.

Iris. The colored part of the eye.

Ischemia. Lack of sufficient blood flow to bring enough oxygen to the muscles or tissues.

Ischial tuberosities. The seat bones.

Iterative. Repeatedly going back and forth between two or more opinions or positions, in order to understand and/or reach a common ground/decision. This definition is not precisely the same as the mathematical definition.

Kyphosis. Backward curve of the spine in the lumbar area, which causes strain on the spinal discs.

Lactic acid. A product of body metabolism which accumulates in muscles that are oxygen-poor, generally because of limited blood flow. Lactic acid buildup is responsible for some sensations of muscle pain.

Lens. The focusing system of the eye.

Light pen. A device which allows writing on a computer screen with a beam of light to which the screen is sensitive.

Lordosis. Forward curve of the spine in the lumbar area that exists naturally when a person is standing up straight. With good ergonomic seating, this curve is preserved.

Lumbar area. The small of the back, just below the waistline.

Luminance. A measure of the amount of light coming from the surface of an object in a specific direction. Measured in footlamberts in the inch-pound (English) system or in candellas per square meter in the metric system. One footlambert is approximately 3.4 candellas per square meter.

Lux (lx). A measure of illuminance in the metric system (approximately 10.8 lux equals one footcandle).

Memory. The capacity of a computer to store information, measured in kilobytes. *Abbreviation*: K.

Menu. Part of a software program which lists possible options (like a restaurant menu).

Metaphor. Explaining something new by likening it to something already known. For example, the workings of the eye can be explained in terms of the workings of a camera, or vice versa. In the context of applying metaphor to computer software, the term is not interpreted as strictly as in English grammar or literature.

Minutes of arc. *See* degree(s) of arc.

Modem. A device which allows computers to communicate over telephone lines.

Monitor (as a noun). The display screen of a VDT.

Monitor (as a verb). To use the computer itself to oversee or check on a worker's computer output.

Mouse. A small, wheeled device, which controls the cursor by its movement on a table.

Musculoskeletal system. The bones and muscles of the body.

Negative contrast. Dark print or other images on a light background. (*Positive contrast* consists of light print on a dark background.) *Polarity of contrast* refers to whether contrast is positive or negative.

Neutral density filters. Filters which uniformly decrease the amount of light that passes through them.

Palm rest. A narrow surface (usually about 5 cm, or 2 inches, deep) located at the keyboard edge that is nearest to the operator and at the same height as the keyboard surface. Used for resting the palm or wrist. Some people use it continuously during keying; others use it only during pauses in keying. Also referred to as a *wrist/palm rest* or simply a *wrist rest*.

Paper copy. Documents or information stored on paper. Also called *hard copy* or *copy*.

Pathology. Disease or damage. *Example*: "No pathology of the eye has been shown to have been caused by working at a VDT."

Pelvis. The hip bones.

Percentile. A statistical term meaning the percentage of persons within the population who have a body dimension of a certain size, or smaller. For example, for a man who is at the 5th percentile with respect to height, 5% of men are shorter than he is. For a 95th percentile man, 95% of men are shorter.

Perception. Reception and processing of information by the senses and the brain.

Phosphor. The glowing material which gives a cathode ray tube (or monitor) its color. Green, amber, and white phosphors are commonly used.

Physiology. The functions and vital processes of living organisms (e.g., metabolism, blood flow, muscle function).

Polarity of contrast. Whether print is light on a dark background (positive contrast) or dark on a light background (negative contrast).

Popliteal area. The area of the leg behind the knee.

Popliteal height. The height from the floor to the crease behind the knee when the leg is vertical. Anthropometric tables give this figure for a barefooted person. Corrected values allow for shoes. *Augmented popliteal height* includes the height of shoes.

Positive contrast. *See* polarity of contrast.

Presbyopia. Inability to focus on objects nearby. This is a normal change in people over the age of 40.

Program (of a computer). *See* software.

Psychology. The science that deals with the mind, mental processes, perception, action, behavior, feelings.

Psychophysiological. Refers to the impact of one's physiology and chemistry (e.g., adrenaline) on behavior.

Psychosocial. Psychological factors as related to interactions among people (the social environment).

Pupil. The opening in the iris of the eye which admits light to the retina.

Raster. The pattern traced by the beam of electrons emitted from the far end of the cathode ray tube of a VDT, which gives rise to the images on the screen.

Reflectance. The percentage of light falling on a surface which is subsequently reflected.

Refresh rate. The time it takes for the electron beam of a CRT to complete one sweep of the screen (raster pattern), re-exciting ("refreshing") the phosphor. Measured in Hertz.

Retina. The light-sensitive area, including rods and cones, behind the lens of the eye.

Reverse video display. A video display in which the characters are dark and the background is light (negative contrast).

Schema. In cognition, hypothetical mental structures which organize knowledge about the world.

Screen. The part of a video display terminal upon which information is displayed visually. Synonymous with *display screen* or *display*.

Seatpan. The seat of a chair, which supports the buttocks.

Smart card. A card like a credit or bank card, which contains a microchip.

Software. A synonym for computer programs. Software determines whether the computer will be used for word processing, spreadsheets, games, etc., at any one time. Many different programs can be used with one computer.

Specular reflectance. Reflectance of light from a mirror-like surface.

Static settings (of a chair). Adjustments which lock the chair into any one of a range of positions.

Static work or static workload. Work done by the muscles which does not result in increased blood flow and breathing, thus allowing for the buildup of lactic acid in the muscles. Sedentary work is an example of static work. (Note: This meaning of *work* is valid in context, but does not correspond to the physicist's definition of the word.)

Stress. The response of the body to demands placed on it. (See Chapter 2.)

Stressor. Any physical or mental situation which elicits the stress response.

Subjective. Resulting from the feelings, temperament, or perception of one person. A person's subjective responses cannot be externally verified (i.e., the person must be asked to describe them).

Syntax. Grammar; rules of expression for communication with computers.

Systems thinking. Thinking about the relationships between all aspects of a workstation, an organization, etc.

Terminal. A keyboard and monitor, usually linked to a central computer.

Theoretical framework. *See* conceptual framework.

Torque. A physical force which produces, or tends to produce, a twisting or rotating motion.

Touch-sensitive screens. Monitors which register commands when they are touched in certain areas.

Typeface. A set of numbers and letters of related shape and form, designed for typesetting. *Also called* a font.

Typewriter return. A surface attachable to an office desk, which is lower than the writing surface and usually angled off to one side, in order to bring the typewriter into a more comfortable level for keying.

User friendly. Taking into account human responses and human errors.

VDU. Visual display unit. Used especially in Europe as a synonym for VDT.

VDT. Video display terminal, including a monitor and a keyboard. This usually means these components are hooked into a central computer. However, in some personal computers/microcomputers, the computer hardware and the keyboard are one unit.

Venous. Having to do with veins and the blood vessels that carry blood back to the heart.

Vertebrae. The small bones which make up the backbone. (*Singular*: vertebra.)

Video display terminal. *See* VDT.

Videotropic response. The tendency of a person not to leave a computer, a VDT, or a television set.

Viewing angle. The angle of the eyes below the horizontal when the operator looks at the center of a VDT screen.

Visual angle. A standardized way of measuring the dimensions of objects that are varying distances from the eye. If you look at this page at arm's length, the visual angle will be less than if you hold it nearer to your nose. The visual angle is related to the size of the characters on the copy or screen. The formula is: visual angle (in minutes of arc) equals 3450 multiplied by character size divided by viewing distance.

Waterfall seatpan. Pronounced rounding down of the front edge of a chair seat, which insures that circulation will not be cut off behind the knees.

Workplace intervention. Making a change in the workplace. It can be, but is not necessarily, part of a research study.

Workstation. Those elements which are in the immediate (reachable) vicinity of the seated operator of a VDT.

Wrist rest or wrist/palm rest. A narrow surface (usually about 5 cm, or 2 inches, deep) located at the keyboard edge that is nearest to the operator and at the same height as the keyboard surface. Used for resting the palm or wrist. Some people use it continuously during keying; others use it only during pauses in keying. Also referred to as a *palm rest*.

Notes

The information in this book is based on a large number of published sources. Certain of these sources have been identified in the text directly by name of author, followed by the year of publication in parentheses. A complete alphabetical list of these sources will be found in the Bibliography. However, in order to enhance the readability and flow of the text, many other sources were not cited directly. In general, these additional references are cited below by author and year of publication. (They will also appear in the Bibliography.) Some shorter newspaper and magazine articles are cited completely in these Notes but do not appear in the Bibliography.

Chapter 1
p. 2. "*Design with humans in mind* . . .": A precise definition of ergonomics/human factors has not been agreed upon by professionals in the field. However, most definitions are quite similar on a *conceptual* level. Standard textbooks include: Grandjean (1982), Kantowitz & Sorkin (1983), Kvalseth (1983), McCormick (1976), Oborne (1982), Wickens (1984).

Chapter 2
p. 10. "*In the mid-1970s* . . .": During this period, many articles devoted to operator problems with VDTs appeared in the popular and trade press. Two examples are Fioravante (1978) and Hebert (1977). See also Makower (1981).

pp. 10-11. "*Examination of VDT workplaces . . . By the early 1980s . . .*": A variety of surveys, field studies, and experiments relating to these issues were carried out. For overviews and summaries of these studies see Dainoff (1982, 1984) and Smith (1984).

p. 10. "*The outcry from VDT workers* . . .": For a European perspective, see Östberg (1984) and Buhmann (1980). In North America, see Canadian Labour Congress (1982), and U.S. Congress Office of Technology Assessment (1985).

"*Yet other workplace surveys* . . .": See, for example, DeGroot & Kamphuis (1983), Gould & Grischkowsky (1984), Starr (1982), Starr et al. (1984).

p. 11. "*. . . Conceptual framework . . .*": See Kuhn (1962).

pp. 14-15. *"Stress"*: There is an enormous literature, both professional and popular, dealing with the concept of stress. Two recent discussions which have an occupational focus are MacLeod (1984) and Quick & Quick (1984).

p. 15. *"Resource allocation"*: An excellent overview can be found in Wickens (1984), chap. 8.

p. 17. *". . . Knowledge . . . is power . . ."*: Quotation is from Francis Bacon, cited in *Oxford Dictionary of Quotations* (2nd ed.) (1953).

p. 18. *"Assessing Scientific Research"*: See Cook & Campbell (1979) or almost any textbook in introductory psychology.

p. 19. *". . . radiation hazards . . ."*: In the testimony of J.D. Millar, Director of the National Institute for Occupational Safety and Health before the Subcommittee on Health and Safety, U.S. House of Representatives, May 15, 1984, is the statement: "We do *not* find VDTs to be a source of dangerous radiation." See also National Research Council (1983).

pp. 19-20. *"Zurich study"*: A complete description of this research may be found in Läubli, Hünting, & Grandjean (1980) and Hünting, Läubli, and Grandjean (1980).

p. 21. *". . . more than 20 studies . . ."*: See Dainoff (1982, 1984) and Arndt (1983).

p. 22. *". . . so potent a psychological force . . ."*: Helender, Billingsley, & Schurick (undated). See also Amick & Celentano (1984).

p. 22. *". . . also reported a number of ergonomic deficiencies . . ."*: For the NIOSH studies, see Stammerjohn et al. (1981). Other differences are reported in the original references to each study.

pp. 23-26. *"NIOSH"*: The first experiment appeared in Dainoff, Fraser, & Taylor (1982) and Dainoff (1983). The second is described in Secrest & Dainoff (1984).

p. 30. *"Productivity . . ."*: This analysis is from Brill et al. (1984), p. 37. An excellent general discussion of human performance and productivity is found in Muckler (1982).

Chapter 3

The quotations "Caution: prolonged sitting may be hazardous to your health," on p. 31, and ". . . beauty is more than upholstery deep . . .," on p. 51, have previously appeared in: M. Dainoff (1984, April). Taking the hazard out of on-the-job sitting. *Facilities Design and Management*, pp. 72-74.

p. 31. *". . . 60% of the adult population . . ."*: This estimate comes from Grandjean (1982), p. 52.

pp. 32-36. *"Sitting involves . . . cause of lower back pain"*: An excellent overview of this material may be found in Oborne (1982), particularly Chapter 9. Other important sources are Branton (1976), Cailliet (1981), Corlett & Eklund (1984), Nachemson (1975), and Mandal (1985).

p. 40. *"Measurements from several laboratories . . ."*: Brunswic (1984), Bendix & Biering-Sorenson (1983).

pp. 42-47. *"However, these anthropometric data bases . . ."*: These issues are discussed in volume 1 of the NASA *Anthropometric Source Book* (Webb Associates, 1978). See also Kroemer (1983a) and Kleeman (1981), chap. 5.

p. 44. ". . . *for a North American population* . . .": There are a large number of individuals and organizations who have published guidelines and recommendations in this area. Helender & Rupp (1984) provide a good overview. In North America, two proposed standards are in preparation at this time; one by the Canadian Standards Association, the second in the U.S. by the Human Factors Society under the auspices of the American National Standards Institute (ANSI). Examples of comprehensive ergonomic guidelines for organizational use include Bell Laboratories (1983), IBM (1984), and Tijerina (1984).

Other useful sources are Kroemer (1983a,b), Kroemer & Price (1982), Miller & Suther (1981), and Sauter, Chapman & Knutson (undated; circa 1985).

p. 49. "*Studies indicate* . . .": Shackel, Chidsey, & Shipley (1976). For a general overview of the issue of seating comfort, see Lueder (1983).

p. 51. "*A field study* . . .": This study, by Kukkonen, Lupojarvi, & Ruhm, was described by Kvalseth (1983). See also DeGroot & Vellinga (1984).

pp. 53-55. "*Elements to Look for* . . .": See notes for p. 44 above.

Chapter 4

pp. 58-60. "*Standards, guidelines* . . .": See Helender & Rupp (1984) and other related references in the Notes to Chapter 3.

p. 60. ". . . *determine the best keyboard slope* . . .": Arndt (1983), Cakir et al. (1980), Grandjean et al. (1983), Helender & Rupp (1984).

pp. 60-62. "*Workstation Recommendations* . . .": These principles are derived from a number of different sources. Particularly useful were: Arndt (1983), Kleeman (1981), Kroemer (1983a,b), Kroemer & Price (1982), National Research Council (1983), Sauter et al. (undated; circa 1985), Tichauer (1973).

p. 62. ". . . *seatpans higher than their popliteal heights* . . .": Sauter & Arndt (1984).

p. 63. "*Experts disagree* . . . *use of footrests*. . .": See, for example, Lueder (1983), p. 702; Bell Laboratories (1983), p. 21. See also DeGroot & Vellinga (1984).

"*Asian woman's popliteal height* . . .": Data is from Miller & Suther (1981).

p. 64. ". . . *upper arm hangs vertically* . . .": See Tichauer (1973).

pp. 65-66. "*Forearm and wrists*": Arndt (1983), Cakir et al. (1980), Cushman (1984), Grandjean et al. (1983), Helender & Rupp (1984).

pp. 66-67. " . . *current key arrangement* . . .": See introductory comment by Cooper (1983).

"*Dvorak keyboard*": See Galitz (1984), pp. 177-178; Norman & Fisher (1982).

p. 68. "*Keyboard layout*": Galitz (1984), pp. 174-183.

p. 68. *"Key characteristics"*: For example, see IBM (1984), Roe et al. (1984).
pp. 68-71. *"Head and neck"*: Arndt (1983), Life & Pheasant (1984), Sauter et al. (undated; circa 1985), and Webb Associates (1978), vol. 1, chap. IV.
p. 69. *"Preferred viewing distance . . ."*: Farrell & Booth (1980), Sec. 3.6; Campbell & Durden (1983).
p. 69. *". . . visual angle . . ."*: For definition, see Riggs (1965); for recommendations, see Snyder (1984).
p. 69. *". . . 10 cm (3.9 inch) tolerance range . . ."*: Vellinga (1984).
p. 70. *". . . possible source of eye fatigue . . ."*: See Stark & Johnston (1984).

Chapter 5

pp. 77-79. *VDTs and visual problems*: See National Research Council (NRC) (1983), and companion papers by Dainoff (1982) and Brown et al. (1982). More recent papers may be found in Grandjean (1984). See also the *Bulletin of the International Scientific Conference on Work with Visual Displays*, Stockholm, 1985.
p. 78. *". . . radiation . . ."*: Much additional material has been published on this topic since the appearance of National Research Council (1983). However, at this writing, there appears to be no compelling reason to change the conclusion contained in that report. See reference to Millar testimony in Notes to Chapter 2.
p. 80. *"Basic Visual Function"*: General references for vision and visual perception may be found in Cornsweet (1970) and Lindsay & Norman (1977). For applications to VDT use, see Bell Laboratories (1983), IBM (1984), National Research Council (1983), Sauter et al. (undated; circa 1985).
p. 85. *"The initials 'VD' . . . visual discomfort"*: Campbell & Durden (1983).
"Permanent Damage": National Research Council (1983), chaps. 1, 3.
pp. 86-87. *"Long-Term Changes"*: National Research Council (1983), chap. 7.
p. 86. *". . . Complicating factors . . . baseline problem . . ."*: Campbell & Durden (1983).
p. 87. *". . . 38% . . . improperly corrected . . ."*: Smith et al. (1983).
pp. 87-88. *"Short-Term Discomfort"*: National Research Council (1983), chap. 7; Stark & Johnston (1984).
p. 87. *". . . stresses in the body as a whole . . ."*: Weston (1962), p. 47.
p. 89. *"Glare and the Vertical Orientation of the Screen"*: Bell Laboratories (1983); Farrell & Booth (1980), Sec. 3.2; National Research Council (1983), chaps. 5, 7.
p. 91. *". . . filters to be effective . . ."*: See, for example, McVey et al. (1984).
pp. 93-94. *". . . upper limit of 25 minutes . . . ratio of 9 to 1 . . ."*: Snyder (1984).
p. 94. *"Direction (Polarity) of Contrast"*: National Research Council (1983), pp. 73-74.
p. 96. *". . . paper copy to be superior . . ."*: Kruk & Muter (1984), Gould & Grischkowsky (1984).

p. 100. "*. . . correlation between motor feedback and visual input . . .*": Gregory (1973) provides a good introduction.
p. 100. "*Videotropic response.*" Term coined by M.J. Dainoff.
p. 101. "*Rest breaks . . .*": See Coe et al. (1980).
   Visual defects: Campbell & Durden (1983), Sauter et al. (undated; circa 1985).
p. 103. "*Ramazzini*": Quote is taken from Campbell & Durden (1983).

Chapter 6
p. 109. "*Privacy*": See Brill et al. (1984), p. 197; Russell & Ward (1982), Parsons (1976).
p. 111. "*. . . frequency and importance ratings . . .*": McCormick (1976), chap. 11.
p. 112. "*Cost of a Person . . . a building*": Brill et al. (1984), pp. 29-31.
p. 113. "*Open Office a Solution . . .*": Brill et al. (1984), pp. 89-166. Also, see Becker (1981), chap. 6, and Parsons (1976) for reviews.
   "*. . . enhanced . . . communication . . .*": Brill et al. (1984), pp. 217-222.
p. 115. "*Financial Costs or Savings . . .*": Brill et al. (1984), pp. 337-352.
p. 117. "*Noise*": For good reviews see: McCormick (1976), chaps. 5, 6, 14, and Kantowitz & Sorkin (1983), chaps. 9, 16. Office Music is discussed in Fox (1983).
p. 121. "*Ambient Lighting*": For good introductory overviews see Bell Telephone Laboratories (1983), Sauter et al. (undated; circa 1985), and IBM (1984). More detailed treatments may be found in Kantowitz & Sorkin (1983), chap. 17; McCormick (1976), chap. 12, and National Research Council (1983), chap. 5.
p. 123. "*Thermal Comfort*": See Grandjean (1982), chap. 17; McCormick (1976), chap. 13; Kantowitz & Sorkin (1983), chap. 19.
p. 125. "*Air Quality and the Tight Building Syndrome*": See Cohen (1984), pp. 7-31, Grandjean (1984), pp. 1-52; and Grandjean (1982), chap. 17.

Chapter 7
p. 136. "*. . . cognitive psychology . . .*": An excellent introduction is found in Lindsay & Norman (1977).
p. 143. "*. . . new techniques are under development . . .*": See Williges (1984) for a brief but comprehensive review.
p. 146. "*. . . recent software review . . .*": Fallows (1985).
p. 146-47. "*Security*": For a brief overview, see Seymour (1985). "Smart cards" are discussed in McIvor (1985).

Chapter 8
p. 149. "*. . . Structure . . . reflects underlying management philosophy . . .*": Baetz (1985), p. 38.
p. 150. "*. . . $11 billion . . .*": Quick & Quick (1984), p. xv.
   "*Workers compensation claims . . .*": MacLeod (1984).
   "*. . . cost of job dissatisfaction . . .*": See also Cascio (1982).

p. 152. *Volvo*: See Gyllenhammar (1977).

"*. . . job enrichment . . .*": For a review, see McCormick & Ilgen (1980), chap. 17.

p. 153. "*Deskilling*": See Cohen (1984).

"*. . . commercial airliner . . .*": See, for example, Weiner (1985).

p. 155. "*Wall Street Journal*": See issue of Monday, June 3, 1985. For a brief example of contrasting views on the subject of monitoring, see *USA Today*, September 6, 1984, p. 8a. A more extensive examination appears in U.S. Congress Office of Technology Assessment (1985).

p. 157. "*. . . secretary's boss . . .*": See, for example, McGee (1984).

"*. . . computerized telephone order entry . . .*": See "Operators' Universal Concern: Job Pressures." *CWA News*, Communication Workers of America, November 1984.

p. 158. "*. . . hostility . . . from 20% . . .*": Fine (1985).

p. 158. "*substitutes for leadership*": See also Manz & Sims (1980). Similar ideas may be found in Baetz (1985), pp. 111-112.

Chapter 9

p. 166. "*These are among the new directions . . .*": We have used Helender (1985) for a discussion of general trends in office automation, and Hillman (1985) for a discussion of artificial intelligence and expert systems, both from an ergonomic perspective. For a broader view of the human issues, see U.S. Congress Office of Technology Assessment (1985).

p. 167. "*the electronic cottage*": Toffler (1981).

"*. . . link will be devoted to socializing . . .*": See Baetz (1985), p. 115.

Appendix I

p. 175. *Interpretation of the Hawthorne effect*: Luthens & Thompson (1981), pp. 15-29.

Appendix II

This table appeared in: Kroemer, K.H.E., & Price, D.L. (1982, July). Ergonomics in the office: Comfortable work stations allow maximum productivity. *Industrial Engineering*. By permission.

Appendix III

p. 187. "*The current state of the art in cylinders . . .*": M.A. Dunlap, Suspa, Incorporated. (1985, February). *Presentation to Health and Safety Committee, BIFMA*.

Bibliography

Note: Professional journals devoted primarily to ergonomic issues include the following: *Human Factors, Ergonomics, Applied Ergonomics,* and *Behaviour and Information Technology.*

Amick, B.C., & Celentano, D.D. (1984). Human factors epidemiology: An integrated approach to the study of health issues in office work. In B.G.F. Cohen (Ed.), *Human aspects in office automation.* Amsterdam: Elsevier.

Andersson, B.J.G., Murphy, R.W., Ortengren, R., & Nachemson, A.L. (1979). The influence of backrest inclination and lumbar support on lumbar lordosis. *Spine, 4,* 52-57.

Argyris, C. (1974, Fall). Personality vs. organization. *Organizational Dynamics,* pp. 3-6.

Arndt, R. (1983). Working posture and musculoskeletal problems of VDT operators — review and reappraisal. *American Industrial Hygiene Association, 44,* 437-446.

Baetz, M.L. (1985). *Planning for people in the electronic office.* Toronto: Holt, Rinehart and Winston of Canada Limited.

Becker, F.D. (1981). *Workspace.* New York: Praeger.

Beldie, S., Pastoor, S., & Schwarz, E. (1983). Fixed vs. variable letter width for televised text. *Human Factors, 25,* 273-277.

Bell Telephone Laboratories, Inc. (1983). *Video display terminals — preliminary guidelines for selection, installation, and use.* Short Hills, N.J.: Author.

Bellucci, R., & Mauli, F. (1984). The effects of visual ergonomics and visual performance upon ocular symptoms during VDT work. In E. Grandjean (Ed.), *Ergonomics and health in modern offices.* London: Taylor & Francis.

Bendix, T., & Biering-Sorensen, F. (1983). Posture of the trunk when sitting on forward inclining seats. *Scandanavian Journal of Rehabilitation Medicine. 15,* 197-203.

Bhatnager, V., Drury, C.G., & Schiro, S.G. (1985). Posture, postural discomfort, and performance. *Human Factors, 27,* 189-199.

Boies, S., Gould, J., Levy, S., Richards, S., & Schoonard, J. (1985). *The 1984 Olympic Message System — A Case Study in System Design.* (IBM Research Report RC 11138 (-50065)). Yorktown Heights, N.Y.: IBM Corporation.

Bouma, H. (1980). Visual reading processes and the quality of text displays. In E. Grandjean & E. Vigliani (Eds.), *Ergonomic aspects of visual display terminals.* London: Taylor & Francis.

Branton, P. (1976). Behavior, body mechanics, and discomfort. In E. Grandjean (Ed.), *Sitting posture.* London: Taylor & Francis.

Brill, M., Marguilis, S., & Konar, E. (1984). *Using office design to increase productivity*. Buffalo Organization for Social and Technological Innovation.

Brown, B., Dismukes, K., & Rinalducci, E.J. (1982). Video display terminals and vision of workers: Summary and overview of a symposium. *Behaviour and Information Technology, 1*, 121-140.

Brunswic, M. (1984). Ergonomics of seat design. *Physiotherapy, 70*, 40-43.

Buhmann, K. (1980). Ergonomic and medical requirements in VDU workplaces and corresponding rules within the Federal Republic of Germany. In E. Grandjean & E. Vigliani (Eds.), *Ergonomic aspects of visual display terminals*. London: Taylor & Francis.

Cailliet, R. (1981). *Low back pain syndrome*. (3rd ed.). Philadelphia: F.A. Davis.

Cakir, A., Hart, D.J., & Stewart, T. (1980). *Video display terminals*. New York: Wiley.

Campbell, F.W., & Durden, K. (1983). The VDT issue. *Opthalmology and Physiological Optics, 3*, 175-192.

Canadian Labour Congress. (1982). *Towards a more humanized technology: Exploring the impact of video display terminals on health and working conditions of Canadian office workers*. Ottawa: CLC-Labour Education and Studies Centre.

Cantoni, S., Colombini, D., Occhipinti, E., Grieco, A., Frigo, C., & Pedotti, A. (1984). In E. Grandjean (Ed.), *Ergonomics and health in modern offices*. London: Taylor & Francis.

Card, S.K., Moran, T.P., & Newell, A.E. (1983). *The psychology of human-computer interaction*. Hillsdale, N.J.: Lawrence Erlbaum Associates, Inc.

Carroll, J. (1982). The adventure of getting to know a computer. *IEEE Computer, 15*, 49-58.

Carroll, J., & Carrithers, C. (1984). Blocking learner error states in a training-wheels system. *Human Factors, 26*, 377-389.

Carroll, J., & Thomas, J. (1982, March/April). Metaphor and the cognitive representation of computing systems. *IEEE Transactions on Systems, Man, and Cybernetics, SMC-12*, 107-116.

Cascio, W.F. (1982). *Costing human resources: The financial impact of behavior in organizations*. Boston: Kent Publishing Company.

Coe, J.B., Cuttle, K., McClellan, W.C., Warden, N.J., & Turner, P.J. (1980). *Visual display units report W/1/80*. Wellington, New Zealand Department of Health.

Cohen, B.G.F. (1984). Organization factors affecting stress in the clerical worker. In B.G.F. Cohen (Ed.), *Human aspects in office automation*. Amsterdam: Elsevier.

Cook, T., & Campbell, D. (1979). *Quasi-experimentation*. Chicago: Rand-McNally.

Cooper, W.E. (Ed.), (1983). *Cognitive aspects of skilled typewriting*. New York: Springer-Verlag.

Corlett, E.N., and Eklund, J.A.E. (1984). How does a backrest work? *Applied Ergonomics, 15.2*, 111-114.

Cornsweet, T. (1970). *Visual perception*. New York: Academic Press.

Cushman, W.H. (1984). Data entry performance and operator preferences for various keyboard heights. In E. Grandjean (Ed.), *Ergonomics and health in modern offices*. London: Taylor & Francis.

Dainoff, M.J. (1982). Occupational stress factors in VDT operation: A review of empirical literature. *Behaviour and Information Technology, 1*, 141-176.

Dainoff, M.J. (1983, December). Video display terminals: The relationship between ergonomic design, health complaints, and operator performance. *Journal of Occupational Health Nursing*, pp. 29-33.

Dainoff, M.J. (1984). Ergonomics of office automation — a conceptual overview. In M. Matthews and R.D.G. Webb (Eds.), *Proceedings of the 1983 International Conference on Occupational Ergonomics. Volume 2: Reviews*. Toronto: Human Factors Association of Canada.

Dainoff, M.J., Fraser, L., & Taylor, B.J. (1982). Visual, musculoskeletal, and performance differences between good and poor VDT workstations. *Proceedings of the Human Factors Society 26th Annual Meeting*, Seattle.

Dainoff, M.J., Happ, A., and Crane, P. (1981). Visual fatigue and occupational stress in VDT operation. *Human Factors, 23*, 421-438.

Daley, R.A., Voisard, B. & Dainoff, M.J. (1985). Evaluation of subjective measures of chair comfort. *Proceedings of the 2nd Midcentral Human Factors/Ergonomics Conference*, Purdue University.

DeGroot, J.P., & Kamphuis, A. (1983). Eyestrain in VDU users: Physical correlates and long term effects. *Human Factors, 4*, 409-414.

DeGroot, J.P., & Vellinga, R. (1984). Practical usage of adjustable features in terminal furniture. In M. Matthews and R.D.G. Webb (Eds.), *Proceedings of the 1983 International Conference on Occupational Ergonomics. Volume 1: Research Reports and Case Studies*. Toronto: Human Factors Association of Canada.

Diffrient, N., Tilley, A.R., & Harmon, D. (1981). *Humanscale*. Cambridge, MA.: MIT Press.

Fallows, J. (1985, October). Software successors. *Atlantic Monthly*, pp. 95-98.

Farrell, R.J., & Booth, J.M. (1980). *Design Handbook for Imagery Interpretation Equipment*. Seattle: Boeing Aerospace Company.

Fine, S. (In press). Terminal paralysis, or showdown at the interface. In D. Shaw (Ed.), *Human aspects of library automation: Helping staff and patrons cope* (Proceedings of the 22nd Annual Clinic on Library Applications of Data Process, 14-16 April 1985). Urbana-Champaign: Graduate School of Library and Information Science, University of Illinois.

Fioravante, J. (1978, March). Warning: Some observers suspect computer terminals may be dangerous to your health. *Bank Systems and Equipment*, pp. 74-77.

Fitts, P. (1951). *Human engineering for an effective air-navigation and traffic-control system*. Columbus, Ohio: Ohio State University Research Foundation. Cited in: Price, H.E. The allocation of functions in systems. *Human Factors, 27*, 33-45.

Fox, J. (1983). Industrial music. In D.J. Oborne and M.M. Gruneberg (Eds.), *The physical environment of work*. Chichester, U.K.: Wiley.

Galitz, W.O. (1984). *Humanizing office automation*. Wellesley, Mass.: QED Information Sciences.

Giuliano, V. (1982). The mechanization of office work. *Scientific American, 247*, 148-164.

Glass, D., Singer, J., & Pennebaker, J. (1977). Behavioral and physiological effects of uncontrollable environmental events. In D. Stokels (Ed.), *Perspectives on environment and behavior*. New York: Plenum.

Gould, J.D., & Grischkowsky, N. (1984). Doing the same work with hardcopy and with CRT computer terminals. *Human Factors, 26*, 323-338.

Gould, J.D., & Lewis, C. (1985). Designing for usability: Key principles and what designers think. *Communications of the ACM, 28*, 300-311.

Grandjean, E. (1980). Ergonomics of VDUs: Review of present knowledge. In E. Grandjean & E. Vigliani (Eds.),

Ergonomic aspects of visual display terminals. London: Taylor & Francis.

Grandjean, E. (1982). *Fitting the task to the man: An ergonomic approach.* London: Taylor & Francis.

Grandjean, E. (1984). Postural problems at office machine work stations. In E. Grandjean (Ed.), *Ergonomics and health in modern offices.* London: Taylor & Francis.

Grandjean, E., Hunting, W., & Pidermann, M. (1983). VDT workstation design: Preferred settings and their effects. *Human Factors, 25,* 161-175.

Gregory, R.L. (1973). *Eye and brain* (2nd ed.). New York: McGraw-Hill.

Gyllenhammar, P.G. (1977, July-August). How Volvo adapts work to people. *Harvard Business Review,* pp. 102-113.

Hebert, J.P. (1977). Caution, CRTs may be eye hazard. *Computerworld, XI,* 29.

Heckel, P. (1984). *The Elements of Friendly Software Design.* New York: Warner.

Helender, M.G. (1985). Emerging office automation systems. *Human Factors, 27,* 3-20.

Helender, M.G., Billingsley, P.A., & Schurick, J.M. (undated). *An evaluation of human factors research on VDTs in the workplace.* Westlake Village, Cal.: Canyon Research Group, Inc.

Helender, M.G., & Rupp, B.A. (1984). An overview of standards and guidelines for visual display terminals. *Applied Ergonomics, 15.3,* 185-195.

Hillman, D.J. (1985). Artificial intelligence. *Human Factors, 27,* 21-32.

Hünting W., Läubli, Th., & Grandjean, E. (1980). Constrained postures of VDU operators. In E. Grandjean and E. Vigliani (Eds.), *Ergonomic aspects of visual display terminals.* London: Taylor & Francis.

IBM Corporation, Human Factors Center. (1984). *Human factors of workstations with display terminals.* San Jose, California: Author.

Kantowitz, B.H., & Sorkin, R.D. (1983). *Human Factors,* New York: Wiley.

Karasek, R.A. (1981). Job decision latitude, job design, and coronary heart disease. In G. Salvendy and M.J. Smith (Eds.), *Machine pacing and occupational stress.* London: Taylor & Francis.

Kerr, S. (1976). Substitutes for leadership. *Proceedings of the American Institute for Decision Sciences.*

Kilbom, A. (1983). Occupational disorders of the musculoskeletal system. *Newsletter of the Swedish National Board of Occupational Safety and Health, 1,* 6-7.

Kleeman, W.B. (1981). *The challenge of interior design.* Boston: CBI Publishing.

Kroemer, K.H.E. (1983a). Engineering anthropometry: Work space and equipment to fit the user. In D.J. Oborne and M.M. Gruneberg (Eds.), *The physical environment at work.* Chichester, U.K.: Wiley.

Kroemer, K.H.E. (1983b). Design parameters for video display terminal workstations. *Journal of Safety Research, 14,* 131-136.

Kroemer, K.H.E., & Price, D.L. (1982). Ergonomics in the office: Comfortable workstations allow maximum productivity. *Industrial Engineering, 14.7,* 24-32.

Kruk, R.S., & Muter, P. (1984). Reading of continuous text on video screens. *Human Factors, 26,* 339-346.

Kuhn, T.S. (1962). *The structure of scientific revolutions.* Chicago: University of Chicago Press.

Kvalseth, T.O. (1983). *Ergonomics of work station design.* London: Butterworth.

Läubli, Th., Hünting, W., & Grandjean, E. (1980). Visual impairments in VDU operators related to environmental conditions. In E. Grandjean and E. Vigliani (Eds.), *Ergonomic aspects of visual display terminals*. London: Taylor & Francis.

Launis, M. (1984). Design of a VDT workstation for customer service. In E. Grandjean (Ed.), *Ergonomics and health in modern offices*. London: Taylor & Francis.

Life, M.A., & Pheasant, S.T. (1984). An integrated approach to the study of posture in keyboard operations. *Applied Ergonomics, 15.2*, 83-90.

Lindsay, D., & Norman, D. (1977). *Human information processing* (2nd ed.). New York: Academic Press.

Lueder, R.K. (1983). Seat comfort: A review of the construct in the office environment. *Human Factors, 25*, 701-711.

Luthens, F., & Thompson, K.R. (1981). *Contemporary readings in organizational behavior*. New York: McGraw-Hill.

MacLeod, A.G.S. (1984). Overview of management concerns and problems in office and clerical work. In Cohen, B.G.F. *Human aspects in office automation*. Amsterdam: Elsevier.

Magnus, P. (1970). *Investigation of troublesome jobs*. Stockholm: The Swedish Board for Technical Development (STU). (In Swedish: cited in Östberg, 1984.)

Makower, J. (1981). *Office hazards*. Washington, D.C.: Tilden.

Mandal, A.C. (1981). The seated man (Homo Sedans), the seated work position, theory and practice. *Applied Ergonomics, 12*, 19-26.

Mandal, A.C. (1985). *The seated man*. Copenhagen: Dafnia Publications.

Manz, C.C., & Sims, H.P. (1980, July). Self-management as a substitute for leadership: A social learning theory perspective. *Academy of Management Review*, pp. 361-367.

Mark, L.S., Vogele, D., & Dainoff, M.J. (1985). Measuring movement at ergonomic workstations. *Proceedings of the 2nd Midcentral Human Factors/Ergonomics Conference*, Purdue University.

McCormick, E.J. (1976). *Human factors in engineering and design* (4th ed.). New York: McGraw-Hill.

McCormick, E.J., & Ilgen, D. (1980). *Industrial psychology* (7th ed.). Englewood Cliffs, N.J.: Prentice-Hall.

McGee, M.W. (1984). Video display terminal user's perspective. In Cohen, B.G.F. *Human aspects in office automation*. Amsterdam: Elsevier.

McIvor, R. (1985). Smart cards. *Scientific American, 253*, 152-159.

McVey, B.W., Clauer, C.K., & Taylor, S.E. (1984). A comparison of anti-glare contrast-enhancement filters for positive and negative image displays under adverse lighting conditions. In E. Grandjean (Ed.), *Ergonomics and health in modern offices*. London: Taylor & Francis.

Miller, I., & Suther, T.W. (1981). Preferred height and angle settings of CRT and keyboard for a display station input task. *Proceedings of the Human Factors Society 25th Annual Meeting*, Los Angeles.

Muckler, F.A. (1982). Evaluating productivity. In M.D. Dunnette & E.A. Fleishman (Eds.), *Human performance and productivity: Human capacity*. Vol. 1. Hillsdale, N.J.: Lawrence Erlbaum Assoc., p. 13.

Nachemson, A. (1975). Towards a better understanding of low-back pain: A review of the mechanics of the lumbar disc. *Rheumatology and Rehabilitation, 14*, 129-143.

National Research Council (NRC). (1983). *Video displays, work, and vision*. Washington, D.C.: National Academy Press.

Norman, D., & Fisher, D. (1982). Why alphabetic keyboards are not easy to use: Keyboard layout doesn't much matter. *Human Factors, 24,* 509-520.

Oborne, D.J. (1982). *Ergonomics at work.* New York: Wiley.

Ong, C.N. (1984). VDT work place design and physical fatigue. A case study in Singapore. In E. Grandjean (Ed.), *Ergonomics and health in modern offices.* London: Taylor & Francis.

Östberg, O. (1984). Work environment issues of Swedish office workers: A union perspective. In B.F.G. Cohen (Ed.), *Human aspects in office automation.* Amsterdam: Elsevier.

Oxford Dictionary of Quotations (2nd ed.) (1953). London: Oxford University Press.

Parsons, M. (1976). Work environments. In I. Altman and J. Wohlwill (Eds.), *Human behavior and environment.* New York: Plenum.

Pustinger, C., Dainoff, M.J., & Smith, M.J. (1985). VDT workstation adjustability: Effects on worker posture, productivity and health complaints. *Proceedings of the 2nd Midcentral Human Factors/Ergonomics Conference,* Purdue University.

Quick, J.C., & Quick, J.D. (1984). *Organizational stress and preventive management.* New York: McGraw-Hill.

Reich, R.T. (1985, September 1). A fork in the road for U.S. labor. *New York Times,* p. E13.

Riggs, L.A. (1965). Visual acuity. In C. Graham (Ed.), *Vision and visual perception.* New York: Wiley.

Roe, C.J., Muto, W.H., & Blake, T. (1984). Feedback and key discrimination on membrane keypads. *Proceedings of the Human Factors Society 28th Annual Meeting.* San Antonio.

Russell, J.A., and Ward, L.M. (1982). Environmental psychology. *Annual Review of Psychology, 33,* 651-688.

Sauter, S.L., & Arndt, R. (1984). Ergonomics in the automated office: Gaps in knowledge and practice. In G. Salvendy (Ed.), *Human-Computer Interaction.* Amsterdam: Elsevier.

Sauter, S.L., Chapman, L.J., & Knutson, S.J. (undated; circa 1985) *Improving VDT work: Causes and control of health concerns in VDT use.* State of Wisconsin: Department of Administration. Available at The Report Store, 910 Massachusetts Street, Lawrence, Kansas.

Schneider, M.F. (1985, January/February). Managerial productivity — quality decision. *Office Ergonomics Review,* pp. 13-14.

Schneider, M.F., & Martin, J. (1984). VDU ergonomics in Ontario Hydro: A case study with emphasis on the method. In M. Matthews and R.D.G. Webb (Eds.), *Proceedings of the 1983 International Conference on Occupational Ergonomics. Volume 1: Research Reports and Case Studies.* Toronto: Human Factors Association of Canada.

Secrest, D., and Dainoff, M. (1984, April 12-14). Performance changes resulting from ergonomic factors in VDT data entry workstation design. In A. Mital (Ed.), *Advances in Ergonomics/Human Factors I,* The First Mid-Central Ergonomics/Human Factors Conference held in Cincinnati, Ohio.

Seymour, J. (1985, April). Locking up your information assets. *Today's Office,* pp. 22-32.

Shackel, K., Chidsey, K.D., and Shipley, P. (1976). The assessment of chair comfort. In E. Grandjean (Ed.), *Sitting Posture.* London: Taylor & Francis.

Smith, M. (1984). Health issues in VDT work. In J. Bennett, D. Case, J. Sandelin, & M. Smith (Eds.), *Visual*

display terminals. Englewood Cliffs, N.J.: Prentice-Hall.
Smith, M.J., Cohen, B. Stammerjohn, L., & Happ, A. (1981). An investigation of health complaints and job stress in video display operations. *Human Factors, 23,* 387-400.
Smith, M.J., Dainoff, M.J., Cohen, B.G.F., & Bierbaum, D. (1983, January). *Health Hazard Report* (HETA 82-329-146). National Institute of Occupational Safety and Health.
Snyder, H.L. (1984). Lighting, glare measurements and legibility of VDTs. In E. Grandjean (Ed.), *Ergonomics and health in modern offices.* London: Taylor & Francis.
Springer, T.J. (1982, June). Redesigning the office. *Computerworld OA*, pp. 33-38.
Stammerjohn, L., Smith, M.J., & Cohen, B.G.F. (1981). Evaluation of workstation design factors in VDT operations. *Human Factors, 23,* 401-412.
Stark, L., & Johnston, P. (1984). Visual fatigue. In J. Bennett, D. Case, J. Sandelin, M. Smith (Eds.), *Visual display terminals.* Englewood Cliffs, N.J.: Prentice-Hall.
Starr, S.J. (1984). Effect of video display terminals in a business office. *Human Factors, 26,* 347-356.
Starr, S.J., Thompson, C.R., & Shute, S.J. (1982). Effects of video display terminals on telephone operators. *Human Factors, 24,* 699-711.
Tapscott, D., Henderson, D., & Greenberg, M. (1985). *Planning for integrated office systems: A strategic approach.* Toronto: Holt, Rinehart and Winston of Canada Limited.
Tichauer, E. (1973). Ergonomic aspects of biomechanics. In *The industrial environment — Its evaluation and control.* Cincinnati, Ohio: National Institute of Occupational Safety and Health.
Tijerina, L. (1984). *Video display terminal workstation ergonomics.* Dublin, Ohio: Online Computer Library Center (OCLC).
Toffler, A. (1981). *The third wave.* New York: Bantam.

United States Congress Office of Technology Assessment. (1985). *Automation of America's offices.* Washington, D.C.

Van Wely, P. (1970). Design and disease. *Applied Ergonomics, 1.5,* 262-269.
Vellinga, R. (1984). Design of a terminal table system. In M. Matthews and R.D.G. Webb (Eds.), *Proceedings of the 1983 International Conference on Occupational Ergonomics. Volume 1: Research Reports and Case Studies.* Toronto: Human Factors Association of Canada.

Webb Associates. (1978). *Anthropometric Source Book: Vols. I and II.* NASA Reference Publication 1024. Yellow Springs, Ohio: Anthropology Research Project.
Weiner, E. (1985). Beyond the sterile cockpit. *Human Factors, 27,* 75-90.
Westgaard, R.H., and Aaras, A. (1980). *Static muscle load and illness among workers doing electro-mechanical assembly work.* Oslo: Institute for Work Physiology.
Weston, H.C. (1962). *Sight, light and work.* London: H.K. Lewis.
Wickens, C.D. (1984). *Engineering psychology and human performance.* Columbus, Ohio: Charles E. Merrill.
Williges, R.C. (1984). Evaluating human-computer interfaces. In M. Matthews and R.D.G. Webb (Eds.), *Proceedings of the 1983 International Conference on Occupational Ergonomics. Volume 2: Reviews.* Toronto: Human Factors Association of Canada.

Zuboff, S. (1982, September-October). New worlds of computer-mediated work. *Harvard Business Review*, pp. 142-182.

Index

Entries marked with an asterisk (*) are defined in the glossary.

Absenteeism, *28–30, 112–16*
* Adaptation (to light and darkness), *83*
Adjustability (flexibility and), *183–95*
Adrenaline, *14*
Air movement and drafts (guidelines for), *124–25*
Air quality, *125–26*
Alternative explanations of data, *18*
* Ambient environment, *107–108, 116–26*
Anthropometric data bases, *42–44*
　Humanscale, *42*
　NASA Anthropometric Source Book, *42*
Anthropometric measurements
　changes with time, *42–43*
　ethnic differences, *42–44, 49*
"Anthropometrically disadvantaged," *43*
Anthropometry, *41–46, 50, 185–95*
Anxiety, *13*
Apple Macintosh, *138*
Architects *8, 31, 57.* See also Facilities planners; Consultants; Designers
Argyris, C., *150*
Assembly line, *150*
　control and, *152*
　deskilling and, *153*
Assessing scientific experiments. See Research results
Assessing scientific research, *21–23, 169–79*
Assessing workstation components (actual task and), *74–75*
Astigmatism, *102*
* Augmented popliteal height, *44–46, 185–95.* See also Popliteal height

Automation
　office, effects of, *149–50*
　support for human decision making, *154, 158*

BOSTI, *112–16, 120–21, 123, 124–25, 177–79*
BOSTI Studies (financial benefits of ergonomic improvements), *28–29*
Back pain, *31.* See also Musculoskeletal problems
　poor posture and, *48*
Backrest tilt angle, *38–41, 102*
Backward tilted posture, benefits of, *38–41*
Baetz, M., *132, 149, 157–59*
Becker, F., *178*
Beldie, S., *98*
Bell Laboratories field study (VDT vs. non-VDT), *21*
Belluci, R., *103*
Bhatnager, V., *48*
Bifocals, *73, 85.* See also Eyeglasses
　load on head and neck, *61, 69*
* Biomechanical criteria, ergonomic design, *62–72*
Blood flow, *47, 54, 63–64, 71*
　"going to sleep," *8, 35*
　impaired, and thigh compression, *63–64*
　and lactic acid buildup, *33–35, 38*
Boies, S., *144*
Bouma, H., *97–98*
Branton, P., *32*
Brill, M., *28–29, 112–16, 177–79.* See also BOSTI
Bucket. See Fatigue
* Bullpen, *29, 114–15*

CRT, Component of VDT, *80*

222

Cantoni, S., *48*
Card, Moran and Newell, *136–39*
Cardiovascular disease
 high demand-low control and, *152*
 stress-related, *150–52*
* Carpal tunnel, serious long-term injury and, *65–66*
Carroll, J., *137–42, 145–46*
Cataracts, *79, 89*
Center of gravity, seated postures and, *36*
Chairs, *31–55*
 assessing on-site, *49–51*
 design, *46–47*
 ergonomic (elements to look for), *53–55*
 repair, *55*
 safety and reliability, *55*
 static electricity and, *54*
 upholstery and, *40, 51–54*
* Character formation, dot matrix elements and, *92–94*
Character shape, legibility and, *96–98*
Character size
 recommended range, *93–94*
 visual angle and, *69–70, 73*
Child-like behaviors, assembly lines and, *150*
Circulation. *See* Blood flow
Coe, J.B., *20*
* Cognitive psychology
 use in software-hardware design, *136–37*
 user-friendly software and, *134–37, 148*
Cognitive theory of the user, software design and, *137–39*
Collection agency, *153–54*
Comfort, *7–10, 30, 47–48*. *See also* Physical discomfort
Communication, *107–14*
 selecting best mode of, *109, 166*
 verbal, nonverbal channels, *108–109*
Comparability, VDT vs. non-VDT, difficulty of assessing, *22–23*
Computer games, *141–42*
Computer networking, *166*
* Computer-human interface (CHI), *131, 134, 138, 148*
Computerized decision making, *153–54*
* Conceptual framwork, *11–18, 21–23*
 environment, *107*

Concern for people, *150*
Consultants, *4, 58, 179*
Consumer of scientific research, manager as, *179*
Continuum of scientific observation, *173*
* Contrast
 character vs. background, *94*
 dark on white vs. white on dark, *84*
 visual display quality and, *81*
Contrast polarity, positive vs. negative, *94*
Contrast ratio, reduction in, from glare, *85*
Contrast reduction, glare and, *89, 104*
Control, *16*
 job decision latitude and, *151–53*
 monitoring and, *156–57*
 noise and, *118–19*
 stress and, *151–53*
 system design, human skills and, *159–60*
 thermal comfort and, *124*
* Control group
 adequate, *171*
 matched populations, *173*
 people as their own controls, *174*
 sample, condition, *170–72*
* Controlled experiment, *18*
Copernicus, *12*
Copyholders, *25, 69, 70–71, 74, 76, 192–95*
Cost/benefit estimates. *See also* Financial benefits
 accuracy of, *116, 179*
 costs, people vs. buildings, *112–13*
* Counterbalanced experiments, *25, 174*
Counterbalanced testing
 chair assessment and, *49–51*
 workstation assessment and, *74–75*

Dainoff, M.J., *19, 23, 47*
Daley, R., *49*
Decision latitude. *See* Job decision latitude
Decision making, computerized support for, *154, 158, 166–67*
Depth of field, *69, 82–84*
* Depth of focus. *See* Depth of field
* Descenders, printed characters, *97*
Design dialogue, *58*
Designers, *8, 57, 58, 177*

architects, vendors,
  communication with, *31. See also*
  Architects; Facilities planners
space planners, behavioral
  programmers, and, *31, 58*
Desk (as software metaphor), *138–40*
Deskilling
  reduced control and, *153–54*
  reduction of discretionary
    authority in, *153–54*
Diffrient, N., *42*
* Disc, measurement of pressure in, *38*
Discs
  lower back pain and, *36–41*
  vertebral or spinal, *35–41*
Distress. *See* Stress
* Dot matrix, *80–81, 92–98*
Dvorak keyboard, keying efficiency
  and, *67*
Dynamic vs. static adjustability of
  chairs, *46–47*
* Dynamic motion of chair, *46–47*
* Dynamic work, *34–35*

Efficiency, *7, 15, 23, 29–30*
"Electronic cottage," *167*
Electronic mail, *161–62*
Electronic performance monitoring.
  See Monitoring
* Electromyography, seated posture
  and, *38*
Employee education
  ergonomic chairs and, *51–52*
  why as well as how, *51–52, 75*
  workstations and, *74–75*
* Enclosure, *29*
  degrees of, *114–15*
  job performance and, *114–15*
Encryption, *147–48*
Energy conservation, tight building
  syndrome and, *126*
Ergonomic changes, physical vs.
  psychological effects, *176*
Ergonomic deficiencies, worksite,
  22–23
Ergonomic intervention
  increase in performance from, *27–29*
  reduction in health complaints
    from, *27*
Ergonomic standards, *10*
* Ergonomics, definition, *2*
Error recovery, *146*
Eternal triangle, *7, 30*
Ethnic mix. *See* Anthropometric
  measurements

* Eustress, *14. See also* Stress
Executive seating, status vs.
  function, *52–53*
Experimental group, sample,
  condition, *170–72*
Experimental research, *169*
* Expert system, *164–67*
Expert vs. novice (user friendliness
  and), *145–46*
Eye
  fatigue, viewing distance and,
    69–71
  movements in reading, legibility
    and, *98–99*
  muscle imbalance (phoria), *102*
  muscles, actions in focussing,
    83–84
  strain, fatigue, *18–27. See also*
    Visual problems
  structure of, *82*
Eyeglasses, *86–87, 100, 104. See also*
  Bifocals
  responsibility for, *102–103*
  task demands and, *102*

Facilities planners (and designers), *8,
  31, 57*
Farsightedness (hypermetropia),
  101–102
Fatigue. *See also* Muscle fatigue
  Grandjean's bucket, *12–17*
Fatigue-stress-resource allocation
  framework, *13, 15–16, 88, 107,
  119, 168*
  predictions from, *23*
Fear response, *11*
Feet and legs, biomechanical
  criteria, *62–63*
Fidgeting, *8*
  decreased performance and, *48*
  poor ergonomic design and, *47–48*
"Fight or flight," *14*
Filters, glare control and, *25, 91–92*
Financial benefits
  bullpen to office system, *115–16*
  enclosure and layout, *115–16*
  of ergonomic improvements,
    28–29
  glare reduction, *123*
  noise and, *120–21*
  relocations and, *115*
  temperature fluctuations and,
    124–25
Fit, *viii, 1–5, 13, 130–31, 148*
Fitts, P., *154, 159*

Flicker, *88, 104, 136*
  fluorescent light and, *95–96*
  peripheral vision and, *95–96*
Footrests, *74, 76, 194–95*
  casters and, *63*
  popliteal height and, *54, 62–63, 73, 184, 194–95*
Forearm angle, *39–41*
Forearm orientation
  deviations from horizontal, *65–66*
  keyboard thickness and, *65–66*
  table height and, *65–66*
Forearms and wrists, biomechanical criteria, *65–66*
Forward tilted posture, benefits of, *38–41*
Framework. See Conceptual framework
Friendly, *131*. See also user friendliness
Frustration tolerance, noise and, *119*
Furniture, optimal vs. suboptimal comparison, *23–28*

Galitz, W., *60, 133, 134, 141–43*
Gas cylinders (pneumatic), *187*
Giuliano, Vincent, *viii*
* Glare, *10, 23, 25, 104, 115*. See also Lighting
  control of, *88–92*
  reduction through control of ambient light, *90*
  and reflection, *121–23*
  vertical orientation of screen and, *89–90*
  from windows and overhead lights, *84–85*
Glass, D., *119*
* Global comparison, *23–26, 172–73*
Goals, organizational, *132*
Gould, J., *143–45*
Grandjean, E., *38–40, 67–68, 170–71*
Grandjean, VDT field study (bank), *19–20*
Grandjean's bucket. See Fatigue
Grandjean's bucket, rest breaks, and the videotropic response, *101*
Green, Barry, *15*
Guidelines and standards. See Standards and guidelines

Hand and arm orientation, *39–41*
Hands, biomechanical criteria, *66–67*

Hawthorne effect, *28, 175–77*
Head and neck
  biomechanical criteria, *68–71*
  strain through repetitive twisting, *68–71*
Health, *7–10, 13, 21, 29–30*. See also Stress; Cardiovascular disease
Health complaints, decrease with improved ergonomic conditions, *22–30*
Health hazard, *23, 31*
  long-term changes in vision and, *87*
  VDT, *18*
Heckel, P., *141–42*
Home, working at, *167*
Home row of keyboard, hand-arm orientation and, *39–41*
Human abilities vs. machine functions, *154, 159–60*
* Human engineering. See Ergonomics, definition
* Human factors. See Ergonomics definition
Humanscale, *42*

IBM, Proofreading comparison, VDTs vs. paper, *21*
IBM-Watson Research Laboratories, *137, 143*
* Illuminance, *122*
Implementing technology, human skills and, *159–60*
Industrial revolution, *149*
Integrated conceptual framework. See Fatigue-stress-resource allocation framework, *15–17*
Integrated workstation system, ergonomic priorities and, *72–75*
Intelligent workstation, *161*
Internal organs, *40*
* Intervention, workplace or field, *174–77*
* Ischemia. See Blood flow
* Ischial tuberosities, *32–35*
* Iterative design, *143–44, 148*
  user-based, *158*

Jitter (character instability), *94*
Job, nature of, *19*
Job decision latitude, job demand and, *151–52*
Job enrichment, redesign of work and, *152–53*
Job satisfaction

dollar estimates of, turnover/ absenteeism, 28–29, 112–16
quality of working life and, 150
Joints, ranges of motion, least effort, 61

Kantowitz, 124
Karasek, R., 151–53, 156
Kerr, S., 158
Keyboard, splitting of, reduction of muscle strain and, 67–68
Keyboard layout, placement of supplementary keys, 68, 73
Keyboard pressure or "feel," 68, 73
Keyboard shape, muscular strain and, 67–68
Kilbom, A., 31
Kleeman, W., 43, 62
"Know thy user," 143–44
Kroemer, E., 43, 181, 190
Kukkonen, 51
* Kyphosis
 lumbar, 36–41
 traditional workstations and, 48
 viewing distance and, 70–71, 101

* Lactic acid, 33–34, 35, 71
Laws. See Legislation
Layout
 office, 107
 and workplace organization, 110–12
Leadership, substitutes for, 158
Legibility, VDTs and paper, 96–98
Legislation, 10, 58
 monitoring and, 155–57
Lighting, 3, 25, 155. See also Glare
 ambient, 121–23
 optimal vs. suboptimal comparison, 23–27
* Light pen, strain on shoulders, 64–65
Line of sight, 25
 optimal, 69, 73
Line spacing, legibility and, 98–99
Link analysis, organization and layout and, 111–12
* Lordosis, lumbar, 35–41, 47, 70
* Lumbar region, of spine, 35–41
Lumbar support, 25, 39. See also Lordosis, lumbar
* Luminance, brightness and, 122

Machine functions vs. human abilities, 154, 159–60

Magnus, P., 34
Management philosophy, 22, 149–50, 154. See also Philosophy, organizational
Mandal, A.C., 39, 40
Manuals, 142, 145–46, 148
 vs. menus, 145–46
Mark, L., 47
Membrane keyboards, problems for long-term keying and, 68
Memory structure, human, 138
* Menus, 145–46, 148
 vs. manuals, 145–46
Message system
 Olympics, 1984, 144
 Store-and-forward, 162
Metaphor, user friendliness and, 137–43, 148
* Metaphors
 choosing effective, 139–40
 films vs. machines, 141–42
 mixed, 140
Model Human Processor, 137–39
* Modems, 167
Monitor glare, control by coatings and filters, 90–92
* Monitoring, 168
 fairness and, 156
 feedback and, 156–57
 legislation and, 155–57
 "productivity spies," 155
 sabotage and, 155
 unions and, 155–57
 video games, sports and, 156
Motion, repetitive, head and neck, harmful effects, 68
* Mouse, 134
 strain on shoulder, 64–65
Movement patterns, beneficial, through job restructuring, 72
Movement of text, visual discomfort and, 99–100
Muscle fatigue, 36, 41, 62
 lactic acid and, 33–34
Muscle work, minimizing, 61–62
* Musculoskeletal problems, 10, 18–27, 102
Musculoskeletal system, 3, 61
Music, office, 121

NASA anthropometric tables. See Webb Associates
NIOSH
 VDT field study, 19

VDT laboratory studies, *23–26*
VDT laboratory studies, fidgeting, *47–48*
Visual problems and, *78*
Nachemson, A., *38*
National Research Council (NRC), radiation from VDTs, *78*
Nearsightedness (myopia), *101–102*
Networking, computer, *166*
New Zealand, VDT field study, *19–20*
No-lose situation, *4*
Noise, *115, 119–21*
Noise, stress, intermittency, and control, *118–21*

OSHA, sound level standards, *118*
Observation, *18*
Observational research, *169*
Older workers, glare and, *89–90*
Olympics, Los Angeles 1984, Voice message system, *144*
Ong, C.N., *27*
Ontario Hydro, *59*
Open office
 dissatisfaction with, *178*
 privacy and communication in, *113–14*
Optical character reader (OCR), *165, 167*
Optical correction, in general population, *86–87*
Optimal workstation vs. suboptimal, *23–26*
Organizational philosophy, *149–50*

Paging, eye movements and, *99–100*
* Palm rest, *66*. See also Wrist rest
Passwords, importance of changing, *147*
* Pelvis, *32–40*
* Percentiles, *43–45*
* Perception, language and, *81*
Perception and memory, computers and, *136–37*
Performance, *48*
Performance, improvement under good ergonomic conditions
 NIOSH study, *23–27*
 Singapore field study, *27*
 Springer study, *27–28*
Performance appraisal, *157–60*
 philosophy and goals, *157–58*

Performance monitoring. *See* Monitoring
Philosophy, organizational
 automation and, *154*
 system goals and, *132, 149–50, 157*. See also Management philosophy
Physical discomfort, *13, 123–27*. See also Comfort
Physical discomfort, cold, heat, humidity, *13, 123–27*
Pioneer, technological revolution, *149*
Pneumatic gas cylinders, *187*
Pollution, air quality and, *125–26*
* Popliteal height, *43–45, 53, 73, 184–85ff.*
 augmented, *44–46*
 heel height of shoes, *45*
 seatpan height and, *62–63*
Portable computers, *164–67*
Postural options in sitting, *41, 191–95*. See also Seated posture
* Presbyopia, bifocals and, *102*
Prisms, visual discomfort and, *100*
Privacy, *29, 107, 112, 168*
 access control and, *110*
 distraction and resource allocation and, *109–110*
 job dissatisfaction and, *109–110*
 visual and auditory, *109–110*
Productivity, *17, 28–30, 168*
 environment and, *107*
 NIOSH laboratory study, *23–27*
Proofreading, VDTs vs. paper, *21, 96*
Proportional spacing (of printed characters), *98*
Prototypes, for software design, *143–44*
Proximate environment, *107–116*
* Psychosocial stress, *150*
Ptolemy, *12*
Pustinger, C., *48*

QWERTY keyboard, keying efficiency and, *66–67*
Quality of working life, *30, 149–60, 168*

Radiation from VDTs, *19, 78*
Ramazzini, B., *103*
* Raster, *80, 83, 88, 95, 99*
Reading speed, dot matrix gaps and, *92–94*

* Reflectance, *123*
* Refresh, VDT screen, *80*
Reich, Robert, *ix*
Repair, ergonomic chairs and, *55*
Repetitive movement, *62, 68*
Research methods, *18*
   observational and experimental, *169*
Research reports, user-oriented vs. technical, *178–79*
Research results, critical review by scientific criteria, *178–79*
Research settings, field and laboratory, *169*
Resistance to automation, *158.* See also Fear response
Resource allocation, *12–17, 21, 85, 88, 168*
   ambient environment and, *117*
   job decision latitude and, *151–53*
Rest breaks, *4, 22*
   as part of ergonomic intervention, *27*
   informal, *20, 101*
   videotropic response and, *100–101*
* Reverse video display
   flicker and, *95*
   glare reduction and, *95*
Safety and reliability, chairs, *55*
Sample size, statistical significance and, *173–74*
San Francisco, VDT study, *19*
Sauter, S., *62*
* Schema, *138–40*
Schneider, M., *59, 179*
Scientific observation, continuum of, *173*
Scientific research, manager as consumer of, *179*
Screen, touch-sensitive, strain on shoulders, *64–65*
Scrolling text, *99–100*
Seated elbow height, *185–95*
Seated eye height, *185–94*
Seated posture
   idiosyncrasies in, due to individual variations, *45–46*
   task specificity and, *41*
* Seatpan height
   excessive, *62*
   impaired blood flow and, *62*
   measuring, *188*
   popliteal height and, *44–45*
   range of adjustment, *44–46*

Seatpan tilt angle, *39–41*
Security, *129–30, 146–48*
   and confidentiality, *165*
Shared logic, *129*
Short-term visual discomfort, eye-brain system and, *87–88*
Showplace/workplace decisions, *51*
Singapore, VDT field study, *27*
Sliding out of chair
   forward tilt, *40*
   railroad passenger, *32*
   upholstery and, *40*
* "Smart card," *147, 165*
Smith, M.J., *19*
Snyder, H., *91, 93*
Social isolation, *167–68*
* Software, *4, 129–48*
   design of, *131–32, 134–39, 141–46, 148, 154*
   games vs. work, *141–42*
Sound level, *3*
   A-weighted decibel, *118*
   permanent damage and, *117–18*
Space reduction, job satisfaction and, *112*
Speech interference, content and predictability, *120–21*
Speech Interference Level (SIL), *120*
Spine, *35–41*
   biomechanical load and posture, *48*
Springer, T.J., *27–28, 175*
Stability vs. motion, *32–35*
Stability, requirement in seated posture, *33*
Standards, ergonomic, *10, 79*
Standards and guidelines
   ANSI/Human Factors Society, *58–59*
   allowable tolerances, *60*
   ambient lighting, *121*
   Canadian Standards Association, *58*
   DIN, *59*
   deviations from optimality, *60*
   disagreements among, *59 60*
   interdependence of elements, *60*
   obsolescence of, *59*
   temperature and humidity, *124*
Starr, S.J., *21*
Static electricity, chairs and, *54*
* Static vs. dynamic adjustability of chairs, *46–47*
* Static workload, *34–35, 61, 64*
Statistical significance, *173*

Storage space, priorities and, *110–12*
Store-and-forward message system, *162*
Strain. *See* Stress
Strength-dependency of ergonomic controls, chairs, *53*
* Stress, *12–17, 130–31, 158, 168*
    diseases, *14, 150, 152*
    psychosocial, *150*
Suboptimal workstation vs. optimal, *23–26*
Supervision
    as support for workers, *158*
    computerized support for, *158*
    open office and, *114–15*
Survival in a technological age, *11*
Sweatshop, *149–50, 167*
* Syntax, of computer commands, *131*
System, biomechanical, *61–62*
* Systems, interdependent, *22*

Tapscott, Henderson and Greenberg, *157–59*
Task design, *4*
Task lights, role in glare control, *76, 90*
Teleconferencing, *163, 166*
Temperature, *3. See also* Thermal comfort
    and humidity (standards and guidelines), *124*
* Theoretical framework. *See* Conceptual framework
Theory of seated posture
    design interpretations of, *46–47*
    deviations from, *44–46*
    testing by applied psychologists, *47–49*
Thermal comfort, *123–25*
Thigh compression
    biomechanical criteria, *63–64*
    desk drawers and, *64*
    waterfall seatpan contour and, *64*
Threat, technological, *21. See also* Fear response
Tight building syndrome, air quality and, *126*
Tobacco smoke, air quality and, *125–26*
Tolerance zone, *69, 82–84*
Training manuals, *142, 145–46, 148*
"Training wheels," transition from novice to expert, *145–46*
Transition to automated office, enthusiasm, creativity and, *159–60*
Trunk, spine, and pelvis, biomechanical criteria, *64*
Turnover, *28–30, 112–16*
Twisting, turning, and smashing, biomechanical criteria, *71–72*
* Typeface (font), acceptability vs. identifiability, *97–98*
* Typewriter returns, *10, 111*

U.S. Civilian Body Dimensions, *42, 181*
Ulnar abduction, keyboard shape and, *67*
Uncorrected vision problems, population level, *101*
Unions
    and labor organizations, *59, 79*
    and monitoring, *155–57*
Upper arm, static load and, vertical orientation and, *64–65*
Upper arms and shoulders, biomechanical criteria, *64–65*
* User friendliness, *129–48*
    determining, *132–35*
    expert vs. novice, *145–46*
    functionality and, *144–45*
    how much is enough?, *144–48*
User-friendly software
    conceptual approach, cognitive psychology and, *134–35*
    design criteria, *143–45*
    documentation by vendors, *135*
    evaluation of, technological vs. conceptual approach, *132–35*
    issues in choosing, *148*
    technological characteristics of, *133–34*

Validity
    assessing, ambiguity in, *177*
    internal vs. external, *169–70*
Van Wely, P., *7, 30*
Vellinga, R., *188–94*
Vendors, *31, 135, 148*
Ventilation, air pollution and, *125*
* Vertebrae, spinal, *35–41*
* Videotropic response, *100–101*
Viewing distance
    determined by character size, *69*
    determined by individual's vision, *69*
    dot matrix blur and, *93*

tilted postures and, *39–41, 190–95*
tolerance zone and ease of focus, *69–71, 82, 191–95*
* Visual angle, definition, *69*
Visual complaints, visual defects vs. ergonomic conditions, *103*
Visual defects, VDT and, *101–103*
Visual function, *80–85*
Visual problems, *18–27.* See also Eye fatigue; Eye strain
   long-term changes and, *86*
   permanent damage and, *86*
   relationship to postural problems, *102*
   short-term discomfort and, *87–88*
   VDT use and, *77–79*
   VDT-non-VDT differences, *79–80*
Voice channel, *165*
Voice recognition program, *161–62*
Volvo, *152*

* Waterfall seatpan, *35, 54, 64, 73*
Webb Associates, *42, 190*
Western Electric (Hawthorne effect), *175–77*
Westgaard, *30*
Window treatments, glare control and, *90*
Windows and overhead lights, orientation to in glare reduction, *92*
Workspace envelope, *107, 111*
Workstation planning, *57–58, 72–76*
Workstations
   flexibility vs. costs, *183*
   on-site trials, importance of, *53, 74–75, 195*
   shared, multi-user, *187*
   VDT, case study, *183–95*
   what to look for in, *75–76*
Wrist angle, critical nature, carpal tunnel, *65–66*
* Wrist rest, *25, 33, 66, 73, 74, 76*

Zuboff, S., *132, 153–54*